I0213173

The Moses Mystery

The Moses Mystery

The Egyptian Origins of the Jewish People

Gary Greenberg

PEREJET PREJJ

© Copyright 1996, 2008, 2021 by Gary Greenberg

All rights reserved. No part of this book may be reproduced in any form, except by a book reviewer who wishes to quote brief passages in connection with a review.

A Pereset Press book
All inquiries should be addressed to:
Pereset Press
P. O. Box 25
New York, NY 10008
Info@PeresetPress.com

Previously published as:
The Moses Mystery: The African origins of the Jewish people
and
The Bible Myth: The African origins of the Jewish people

First Pereset Press printing in 2008.

ISBN: 978-0-9814966-9-6
Library of Congress Control Number: 2021912187

Cover design by JoAnne Chernow

This book is dedicated to the
memory of my father, Emanuel Greenberg

Contents

Tables

Notes on Egyptian Terminology

In any effort to write a history of Egypt, one is inevitably faced with the problem of how to transliterate Egyptian names into English. Egyptologists have no agreed-upon convention for doing so. The chief difficulty is the lack of vowels in ancient Egyptian. This leads, for instance, to many writers referring to a particular Egyptian deity as Amen while others use Amun, and still others prefer Amon.

Then there is the matter of Greek. Many early Egyptologists obtained much of their information from the classical Greek writers, who transliterated Egyptian names into their own tongue. Since these were the first versions of the known names, many Egyptologists continued to use the Greek renditions and still do today. So, for example, Egypt's famous Fourth Dynasty pyramid builders, Khufwey, Khafre, and Menkaure, are better known by their Greek variations—Cheops, Chephren, and Mycerinus.

For the purposes of this manuscript, when engaged in my own commentary, I will generally adhere to the usage followed by Sir Alan Gardiner in his *Egypt of the Pharaohs*. When quoting from the works of another writer, I will retain that writer's usage.

Acknowledgments

I want to thank Professor Robert Stieglitz of Rutgers University for agreeing to review several draft versions of this manuscript and giving me the advantage of his many criticisms and insights. I also want to thank Professor Martin Bernal of Cornell University, author of *Black Athena,* for reading and commenting on a draft version of this manuscript.

These acknowledgments should not be taken as an indication that either gentleman endorses any particular portion of this work.

On page 57, for the paragraph beginning with "The time frame established" substitute the following paragraph.

The time frame established, an approximate date for the ninth year of Amenhotep I could be determined, but first another small matter had to be resolved. Where did the Sothic sighting take place? The two proposed options were Memphis (or nearby Heliopolis) and Thebes, the country's two most important cities. Because of the large distance between these two locations, astronomical requirements produce two different sets of possible dates for the 9th year of Amenhotep I. If the event occurred in Thebes, then the 9th year fell somewhere between 1525 and 1517, with most proponents of that view favoring 1517-18;[36] if in Memphis (or nearby Heliopolis), then the 9th year fell between 1544 and 1537, with most proponents of that conclusion favoring about 1542-44.[37]

On page 58, for the paragraph beginning with "The Thutmose references" substitute the following paragraph.

The Thutmose references to the lunar calendar allowed for two possible years in which that king could have ascended to the throne, 1504 or 1490.[38] Thutmose III ruled for fifty-four years and the Sothic date for his reign was not tied to any specific year. However, if the Sothic sighting for Amenhotep I was from Thebes, then the 1504 starting date for Thutmose III is improbable. On the other hand, if the Sothic sighting for Amenhotep I was from Memphis, then a 1490 starting date for Thutmose III is unlikely, although not impossible. Because of the continuing debate over the Memphis–Thebes issue, Egyptologists still disagree over which of the two starting dates for Thutmose III is correct.

On page 115, for the paragraph beginning with "The chief problem" substitute the following paragraph.

The chief problem with such a view about Joseph and the administration that he served is that it doesn't coincide with the Genesis chronology. Joseph was born in 1564 B.C. and became prime minister in his thirtieth year, in 1534 B.C.[16] Since Joseph served for at least fourteen years and the Hyksos kings controlled Egypt until no later than the fourth year of the Eighteenth Dynasty, a Joseph-Hyksos administration would require a starting date for the Eighteenth Dynasty no earlier than 1525 B.C. Such a date is inconsistent with all acceptable theories about when that dynasty began, all of which require an earlier date. It is not possible, under the Genesis chronology, for Joseph to have served in a Hyksos administration. If he ever existed, he would have risen to power during the Eighteenth Dynasty, and there ought to have been some records of his existence, unless the story of his political influence is highly exaggerated.

The Moses Mystery

1

The Problem of Israel's Origins

Who were the earliest Israelites? Where did they come from, and under what circumstances did they rise to power in Canaan? These questions, which bear on the intellectual origins of Western civilization, engage the finest minds in biblical studies. But the answers, like Tantalus's fruit, remain just out of reach.

The Bible tells us that the Hebrew nation originated with Abraham, in Mesopotamia—Ur of the Chaldees, to be specific.[1] From Ur, he and his family traveled to Haran, and from there to Canaan, where God promised him that his descendants would rule over the land. This covenant passed on to his son Isaac, and then to Isaac's son Jacob (later called Israel). Jacob had twelve sons, and one of them, Joseph, became Prime Minister of Egypt. At Joseph's invitation, Jacob and his family, less than seventy males in all, left Canaan and moved to Egypt. At first they were warmly received, but as their number rapidly swelled the goodwill turned to fear and anger. Israel soon found itself condemned to forced labor. Eventually, a hero named Moses arose from the enslaved ranks and challenged the mighty pharaoh to a duel of gods. Egypt's multitude of false idols were no match for the one true god of Moses, and the Israelite hero triumphantly led his people out of that country and toward the promised land of Canaan. Just forty years later, the Israelites marched into their new homeland and, by force of arms, imposed their territorial claims on the native population. Unfortunately, there is not a shred of evidence outside the Bible to corroborate these claims.

1

What Scholars Believe

Currently, biblical scholars recognize three possible scenarios explaining Israel's rise to power in Canaan:
- the "conquest" theory, which posits that Israel came in from the outside and conquered the land
- the "peaceful settlement" theory, which argues that Israelites entered gradually, settling in the sparsely populated areas of the central highlands
- the "peasant revolt" or "social revolution" theory, which contends that Canaanites rose up against their overlords[2]

Despite this wide range of disagreement, there are certain related matters, consistent with the biblical account, upon which there is virtual unanimity. The consensus holds that prior to the Hebrew monarchy, Israel was bound together in a confederation of Semitic tribes. This political arrangement supposedly evolved over several centuries from associations of Semite-speaking groups of pastoral nomads. Scholars also believe that before Israel became a power in Canaan at least some portion of the Hebrew population, if not all of it, journeyed into Egypt and lived there under hostile circumstances. In addition, historians agree that the crucial stages occurred in the twelfth or eleventh century B.C., when hundreds of new settlements were founded in the hill country of central Canaan, although there is no specific evidence connecting any of these settlements to the Israelites. Certain questions persist.

Where Is the Evidence?

How do we know, independent of the Bible, that Israel's presence in Egypt was preceded by an earlier presence in Palestine? Why is there no archaeological record of Israel or the Hebrew people prior to the thirteenth century B.C.? Why is there no extrabiblical evidence linking any specific Semitic tribes to the Hebrew people? And why did the so-called ten lost tribes disappear from history without an archaeological trace of their existence?

For Israel's history before the thirteenth century we have only the biblical account, but that rests on a shaky foundation. Modern scholars now recognize that the early books of the Bible weren't fully edited until after the seventh century B.C., and perhaps centuries later. (There is no extant portion of biblical text dated earlier than the third century B.C.) The final version attempted to weave a seamless narrative out of a diverse collection of contradictory historical claims that reflected clashing political philosophies and opposing religious doctrines. The resulting compilation indicates numerous compromises of the truth.

Even if we assume that the Bible is derived from earlier sources yet to be discovered, it still describes events that occurred more than a thousand years before its completion, and in those ancient times few peoples had a strong tradition of historical writing and perspective. Much of what passed for history consisted of myth, legend, and rumor, elements of which are pervasive throughout the biblical text. (Herodotus, widely considered the father of historical writing, dates to the fifth century B.C.—approximately the same time that the early books of the Bible were edited into their final form—and he drew substantially on myths and rumors for much of what he recorded.) Though several nations had written records in the second, third, and fourth millennia B.C. from which modern historians can draw conclusions, there is no evidence that Israel was among them.

Quite simply, where a group of people lived in the sixth century B.C., what language it spoke, and what it believed about its historical roots a thousand years earlier, does not, without independent corroboration, prove where it lived a thousand years earlier, what language it *originally* spoke, and what took place in its formative years. Certainly, little in the biblical text would have been outside the knowledge of learned Hebrew scribes in the sixth century B.C. Furthermore, the many anachronistic phrases in the early books of the Bible point to a very late editing. This is not to say that in this later time the Hebrews did not speak a Semitic language or strongly identify with Semitic culture. We just do not know that this was always so.

A New Model for Israel's Origins

In this book I offer a radical new solution to the mystery of Israel's origins, one that places its earliest roots in fourteenth-century B.C. Egypt during the reign of the monotheistic pharaoh Akhenaten. I call this the Atenist theory, after the unique deity that he worshiped. It holds that the refugees departing Egypt during what later became known as the Exodus were native Egyptians, devoted followers of the pharaoh Akhenaten.

This king's monotheistic religious reforms triggered massive resentment throughout Egypt. Less than two decades after Akhenaten's death Pharaoh Horemheb launched an aggressive counterrevolution aimed at suppressing all memory of his hated predecessor. Akhenaten's loyal followers suffered greatly. They were removed from office, stripped of honor and property, and in many instances were banished from the country. These persecuted Egyptians united together, rose in rebellion, and formed the House of Israel.

Akhenaten

The pharaoh Akhenaten, ninth king of the Eighteenth Dynasty, ruled Egypt for seventeen years in the middle of the fourteenth century B.C.[3] A monotheist militantly devoted to the worship of Re-Herakhty, the sun god whom he believed to be manifest in the form of Aten, the solar disk, he subscribed to a revolutionary religious doctrine that allowed no competition. Especially offensive to him was the worship of Amen, chief deity of Thebes and widely celebrated as the king of the gods. So strong was his animosity, that in an act of theological intolerance never before experienced in that nation's millennia-long history, he dispatched agents throughout the land to shut down the god's temples and excise the offensive name from walls, tombs, statues, and inscriptions.

Another target of the king's wrath was the popular god Osiris, judge of the afterlife. Under Akhenaten, the Osirian funerary practices so central to the Egyptian way of life were purged of all polytheistic symbolism. After the fifth year of his reign, the plural form for *god* no longer appeared in any writing of that time. In keeping with his proscription against graven images, the scribes sometimes substituted phonetic spelling for the anthropomorphic and theriomorphic signs used in script.[4]

Akhenaten's monotheism did not take root, and Egypt did not remember him kindly. In fact, they did not remember him at all. Pharaoh Horemheb systematically destroyed all public evidence of the heretic's existence. Workers chiseled out Akhenaten's identifying hieroglyphs wherever they were found. They demolished his newly built capital city and quarried stones for new building projects in other parts of the country. They even omitted his name from the lists of kings. He had become a nonperson, the nation doing all it could to forget that he ever lived. Ironically, today he is one of the best known of all pharaohs.

The modern world did not learn of Akhenaten's existence until the late nineteenth century, when teams of archaeologists visited the ruins of an unidentified city in an area now known as Amarna. These remains were what was left of the king's demolished capital city. On some of the walls, portrayed in an artistic style considered an unusual departure from traditional Egyptian portraiture, they found the deformed image of an unknown pharaoh and his beautiful queen. The hieroglyphs indicated that this strange monarch was named Akhenaten.

Continued exploration of this city produced a number of informative discoveries. These included the famous Amarna letters, clay tablets containing vivid reports of the turbulent state of foreign relations in the time of both Akhenaten and his father, Amenhotep III. In other Egyptian cities excavators discovered not only other structures attributed to this reign but also many of the stones transported from Akhenaten's capital city, some with fragments of revealing text. Before long, a sketchy profile of this monotheistic revolutionary took shape.

At first his reputation soared. Historians hailed him as "the first individual," a religious reformer, a great thinker, witness to the truth, a magnificent poet, an artistic revolutionary, and even the forerunner to Moses. But even the most aggressive advocates of a link between Moses and Akhenaten still adhered to the Semitic model of Israel's roots.

Sigmund Freud, in *Moses and Monotheism*, argued that Moses was an Egyptian noble who followed the Atenist beliefs of the heretic pharaoh, and he even identified Aten with Adonai, a name the Hebrews use for God. On the issue of the Hebrew people, however, he could only speculate as to how Moses came to be the leader of Semitic tribes. He suggested that Moses must have served as an Egyptian governor who became sympathetic to the Hebrew plight.

Thomas Mann, in his novel *Joseph the Provider*, reflected much of the speculation in the early years of Akhenaten's discovery, making Akhenaten the pharaoh who elevated Joseph to the position of prime minister of Egypt. In all other respects, however, Mann adopted the traditional biblical account.

In recent years Akhenaten's luster has worn thin. Today many Egyptologists dismiss him as a voluptuary, an intellectual light-weight, an atheist, and, ultimately, a maniac.[5] They sharply reject any connection between Akhenaten and Moses. Summing up the view of most Egyptologists, Donald B. Redford, Director of the Akhenaten Temple Project and one of the chief students of the Amarna Age (as Akhenaten's reign is known), writes, "A vast gulf is fixed between the rigid, coercive, rarified monotheism of the pharaoh and Hebrew henotheism [worship of one god exclusively]; which in any case we see through the distorted prism of texts written seven hundred years after Akhenaten's death."[6] When reciting the history of Akhenaten's monotheism, one historian after another adds similar disclaimers.

This sentiment, so widely endorsed, raises a question. If our view of the early Hebrew religion is distorted through the prism of texts written seven hundred years after the death of Akhenaten (such as the Bible, which received its present written form no earlier than the sixth century B.C.), how can it easily be concluded that the original religious views of Moses were any less a rigid, coercive, rarefied monotheism than that of Akhenaten?

Horemheb

The pharaoh responsible for waging the campaign against Akhenaten's memory was Horemheb, who came to the throne about fourteen years after Akhenaten's death. He demolished Akhenaten's buildings, erased the heretic's name from monuments, and perse-cuted the remnant of Akhenaten's following. Those holding any form of public office or important position were denounced as corrupt and ineffective. He removed them from office, punished many of them, and, in some cases, banished them from Egypt. The destruction of Akhenaten's capital city must have displaced tens of thousands of inhabitants, many of them priests, soldiers, and members of aristo-cratic families.

Horemheb had no royal blood. A popular general, he came to the throne when the royal blood line ended. He also left no blood heirs. In the year before he died, he appointed Ramesses I, another mili-tary figure, as his coregent. Ramesses outlived Horemheb by less than three years, and during his brief reign appointed his son, Sethos I, as coregent. Egyptologists mark the death of Horemheb as the dividing line between the Eighteenth and Nineteenth dynasties of Egypt.

Moses

In this book I will argue that Moses was the chief priest of the Aten cult and that at the time of Akhenaten's death Moses fled from Egypt to avoid execution. Upon Horemheb's death he returned to Egypt and attempted a military coup, the purpose of which was to restore the Aten cult to the throne. His allies included the persecuted remnant of Akhenaten's following, large numbers of badly treated sick and diseased Egyptians, assorted opponents of Ramesses I, and an army belonging to the Canaanite kingdom of Shechem, whose rulers were openly hostile to Egypt's demands for submission.

Moses's actions brought the nation to the brink of civil war. The confrontation ended with a negotiated truce that guaranteed the insurgent army safe passage out of the country. This truce and safe passage out of Egypt was the Exodus.

As the centuries passed, the refugees, like most immigrant groups, identified increasingly with the language, culture, and traditions of their new neighbors—and at the same time lost touch with their own roots. As the biblical authors repeatedly wrote, Canaanite culture had a powerful pull on the Israelites, and they frequently succumbed to its enticements. Despite unrelenting apostasy, however, one truth remained with them: a god like no other had delivered them from their oppression in Egypt.

Corollaries

This new model of Israel's origins has several corollaries:

1. Israel's appearance in Canaan occurred suddenly in the late fourteenth or early thirteenth century B.C., and not after several centuries of evolution from tribes of Semite-speaking nomads.

2. The first Israelites spoke Egyptian and adhered to Egyptian cultural practices and beliefs.

3. No confederation of Semitic tribes preceded the Hebrew monarchy.

4. The "ten lost tribes" disappeared not because of the Assyrian conquest but because they never existed.

Dating the Exodus

When did Israel leave Egypt and under what circumstances did it do so? These are the central questions that we must answer before the Atenist theory can be validated, but testimony is lacking. Outside the Bible there is no evidence that the Exodus even occurred. It is only because of the fervency with which ancient Israel proclaimed such a demeaning origin that historians give any credit at all to the biblical account.

Within academic circles these questions provoke heated argument. There is nothing inherently implausible in dating the Exodus to just after the end of Horemheb's reign. Doing so, though, raises a host of problems for those who deny a connection between Moses and Akhenaten, and most modern scholars deny such a connection. Consequently, all popular solutions to the Exodus problem carefully place a chronological wall between these two innovative thinkers.

The Majority View

The majority view dates the Exodus to the middle of the reign of Ramesses II, at least seventy to eighty years after Akhenaten's death and outside the range acceptable for the Atenist model. In support of this position, proponents argue that the Exodus must have occurred about the time of the onset of the previously mentioned Canaanite settlements in the twelfth and eleventh centuries B.C.

In the previous century most scholars believed that the Exodus occurred sometime during the reign of Merneptah, successor to Ramesses II, but an archaeological find known as the Merneptah victory stele (see page 13) required that the Exodus precede his reign. Also in favor of Ramesses II being the pharaoh of the Exodus is that there were many years of peace in the latter part of his sixty-seven-year rule, and such a condition suggests a likely time frame in which the Hebrews could have wandered in the wilderness without Egyptian retribution.

Pi-Ramesse

Perhaps the most important piece of evidence cited in favor of Ramesses II being the pharaoh of the Exodus is the biblical claim that when the pharaoh ordered the enslavement of the Hebrew people he set them to work at the city of Raamses.[7] Scholars uniformly accept that the biblical city of Raamses corresponds to the Egyptian city of Pi-Ramesse, the royal residence of Ramesses II.

What makes Pi-Ramesse intriguing is that the city didn't receive that name until the reign of Ramesses II. Prior to that it was known as Avaris, which had been the capital city and stronghold of the earlier Hyksos kings. Biblical scholars argue that if the Hebrews worked in the city of Raamses and that name first came into existence during the reign of Ramesses II, then the Exodus must have occurred no earlier than the reign of this pharaoh. In addition, based on the Merneptah victory stele, scholars recognize that the Exodus had to occur prior to the reign of Pharaoh Merneptah, the immediate successor to Ramesses II. The scholars say that such a sequence of events indicates that the Exodus could only have happened during the reign of Ramesses II.

That argument has a number of flaws. First, according to the Bible, the pharaoh who set the Hebrews to work on Raamses could not have been the pharaoh of the Exodus: His actions occurred before the birth of Moses, and the Exodus occurred in Moses's eightieth year. Ramesses II only ruled for sixty-seven years, not long enough to encompass both the birth of Moses and the Exodus.

Second, again according to the Bible, while Moses was in exile from Egypt the pharaoh on the throne died and a new one came to power,[8] this one being the pharaoh of the Exodus. So if Ramesses II had to be on the throne for the work order at Raamses, then one of his successors had to be the pharaoh of the Exodus. But because of the previously mentioned problem with the Merneptah victory stele, an Exodus in the reign of a successor to Ramesses II has been almost universally rejected.

Third and most important, the Bible connects the city of Raamses with Joseph, who

> placed his father and his brethren, and gave them a possession
> in the land of Egypt, in the best of the land, in the land of
> Rameses, as Pharaoh had commanded.[9]

Following the logic of the biblical scholars, Joseph would have had to have lived in the reign of Ramesses II. Since the pharaoh of the enslavement acted after Joseph died, both the pharaoh of the enslavement *and* the pharaoh of the Exodus would have to have been successors to Ramesses II, which is even more objectionable.

What these conflicts show is that the author of the biblical passages referring to Raamses wrote at a time when the city of Avaris had become known by the name Pi-Ramesse. This could have been anytime after the reign of Ramesses II. The events described as happening there could have occurred before the name change in the reign of Ramesses II, but the author could have substituted the name he knew at the time for the original name of Avaris. Later, when we consider Egyptian accounts of the Exodus, we will see that Egyptian historians placed the people involved in the Exodus in the city of Avaris rather than in Pi-Ramesse.

Other Objections to Ramesses II

In arguing against placing the Exodus in the reign of Ramesses II, critics note that he was a strong military leader who had a significant presence in Palestine. (He engaged the powerful Hittites in a major military battle as far north as Syria.) How could the Israelites have successfully resisted such a powerful emperor and there be no record of the confrontation? Even if the Egyptians had suffered some sort of military defeat, from historical records we know that they were not averse to lying about what occurred and claiming victory. "An expulsion of alien forces" is how they might have put it, if the Israelites had not been Egyptians.

For the Hebrews to have avoided an Egyptian reprisal so soon after the Exodus would have required a much weaker Egypt. Such a situation was evident in the reign of Horemheb, whose final days on the throne preceded Ramesses II by less than fifteen years. Under his predecessors, beginning with Akhenaten about a quarter of a century earlier, Egyptian hegemony in Canaan and Syria had been severely eroded by the expanding influence of the Hittites and the rebelliousness of many subject kings. Little is known about Horemheb's foreign policy activities, but no evidence indicates that he significantly reinstated Egyptian authority. Furthermore, other evidence suggests that he abandoned a series of Palestinian fortresses, which indicates a weak Egyptian presence during his reign.

Interestingly, if the Exodus represented a rebellion by the remnants of Akhenaten's following it would explain why there are no public Egyptian records of the confrontation between the two sides: The pharaohs meant to wipe out any record of Akhenaten's existence. Memorializing such a confrontation in public displays, even by those claiming victory over the heretic, would only perpetuate memories of the hated king. But this does not mean that private reports or disguised accounts didn't exist, and in later chapters we will examine evidence of what such records had to say about this affair.

Minority Views

There are also some strong minority opinions about the date of the Exodus, all of which place it well before the reign of Akhenaten. One such theory, partially based on powerful volcanic eruptions in nearby Crete, dates the Exodus to about 1450 B.C. Some scholars suggest that these powerful explosions caused the parting of the sea and the pillars of fire and smoke described in the biblical account. Until recently most archaeologists thought this eruption took place around 1450, but new evidence indicates it occurred about 1645 B.C., well before any acceptable date for the Exodus.[10]

The year 1450 is also troublesome for other reasons. Egypt was then at the height of its power, its authority extending deep into Syria and lasting almost another hundred years. It is hard to believe that a rebel nation could successfully resist Egypt's superior military resources or that records of the time, in Egypt and elsewhere, would omit any mention of such a notable achievement.

Another theory, once widely held but now much less so, holds that the Exodus corresponded to the expulsion of the Hyksos kings at the start of the Eighteenth Dynasty, a date in the mid–sixteenth century B.C. The Hyksos were Asian chieftains, probably of Semitic background, who, between the eighteenth and sixteenth centuries, ruled considerable portions of Egyptian territory. Josephus, the Jewish historian of the first century A.D., was the first to identify the expulsion of the Hyksos with the Exodus, and his argument was influential for much of later history. The problem with such an early date is that it creates a post-Exodus period of over three hundred years in which Israel does not appear in any historical record.

Contradictory Biblical Evidence

Dating the Exodus is problematic because evidence of its occurrence appears exclusively in the Bible, and what little it tells is contradictory. Exodus 12:40–41, for example, places the Exodus 430 years after the start of Israel's sojourn in Egypt (i.e., beginning with Jacob's arrival), whereas Genesis 15:13–14 indicates that four hundred years transpired from the birth of Isaac to the end of the bondage. Both claims cannot be true. Jacob was born in Isaac's 60th year,[11] and he didn't arrive in Egypt until his 130th year.[12] If the sojourn lasted 430 years, then the Exodus would have to have occurred 620 years after Isaac's birth.[13] On the other hand, if the Exodus occurred 400 years after Isaac was born, then the sojourn could only have been 210 years long.[14] Other biblical passages raise additional problems.

Even if we favored one biblical claim over another, what historical event would permit us to anchor that claim to a specific date? In 1 Kings 6:1 there is the assertion that the Exodus occurred 480 years before Solomon started work on the temple. This is somewhat corroborated by Judges 11:26, which suggests that Jephthah judged Israel three hundred years after the Exodus. Since historians date Solomon's ascension between c. 970 and 950 B.C., that claim would yield a potential Exodus date between 1450 and 1430 B.C.

However, because of the aforementioned problems with such a date, most scholars maintain that the expression "480 years" derives from a misunderstanding. According to this view, the biblical author meant to describe twelve generations of Israelites (since 1 Chronicles 6 shows twelve generations from the Exodus to Solomon) and assigned forty years to each generation. But, the argument continues, forty years are too many for a generation. Proponents of this argument say twenty-five years would make a better fit, resulting in a total span of three hundred years. Such a procedure would date the Exodus between 1270 and 1250 B.C., during the reign of Ramesses II, right where the majority would like it.

That there is no reference to a generation lasting forty, twenty-five, or any other number of years, does not dissuade proponents of this surgical reconstruction. Nor can we find any convincing proof that the biblical author meant twelve generations instead of 480 years. In fact, the number of years assigned to a generation is wholly arbitrary. In this case, scholars chose twenty-five years because it conveniently placed the Exodus exactly where the majority would have it.

This solution also ignores another problem. There is no extrabiblical evidence that David, Solomon, or the vast and glorious empire over which they ruled ever existed. That a Hebrew nation existed cannot be denied, and most certainly it had a king. The name Solomon, however, is simply an adopted title meaning "peaceable."[15] It could have been a title adopted by many Hebrew kings.

If Solomon ever had such an extensive kingdom as described in the Bible, it seems to have escaped the notice of both its subjects and its neighbors—the Phoenicians, Egyptians, Assyrians, Babylonians, Amorites, Canaanites, Edomites, and Moabites. All of these nations have remained mute on the subject of this kingdom. History contains many rumors about mighty kingdoms that never existed, but rarely does one hear nothing from contemporaries of a great kingdom that *did* exist. Such an ephemeral kingdom cannot serve as an anchor for biblical dating.

Also, the date proposed by scholars for Solomon's reign conflicts with biblical chronology. As commentators have noted, if you add up the length of each of Solomon's successors' reigns, the total time from the year he began building the temple to its destruction is 430 years. Since independent sources permit us to date the destruction of the temple to 587 B.C., the biblical account would require that Solomon's initial building program begin in 1017, about sixty years earlier than scholars would allow.[16]

Arguing against this earlier date, historians claim that the 430 years from the beginning of the temple to its destruction is the same duration as the Hebrew sojourn in Egypt, and that the numbers have been juggled to create a parallel history in post-Exodus times. This may be a legitimate attack on the post-Exodus chronology, but it simply cuts Solomon loose from any chronological anchor. Since we can't accurately date the start of Solomon's reign, we can't use that to date the Exodus.

The Earliest Archaeological Evidence for Israel

The Merneptah Stele

Although history does not tell us of the Exodus, it does supply some help in setting the latest possible date. The earliest nonbiblical reference to the name Israel appears on an Egyptian stele dating to the latter half of the thirteenth century B.C., about 100 to 125 years after Akhenaten's death. It is unusual in that Egyptians never used the name again.[17] One has to skip forward almost four hundred years, completely bypassing the reigns of David and Solomon, before its next appearance outside the Bible.[18]

Commemorating Pharaoh Merneptah's victory over the combined forces of Libya and the Sea Peoples, the monument preserves an effusive hymn full of national joy and enemy disgrace. Tucked away near the very end is this poem:

The princes are prostrate, saying: "Mercy!"
Not one raises his head among the Nine Bows.
Desolation is for Tehenu; Hatti is pacified;
Plundered is the Canaan with every evil;
Carried off is Ashkelon; seized upon is Gezer;
Yanoam is made as that which does not exist;
Israel is laid waste, his seed is not;
Hurru is become a widow for Egypt!
All lands together, they are pacified;
Everyone who was restless, he has been bound.[19]

The conquests claimed have no connection to the Libyan war, and they depict no historical truth.[20] Their inclusion serves only as a poetic attempt to portray Merneptah as a grand warrior.

A curious feature of this inscription is that Israel is the only name with a grammatical determinative signifying *people* instead of *land*. To almost all biblical scholars the grammar suggests that here we have a picture of ancient Israel in its post-Exodus, pre-Conquest stage.[21] This discovery caused quite a shock to the academic world of 1896, the year in which the monument was discovered. At that time most biblical and Egyptological scholars identified Merneptah as the pharaoh of the Exodus. On this new evidence historians had to date the event to an earlier time.[22] But when?

If the Exodus happened not much earlier than the start of Ramesses II, then Moses and Akhenaten would become childhood pals, educated together and receiving their religious training in the great Egyptian temple of Annu (in Greek, Heliopolis; in the Bible, On). If scholars wanted to separate these two revolutionaries (and they did), they had to date the Exodus either late in the reign of Ramesses II or set it at least two centuries earlier.

The Merneptah inscription also lends support to my claim that Israel emerged suddenly in the fourteenth century B.C., as opposed to the current view that Israel evolved over several centuries from nomadic tribes of Semite-speaking peoples. Prior to the Merneptah inscription, no record exists of either Israel or any of the tribes that made up the Israelite tribal confederation. Where did this Israel come from? What territory did it occupy? Why doesn't it have any history before this? The absence of answers suggests that Israel was a newcomer.

The inscription does not tell us what language Israel spoke, but it does imply that Israel, despite its lack of identification with a specific territory, stood as a powerful military force. The text places it among several major political entities. (Hatti was the Hittite kingdom; Hurru was the Hurrian kingdom; Ashkelon and Gezer were two of the most substantial city-states in Canaan.) The context suggests that it wouldn't have been listed if it hadn't been thought worthy of mention as a defeated force. Its presence as a large powerful force without a territory of its own suggests that *this* Israel came from somewhere else.[23]

It could not have arrived there much earlier than the middle of the reign of Ramesses II, otherwise it would likely have been identified with the territory where it was found. This suggests it arrived within forty years of the death of Horemheb, a time frame that would be consistent with both the biblical claim that Israel entered Canaan about forty years after the Exodus and the Atenist theory that the Exodus occurred shortly after the death of Horemheb.

It is also interesting that the very first mention of the name Israel occurs in Egyptian writing; it does not appear again in the historical record for almost four hundred years afterward.

The evidence suggests, then, that at a time consistent with both biblical chronology and the Atenist model, Israel, previously unknown in the historical record, suddenly appeared in Canaan or its neighboring territories with a powerful military force. What we do not have is evidence that at that time this Israel was a Semitic-speaking people or ever inhabited Asia prior to its departure from Egypt.

Jacob-Her

Concerning the last point, some comments about certain archaeological finds are in order. As early as the seventeenth century B.C., Semitic-speaking tribes and groups moved into the Nile Delta. It is from these groups that the Hyksos chieftains probably emerged, and these immigrants probably served as the base of later Hyksos power.

Scarabs, small beetle-shaped sculptures with inscriptions, from this era show many chieftains with Semitic names, two of whom were Jacob-Her and Anat-Her. Linguists do not know what the *her* element stands for, but Anat was a well-known Palestinian goddess.[24] Scholars are quick to see the name Jacob on the other scarab and speculate about its connection to the biblical Jacob. That the names are similar is true, but by analogy to the Anat-her inscription, Jacob could have been the name of a Palestinian god. At most, it only proves that the name Jacob existed in ancient times. No evidence connects Jacob-her in any way to the biblical Jacob.

Habiru/Hebrew

In these early times the archaeological records make frequent reference to a class of people known as Habiru or 'Apiru, many of whom were enslaved in Egypt. The term seems to be a classification or slang expression for mercenaries, servants, and outlaws, a term of derogation often translated as "people of the dust." Many scholars see in *Habiru* a source for the name Hebrew, and opinion on this changes from time to time. On the basis of complicated philological issues, scholars generally reject the connection.

In any event, the Habiru were not an ethnic group. Studies of Habiru names show that they contained both Semitic and Indo-European elements. If *Hebrew* is derived from *Habiru*, it would most certainly be a post-Exodus derivation used to describe the Israelites at a time when they were not yet settled in a territory and therefore exhibiting characteristics associated with the Habiru class. The name Hebrew, as a term for the Israelites, is not attested to until late in the first millennium B.C.

The Patriarchal History

If ancient Israel originated in the aftermath of Akhenaten's religious revolution, we must also account for the patriarchal history—the stories of Abraham, Isaac, and Jacob. These stories not only took place centuries before Akhenaten, they also place the Hebrew ancestors in Canaan, not Egypt. These accounts present vivid portraits of colorful characters; they exhibit wide ranges of emotion and personality, display virtues and flaws, describe many highly interesting activities, and tell of exciting events. They seem to have few, if any, counterparts in Canaanite-Mesopotamian mythology.

Where did such fully developed histories come from? Does this vast amount of narrative detail suggest that the biblical authors drew upon folk histories of real characters? There is so much personality in these stories that many scholars find it hard to believe that these patriarchal families were made up out of whole cloth. One need not believe all the events occurred to be tempted by such a view.

Nevertheless, the patriarchal history is false. Consider, for example, this problem: The book of Genesis ends with the death of Joseph, and the story picks up in the book of Exodus with the birth of Moses. This transition encompasses several generations and, allegedly, several centuries. In this time Israel grew from a handful of people to over 600,000 males and their families. All we are told about this transition is that the pharaoh feared the Israelites and reduced them to slavery in order to eliminate any potential threat.

It is precisely this gap in the history of Israel that is responsible for all the debates about the date of the Exodus. Why does the Bible have such a detailed history of Israel's ancestors, from the Creation to the death of Joseph, and such a detailed history of Israel, from the birth of Moses to the end years of biblical history, and virtually no description of what occurred in the centuries in between?

One feels compelled to ask: In the several hundred years during which Israel allegedly grew from a small family to a mighty kingdom and to an enslaved nation, did nothing of interest happen? Were there no tales worth remembering, no accounts of heroism, no stories of inspiration, no tales of faith challenged or lost, no good or bad deeds of note?

Furthermore, at the end of the patriarchal history, Jacob set the stage for massive conflict and intrigue in this period of missing history.[25] He denied the birthright to his three oldest sons, accusing them of dastardly deeds, and appointed the tribe of Joseph, his eleventh son, as his heir. But, to Joseph's dismay, the inheritance went to Joseph's younger son, Ephraim, rather than his oldest son, Manasseh. To top it off, after giving the crown to Ephraim, Jacob then announced that the scepter would not depart from Judah, his fourth oldest son. Who was supposed to rule Israel, Ephraim or Judah?

How did these events affect the children of Israel and their descendants? How did the sons and the families handle these decisions? Was there anger, joy, resistance, rebellion, or acceptance? What went on in those centuries? Why would there be a biblical dark age in the eyes of the scribal redactors when everything before and after is so clearly illuminated?

The answer is that the events that supposedly preceded the dark ages never occurred. True biblical history begins with the Exodus, and the patriarchal history is myth, pure and simple. In some of the following chapters I will set forth the exact mythological sources from which most of the patriarchal history is derived.

By way of preview, however, let me briefly outline the argument. Patriarchal history draws upon Egyptian mythology. Abraham, Isaac, Jacob, and their key family members correspond to a family of popular Egyptian deities associated with the Egyptian god Osiris. Most of the events depicted in the patriarchal accounts come directly from Egyptian literary sources and themes, and I will examine the precise mythological incidents that gave rise to the biblical sources. If this evidence is as obvious as I suggest, the reader may well be tempted to ask why biblical scholars and Egyptologists failed to uncover these connections. There are a number of reasons for such oversights.

When the Israelites came out of Egypt, the people brought with them the many stories about Egyptian gods and goddesses, stories they believed to be true histories of their country. But because the Israelites were militantly monotheistic, with a strong prejudice against the god Osiris, the deities were transformed into human ancestors. As with any immigrant group, after centuries of immersion in new cultures and surroundings, the settlers adopted the traditions and beliefs of their new neighbors, often integrating their old beliefs with the newly learned traditions. And as the biblical prophets make clear, over and over, Canaanite culture exerted a mighty force over the Israelites.

The Egyptian deities, already transformed from gods to heroic human ancestors, came to look less and less like Egyptians and more and more like Canaanites. Atenist religious views melded with local traditions. Over the centuries numerous political and religious feuds developed, and old stories were retold in order to favor one group over another. Then came conquest and destruction. Most of Israel disappeared from history after the Assyrian conquests. Those Israelites remaining were captured by Babylon and force-fed Babylonian culture and history. Shortly thereafter, the Hebrews were liberated from Babylon by the Persians, and close cultural contact between the two nations existed.[26]

In the morass of conflict, Israel lost touch with its Egyptian roots. By the time modern scholars came to review its history, the long religiously orthodox image of Israel as firmly rooted among Semitic tribes wandering in Canaan and Mesopotamia was fixed in the Western mind. Biblical scholars saw no need to apply to Egypt the scholarly intensity of research reserved for the Semitic world. Israel was Canaanite. Biblical history was assumed true, at least in its outline. That the biblical scribes and redactors could have committed such a major error in location never entered the biblical mind.

The Twelve Tribes

Closely associated with the problem of the patriarchal history is that of the Twelve Tribes. Biblically, they also originated in the pre-Egyptian period of Genesis, but their story carries forward from the patriarchal period to the post-Exodus era. However, no archaeological evidence demonstrates that this tribal coalition ever existed, and, given the alleged history of the Israelites in Egypt, we should not expect to find any such evidence.

The Israelites allegedly entered Egypt with only about seventy males. According to the Bible, they lived mostly in the small territorial area of Goshen. But they left Egypt with over 600,000 males and their families.

It seems inconceivable that over this time, in a small territory, such a large number of people could have maintained anything like a tribal structure. By that time intermarriage alone, a practice common in biblical genealogy, would certainly have wiped out anything resembling clear linear family divisions. The biblical Israel emerging out of Egypt would have been divided along class, religious, and political lines, not the artificial tribal structure that implies small isolated family clans. How does it happen, then, that this fictional tribal history spans both the mythological and historical portions of Israel's history?

Several factors influenced this development. As the evidence in the following chapters develops, we will see that the original idea of twelve tribes, or, more specifically, twelve political entities, originated in Egyptian traditions. After they left Egypt, other factors came into play.

At first the Egyptian emigrants dwelled peacefully in southern Jordan. Then they moved north into central Jordan and west into central Canaan, settling into what was then unoccupied territory. While the Bible alleges that Israel conquered Canaan at this time (although elsewhere it casts doubt on this proposition), the territory was already in the throes of a military invasion by a powerful outside force known as the Sea Peoples. Mostly a coalition of Greek warriors seeking a new homeland, the invaders established themselves in several city-states along the Canaanite coast and in the northern Canaan territories. Their aggressiveness led to several direct confrontations with the Egyptians on Egyptian territory. (One such engagement is described in the previously mentioned Merneptah stele.)

The most powerful and famous of these invaders were the Philistines, who soon threatened all the residents of Canaan, including their former Greek allies who had settled in other city-states. In order to halt the Philistine advance, I propose that the Israelites formed a confederation with the other Sea People states and local Canaanites, and out of this confederation came a new nation of Israel.

At this time, I argue, Judah did not exist. The Judaeans only entered the picture at the time of David, a Hebrew mercenary who worked with and was trained by the Philistine warlords. David used his newly acquired military skills to form an effective military force and seized control of much of the territory belonging to the Israelite alliance. He declared himself king and established the House of Judah. It was in the time of David that many of the stories pitting Judah against Ephraim and other tribes came into being.

The Canaanite conquest served mostly as a Davidic myth to justify Judaean control over the alliance. It relied more on tales of the Sea Peoples' invasion than it did on any Israelite actions. These stories of conquest found their way into the biblical corpus, and several verses indicate that only Judah succeeded in conquering its designated territories. The other tribes allegedly floundered in their efforts, indicating that only Judah was justified in serving as head of the federation.

Outline of the Argument to Be Presented

It is one thing to point out that there is no evidence corroborating the biblical account of Israel's early years; it is quite another to substitute whatever theory one wants. After all, without evidence to the contrary, it is possible that the broad outlines of biblical history are correct. To argue that Moses and Akhenaten were theological comrades-in-arms and that the first Hebrews were Akhenaten's persecuted followers simply because it is theoretically possible does not make it so. Such coincidences provide no solid proof for challenging what almost all biblical scholars believe to be true. We need hard evidence, irrefutable arguments that prove the case. I provide that evidence in the following chapters.

Chapter 2 will examine the famous and puzzling birth-and-death chronology in Genesis 5 and 11. These passages, which provide a continuous chronological link between the births and deaths of twenty-three generations, beginning with Adam at the dawn of Creation and ending with the birth of Abraham in the early part of the second millennium B.C., generate much controversy. Scholars casually dismiss this chronology as worthless, but in later chapters I will show that it provides a highly accurate record of Egyptian dynastic history.

Chapter 3 provides the background material necessary to understand Egyptian chronology and the problems associated with establishing an accurate history of Egyptian dynasties and kings.

Chapters 4 through 7 cross-reference the Genesis chronology with Egyptian dynastic history. The evidence shows that the Genesis birth and death dates derive from Egyptian king lists and provide an exact one-to-one correlation with the starting dates for Egyptian dynasties and several important Egyptian kings. These correlations begin with the foundation of the First Dynasty (c. 3100 B.C.) and end with the start of the Eighteenth Dynasty, over 1,500 years later. This chronological record enables us to place the mysterious events surrounding the Exodus in their proper historical context.

Chapter 8 reviews the various problems associated with dating the Exodus from biblical data. Then, using correspondencing Genesis and Egyptian dates, it places the biblical data into chronological context and resolves the many contradictions. My analysis places the Exodus in 1315 B.C., during the coregency of Ramesses I and Sethos I. Such a date means that Moses and Akhenaten were children together, raised and educated at the same time in the royal household of King Amenhotep III.

Chapter 9 provides an overview of historical matters associated with Pharaoh Akhenaten, including the nature of his revolution, the deterioration of Egypt's foreign empire under his reign, and the counter-revolution undertaken by Horemheb.

Chapter 10 moves from the biblical accounts of the Exodus and looks at the event through Egyptian eyes, examining ancient Egyptian texts and the writings of other classical historians. The Egyptian materials parallel the biblical story in many areas but reverse the roles of Moses and the pharaoh, making Moses the cruel ruler and Pharaoh the young child who was hidden away and later returned to liberate his people. Reducing the parallel themes to their essential elements, we learn how Egyptian mythological and literary motifs helped shape the biblical story of Moses. Placing the Egyptian and classical histories alongside the biblical accounts, we learn that upon Horemheb's death Moses launched a military campaign aimed at restoring the Atenists to the throne, but failed in the effort and led his followers out of Egypt.

Chapters 11 through 13 place the patriarchal history in mythological perspective. The evidence shows how the early Israelites adapted Egyptian myths about the god Osiris and his family and transformed them into stories about distant human ancestors, removing them from the magical realm of Egyptian religion and placing them in the hands of the one and only God of Israel. The chapters trace most of the major events in the lives of the Hebrew patriarchs and set forth many of the Egyptian myths and stories upon which the biblical accounts were based.

Chapter 14 examines the matter of the Twelve Tribes of Israel. There we find that even the biblical writers were unsure of how many tribes existed or whether or not they conquered Canaan. The evidence shows that the Exodus group originally included only the two Rachel tribes of Joseph and Benjamin, and that at a later time the Rachel group united with remnants of the Greek Sea Peoples and other non-Hebrew Canaanites to form an alliance against Philistine encroachment. This new alliance became the House of Israel, but it still did not include the Twelve Tribes. At least three alleged tribes, including Judah, Manasseh, and Gad (and perhaps more) did not yet exist. I also examine some Egyptian stories that may have been responsible for the idea that Jacob had twelve sons and that these sons formed a political alliance.

Chapter 15 summarizes the evidence. It shows that Moses served as chief Priest to Pharaoh Akhenaten, ancient Israel originated in the political turmoil following Akhenaten's death, Genesis chronology draws upon Egyptian king lists, patriarchal history derives from Egyptian mythology, and the Twelve Tribes of Israel never existed.

2

The Genesis Birth-and-Death Chronology

The Book of Genesis contains numerous genealogical trees tracing the histories and families of many nations and people. One of these contains some rather unusual information. While the other family trees just list the sequences of births, this particular tree, encompassing some twenty-six generations over several millennia, provides a chronological record of birth and death that begins with the birth of Adam at the dawn of Creation, continues past Noah's Flood, and ends with the death of Joseph, the final event in Genesis.

The people mentioned in this chronology lived lives of extraordinary lengths. Adam, for example, lived for 930 years. And Joseph, the shortest life of all those listed, died at the age of 110. As a general rule, those born closer to Creation lived substantially longer lives than those born later.

The bulk of this chronology appears in Genesis 5 and 11. The former includes births and deaths that occurred before the Flood, and the latter, ending with the birth of Abraham, lists only births and deaths that occurred after the Flood. Other biblical passages permit us to extend the chronology from Abraham's birth to the death of Joseph.

Because this chronology begins in the mythic period of Creation and continues through Noah's Flood, scholars routinely dismissed it as a fabrication. Nevertheless, historians still accept that the chronology may be modeled after other Middle Eastern king lists.[1]

Both the Egyptians and the Babylonians produced ancient king lists, and in both cultures the earliest kings belonged to a mythological period, with many of them each ruling for thousands of years. In both cultures, however, these lists proceeded from a mythological to a historical period, accurately recording a succession of true kings. Historians have had no trouble separating the lists into mythological and historical portions.

The biblical chronology, however, presents something of an anomaly. While it too begins in the mythological period, with several long-lived ancestors, it continues well into the historical era, late into the second millennium B.C., but the people named in this later time still seem to occupy a mythological status, living far longer than any believable human life span, often hundreds of years. Also, none of the people named have turned up in any records as actual rulers among the Hebrews or any other Semitic-speaking nation.

While there is much speculation and writing about the meaning and origin of this chronology, other than the belief that it is modeled after Babylonian-style king lists, no answers have yet come forward that satisfy the scholarly community. Despite the fact that it crosses deeply into the historical era, from which there is much archaeological data, scholars dismiss the entire chronology as fiction. Still, while rejecting the credibility of this list, many scholars still believe that the Genesis patriarchal history (Abraham, Isaac, and Jacob) derives from some historical memories about real people, and that the time frame associated with those memories coincides with the second millennium time frame in Genesis.

In the following few chapters we will follow a different trail. According to the Bible, Moses grew up in the Egyptian royal household. As a royal prince, he would have received the finest education available to an Egyptian. Any perspective he would have had on ancient history before his time would have been deeply influenced by his Egyptian education. His research libraries would have been in the Egyptian temples. His world view would most likely have been Egyptian rather than Canaanite or Mesopotamian. Perhaps, then, a solution to the chronological puzzle lies within Egyptian history rather than Asian.

In this chapter we will take a closer look at the Genesis chronology. In the next chapter we will investigate Egyptian dynastic chronology. Then, in chapters 4 through 7, we will place the two chronologies side by side. Evidence will show that the Genesis birth-and-death chronology is derived from Egyptian king lists and provides a reasonably accurate historical record from which we can draw useful conclusions.

The Documentary Hypothesis

Not so long ago serious scholars considered the Genesis chronology essential to understanding ancient history. Creation and the Flood were routinely accepted as events that happened within the time frame allotted by the Bible. The first five books were routinely accepted as the product of a divinely inspired Moses.

As recently as the seventeenth century, as brilliant a scientist as Sir Isaac Newton devoted much of his energy to writing *The Chronology of Ancient Kingdoms Amended,* in which he attempted to conform the histories of different nations to the chronological claims of Genesis. While it is understandable that early students of the Bible, such as the Hellenistic Jew Demetrius, might carefully comb it for every chronological clue to world history, scientists such as Newton doing so strikes an odd note in today's society. However, in Newton's time geology and archaeology had not yet advanced into disciplined sciences, and two hundred years separated Newton from Darwin's theory of evolution. Then, belief in Creation and the Flood did not require any suspension of scientific understanding.

Newton, like most of his contemporaries, also believed that the first five books of the Bible, (Genesis, Exodus, Leviticus, Numbers, and Deuteronomy, known collectively as the Torah in Hebrew and the Pentateuch in Greek) were written by a divinely inspired Moses. What few voices that could be heard in opposition were dismissed as heretics. The first important scholar to argue openly against the prevailing view was the sixteenth-century British philosopher Thomas Hobbes, who gathered a large body of facts and statements inconsistent with the principle of Mosaic authorship.[2] Only a few years later, Spinoza, the Dutch philosopher, and Isaac de la Peyrere, a French Calvinist, independently published similar assertions. De la Peyrere was arrested and forced to recant; Spinoza was condemned by Jews, Catholics, and Protestants.

In challenging the idea that Moses was the sole author of the Torah, these critics noted that several passages attributed to his hand claim that certain things were still true "to this day," indicating that they were written well after Moses died.[3] Consider this example: In Deuteronomy 3:14, we are told that Jair, a son of Manasseh, captured the territory of Argob and called it Bashanhavothjair. The details are placed in the mouth of Moses and tell part of the story of Israel's wanderings in the wilderness. But after stating that Jair renamed the territory, the author adds that the city is still called by the new name "unto this day." If the naming of the city occurred during Moses's lifetime, why would the author point out that this new name is still used "unto this day"? It is obvious that the passage was written long after the death of Moses, and that the author used the fictitious device of making Moses the author of the narrative.

Perhaps the most powerful argument against Moses being the sole author of the first five books of the Bible is that the text describes his death, a fact that seems out of place in a book attributed to his hand. Those defending its sole authorship by Moses argue that the passage about his death is just a prophetic rendering of the future. But Deuteronomy 34:6 makes the odd claim that Moses is buried in Moab and that the location of his grave is unknown "unto this day," a clear indication that the passage was written long after Moses died.

In the seventeenth and eighteenth centuries, scholars paid increasing attention to the interesting problem of biblical doublets—the retelling of the same story with slight variations in details. To list just a few, there were two stories of Creation, two stories of the covenant between God and Abraham, two stories in which Abraham told a foreign king that his wife was his sister, two stories of Abraham naming Isaac, and two stories about how many animals were taken aboard Noah's ark. Even in translation, many of these variations and conflicts were obvious.

The first two chapters of Genesis illustrate this problem. Genesis 1 places the arrival of man and woman after the creation of other creatures and plant life, but in Genesis 2 man appears before creatures and plant life, and woman appears afterward. The orthodox dismiss such claims of inconsistency by arguing that what seemed to be contradictions were only subtle lessons that required proper exegesis and explanation. And if that meant wrenching the plain meaning out of context and beyond recognition, so be it. In line with this view, they argued that Genesis 2 did not contradict Genesis 1; it only supplemented the first story with additional details about what happened between the arrival of Adam and the arrival of Eve. That this explanation entirely fails to resolve the contradiction is apparently of no moment, as if the making of a clever argument is as legitimate as the making of a logical one.

By the latter part of the nineteenth century this debate took on new dimensions. Analysis of the doublets showed a startling pattern. After separating them into parallel sets of stories, each was found to use different names to refer to God. One always used the divine name *Jahweh*, the other used the more common name Elohim. What's more, if the sets were separated and the Jahweh and Elohim passages were studied independently, one found characteristic themes and styles distinguishing the two accounts, suggesting that two different manuscripts had been merged into one. The Jahweh source was called "J" and the Elohim source was referred to as "E."

Further research into the two-document theory yielded other new discoveries. The Bible combined not two source documents but *four*. Analysis of the E document showed that most of it was derived from a third source concerned mostly with matters relating to the priesthood and the laws. Because of its priestly nature, this third source was called "P." The fourth source, known as "D," seemed confined to the Book of Deuteronomy.

There was also the matter of the Genesis chronology. Located primarily in chapters 5 and 11, it bears a stylistic resemblance to the P source, but some scholars think it may originally have belonged to a fifth source dubbed the Book of Generations.[4] The claim that the Five Books of Moses were assembled from earlier source documents is referred to by scholars as the Documentary Hypothesis. Today, hardly a biblical scholar in the world actively working on the problem would claim that Moses or any other single individual wrote the Torah.[5]

Dating the Sources

Determining when these source texts were written presents another interesting problem. Hampered by the lack of extant manuscripts dated earlier than the fourth century B.C., historians attempt to extract meaningful data by examining the separate sources for clues about issues and events that could have only occurred within certain time frames, such as references to external events having independent corroboration.[6] Richard Elliot Friedman, who has studied this question extensively, draws the following conclusions: The J author wrote between 922 and 722 B.C., before the Assyrian destruction of the northern kingdom of Israel[7]; E appeared between 848 and 722 B.C., also before the Assyrian conquest;[8] D belongs to the reign of Josiah, king of Judah about 622 B.C.;[9] and P appeared between 722 and 609 B.C.[10] D and P, therefore, date to after the Assyrian conquest but before the Babylonian conquest. As to the Genesis chronology, no one can satisfactorily explain when it came into existence, what it means, or what its original source was.

Still, determining the theoretical dates of the sources does not tell us when the manuscripts were edited and redacted into their present form. It is widely accepted, though not universally, that the Torah was completed no earlier than the sixth century B.C., and very probably in the fifth century B.C., though not without a significant amount of editing.

It should also be noted that this final editing was not a mere compilation or collation of alternative histories. It was a major reconstruction, an attempt to weave a seamless narrative out of these conflicting threads. In a few short paragraphs one cannot begin to do justice to the wealth of scholarly research, analysis, and debate aimed at recovering the original meanings and contexts.

Left unexamined here are the nature of the political, religious, and philosophical arguments that stirred the passions of the source authors, as well as more esoteric issues concerning additional sources, coauthors, and sequential authors. Most of the conflicts stem from disputes that reflect either the post-Solomon split between the kingdom of Israel and the kingdom of Judah, the political feuds between opposing political factions, or the struggles of various factions for control of the priesthood. Suffice it to say that the bitterness inherent in the opposing views found its way into altered histories, distorted records, and out-and-out character assassinations aimed at many of the Hebrews' earliest heroes.

As late as the authorship of these sources may have been, large portions of the material were certainly based on still earlier texts and beliefs. The common history shared by all the sources demonstrates the prior existence of a communal experience or tradition central to the beliefs of the later authors. Textual differences often reflect the shadings of political dispute, not disagreements over historical authenticity. The Bible itself makes reference to earlier source works. Joshua 10:14, for example, mentions a Book of Jasher, and the Second Book of Kings repeatedly refers to books that chronicle the kings of Judah and Israel. None of these books has yet been found, nor can we say what was in them independent of the alleged biblical epitomes, but the context leaves little doubt that earlier sources existed.

Catastrophism Versus Evolution

The nineteenth century witnessed not only the emergence of the Documentary Hypothesis but also of important scientific doctrines that cast additional doubt on the reliability of the Genesis chronology. The most important was Darwin's theory of evolution, which called into question the entire biblical account of the Creation, Flood, and succeeding development of biological life. If change took millions of years to work through the genetic chain, as implied by the theory of evolution, then Creation couldn't have occurred only a few thousand years earlier.

The theory of evolution also challenged the then-prevailing scientific doctrine of Catastrophism. This doctrine held that major changes in the earth's structure were due to cataclysmic events, earthquakes, tidal waves, and crashing comets—a theory scientifically consistent with biblical Creation. But with the march of the theory of evolution, Catastrophism quickly fell by the wayside.

Another nineteenth-century challenge to the Genesis chronology came through the emergence of archaeology as a scientific discipline. Because of their interest in biblical studies, archaeologists devoted much of their attention to the lands mentioned in the Bible. This led to the discovery of evidence that often contradicted biblical claims. Jericho, for instance, was uninhabited at the time Joshua could have reasonably been expected to have brought the walls tumbling down.

The convergence of these academic streams overflowed the banks of fundamentalist biblical inerrancy, consigning much of Genesis to the realm of myth, including the Genesis chronology. Ironically, recent advances in Egyptian archaeology enable us to demonstrate that the Genesis chronology is derived from a historically accurate chronology of Egyptian dynasties.

Dating Creation

Before we turn to the matter of correlating the Genesis chronology with the Egyptian king lists, we must first resolve two questions: Which of several Genesis chronologies should be followed, and what starting date should be used for Creation? We have at least three different Genesis chronologies: the "Masoretic" Hebrew version, from which the King James Bible derives; the Septuagint version, a Greek translation of an earlier unpreserved Hebrew text; and the Samaritan version, an alternative rendition of the Hebrew text. Among these texts, there is a significant discrepancy over the number of years between the Creation and the Flood. The Septuagint records a longer period of time than the Masoretic, primarily because the birth dates of several pre-Flood patriarchs are pushed back by a century, causing several additional centuries to separate the Creation from the Flood. The Samaritan version gives shorter time spans than the other two.

Scholars generally accept the Masoretic version as the most accurate reproduction of the original biblical manuscript, and that is the one followed in this book. However, there is one instance in which I will refer to a life span in the Septuagint version. While the Septuagint and the Masoretic texts disagree about when, in an ancestor's life, a certain child was born, in almost every instance they agree on the overall length of the ancestor's life span. The one important exception is the life span of Lamech, the father of Noah. The Masoretic text says that he lived 777 years, but the Septuagint gives him a duration of 753 years. We have no way of knowing which is the original life span, so in the course of my analysis I will also use the Septuagint's 753 years. When I use the Septuagint figure I will identify Lamech as Lamech (lxx).

This still leaves the question of what starting date to use for Creation. Jews who follow the Masoretic text date Creation to 3761 B.C.; Luther, using the same text, concluded in his *Supputatio annorum mundi* that Creation occurred in 3960 B.C.; and James Ussher, the seventeenth-century archbishop of Amargh, also using the Masoretic text, was convinced that the date was 4004 B.C. The last is suspect because biblical scholars in Ussher's time believed that Christ was born in 4 B.C., and Ussher's Creation date conveniently falls exactly 4,000 years earlier. These small variations in interpretation are primarily the result of the previously noted biblical inconsistencies concerning the date of the Exodus. My work uses the traditional Jewish date of 3761 B.C.

Unrecognized Egyptian Influences

Until now, studies of pre-Exodus biblical chronology suffered from a form of tunnel vision—the unswerving view that Israel emerged in either Mesopotamia or Canaan. The astonishing surface similarities between the Genesis Flood myth and that of the Babylonians certainly suggested that this was the correct approach, and analyses of Genesis were always based on cross-references of the histories, myths, and cultures of these Asiatic regions. Biblical scholars generally consider the Genesis chronology little more than an imitation of Near Eastern king lists, without any historic validity of its own. As some have argued, attributing long lives to ancient ancestors in the ancient Near East, as in the Sumerian and Babylonian king lists, demonstrated the semi-divine nature of an individual; the Genesis author, they suggest, simply adopted this practice with respect to the early patriarchs.[11]

This view so dominates biblical scholarship that no one seems to have thought to compare the Genesis chronology with Egyptian chronology, even though prior to the Exodus the Israelites allegedly spent hundreds of years in Egypt. Moses's own perspective on the unfolding of history would have been Egyptian, not Canaanite or Mesopotamian.

Despite small disagreements in several areas of chronological reconstruction, Egyptologists have currently established a reliable model of Egyptian dynastic history, enabling them to determine the starting date of each dynasty within a few years of its occurrence, as well as the dates most kings came to the throne. Later chapters will show that the Genesis birth and death dates, counting from the year of Creation, unquestionably derive from Egyptian king lists and were intended to mark off a chronological history of the world, from the Creation to the Exodus, as the Egyptians knew it. But why should the historians and scholars have overlooked such an obvious connection?

Three reasons explain this failing. First, there are not many academics who are experts in both Egyptian and biblical studies, and of those who did exist, many lived at a time when the Egyptian chronology was still in a high state of flux. Second, most Egyptologists and many biblical scholars tended to utilize biblical Creation dates other than the traditional Jewish date of 3761, preferring instead dates such as Bishop Ussher's 4,004, or Luther's 3960. Using the wrong Creation date causes a misalignment between the Genesis chronology and the Egyptian chronology, making it almost impossible to see the actual one-to-one correspondences between the two lists. Third, biblical scholars consider Egyptian culture alien to the biblical experience.

Genesis 5 and 11

Beginning with Adam, Genesis records a series of births and deaths in such a way that we can tell how many years after Adam's birth each child was born and how long the parent lived. Adam, for instance, lived 930 years, and when he was 130 years old he had a son named Seth. By dating Adam's birth to the year of Creation, 3761, we can assign an absolute date for each of the births and deaths recorded. For example, Adam died in 2831, *after* the founding of Egypt's First Dynasty. By tracing all the chronological links between Adam and Joseph, we can date Joseph's death to 1454 B.C., a date that will be most helpful in resolving many of the problems in dating the Exodus.

Table 2.1
The Birth-and-Death Chronology in Genesis 5

Generation	Years After Creation	Age at Birth of Son	Life Span	Birth Year	Death Year
Adam	0	130	930	3761	2831
Seth	130	105	912	3631	2719
Enos	235	90	905	3526	2621
Cainan	325	70	910	3436	2526
Mahalaleel	395	65	895	3366	2471
Jared	460	162	962	3301	2339
Enoch	622	65	365	3139	2774
Methuselah	687	187	969	3074	2105
Lamech	874	182	777	2887	2110
Lamech(lxx)			753		2134
Noah	1056	500		2705	
Shem	1556			2205	

Dates are B.C. Adam's birth is placed in 3761, the date of Creation in Jewish tradition. The entry for Lamech (lxx) comes from the Septuagint version of the chronology, which gives him a different life span than does the Masoretic text.

Genesis 5

Genesis 5 spans eleven generations and 1,656 years, from the birth of Adam in 3761 B.C. (the year of the Creation) to the death of

Methuselah, who died in 2105, five years after his son Lamech. Table 2.1 summarizes the chronological information along with the death date of Lamech (lxx). (Note the omission of both Noah's and Shem's dates of death. This is because Genesis 5 only records births and deaths that occurred before the Flood, and Noah and Shem both died afterward.)

Genesis 7:6 places the Flood in Noah's 600th year, which gives it a date of 2105 B.C. From table 2.1 you can see that this is the same year in which Methuselah died. Additionally, Genesis 9:28–29 notes that Noah lived 350 years after the flood, giving him a death date of 1755[12] (and making him a contemporary of Abraham). Genesis 11 gives us Shem's death date.

The Genesis 5 chronology runs as follows:

1   This is the book of the generations of Adam. In the day that God created man, in the likeness of God made he him;
2   Male and female created he them; and blessed them, and called their name Adam, in the day when they were created.
3   And Adam lived an hundred and thirty years, and begat a son in his own likeness, after his image; and called his name Seth:
4   And the days of Adam after he had begotten Seth were eight hundred years: and he begat sons and daughters:
5   And all the days that Adam lived were nine hundred and thirty years: and he died.
6   And Seth lived an hundred and five years, and begat Enos:
7   And Seth lived after he begat Enos eight hundred and seven years, and begat sons and daughters:
8   And all the days of Seth were nine hundred and twelve years: and he died.
9   And Enos lived ninety years, and begat Cainan:
10 And Enos lived after he begat Cainan eight hundred and fifteen years, and begat sons and daughters:
11 And all the days of Enos were nine hundred and five years: and he died.
12 And Cainan lived seventy years, and begat Mahalaleel:
13 And Cainan lived after he begat Mahalaleel eight hundred and forty years, and begat sons and daughters:
14 And all the days of Cainan were nine hundred and ten years: and he died.

15 And Mahalaleel lived sixty and five years, and begat Jared:

16 And Mahalaleel lived after he begat Jared eight hundred and thirty years, and begat sons and daughters:

17 And all the days of Mahalaleel were eight hundred ninety and five years: and he died.

18 And Jared lived an hundred sixty and two years, and he begat Enoch:

19 And Jared lived after he begat Enoch eight hundred years, and begat sons and daughters:

20 And all the days of Jared were nine hundred sixty and two years: and he died.

21 And Enoch lived sixty and five years, and begat Methuselah:

22 And Enoch walked with God after he begat Methuselah three hundred years, and begat sons and daughters:

23 And all the days of Enoch were three hundred sixty and five years:

24 And Enoch walked with God: and he was not; for God took him.

25 And Methuselah lived an hundred eighty and seven years, and begat Lamech:

26 And Methuselah lived after he begat Lamech seven hundred eighty and two years, and begat sons and daughters:

27 And all the days of Methuselah were nine hundred sixty and nine years: and he died.

28 And Lamech lived an hundred eighty and two years, and begat a son:

29 And he called his name Noah, saying, This same shall comfort us concerning our work and toil of our hands, because of the ground which the LORD hath cursed.

30 And Lamech lived after he begat Noah five hundred ninety and five years, and begat sons and daughters:

31 And all the days of Lamech were seven hundred seventy and seven years: and he died.

32 And Noah was five hundred years old: and Noah begat Shem, Ham, and Japheth.

Genesis 11

After some interruption for the story of Noah's Flood and the events immediately thereafter, the Genesis chronology resumes at

Genesis 11:10. Table 2.2 summarizes the chronological information it contains.

Table 2.2
The Birth-and-Death Chronology in Genesis 11

Generation	Years After Creation	Age at Birth of Son	Life Span	Birth Year	Death Year
Shem	1556	100	600	2205	1605
Arphaxad	1656	35	438	2105	1667
Salah	1691	30	433	2070	1637
Eber	1721	34	464	2040	1576
Peleg	1755	30	239	2006	1767
Reu	1785	32	239	1976	1737
Serug	1817	30	230	1944	1714
Nahor	1847	29	148	1914	1766
Terah	1876	70	205	1885	1680
Abram	1946			1815	

Birth and death dates are B.C.

The relevant text runs as follows:

10 These are the generations of Shem: Shem was an hundred years old, and begat Arphaxad two years after the flood:
11 And Shem lived after he begat Arphaxad five hundred years, and begat sons and daughters.
12 And Arphaxad lived five and thirty years, and begat Salah:
13 And Arphaxad lived after he begat Salah four hundred and three years, and begat sons and daughters.
14 And Salah lived thirty years, and begat Eber:
15 And Salah lived after he begat Eber four hundred and three years, and begat sons and daughters.
16 And Eber lived four and thirty years, and begat Peleg:
17 And Eber lived after he begat Peleg four hundred and thirty years, and begat sons and daughters.
18 And Peleg lived thirty years, and begat Reu:
19 And Peleg lived after he begat Reu two hundred and nine years, and begat sons and daughters.
20 And Reu lived two and thirty years, and begat Serug:
21 And Reu lived after he begat Serug two hundred and seven years, and begat sons and daughters.

22 And Serug lived thirty years, and begat Nahor:
23 And Serug lived after he begat Nahor two hundred years, and begat sons and daughters.
24 And Nahor lived nine and twenty years, and begat Terah:
25 And Nahor lived after he begat Terah an hundred and nineteen years, and begat sons and daughters.
26 And Terah lived seventy years, and begat Abram, Nahor, and Haran.

. . .

32 And the days of Terah were two hundred and five years; and Terah died in Haran.

Inconsistencies Between Genesis 5 and 11

Before proceeding further, we should take note of a small inconsistency between Genesis 5 and 11. Genesis 11:10 says that Arphaxad was born two years after the Flood, in Shem's one hundredth year, but Genesis 5:32 says Shem was born in Noah's five hundredth year, 2205 B.C., which makes his one hundredth year 2105, the year of the Flood. The two passages contradict each other, leaving the pre-Flood and post-Flood lists out of sync by two years.

Biblical exegesis cannot explain away this metaphysical impossibility, but textual analysis offers us a clue as to how it came about. If you compare a typical birth passage in Genesis 5 to a typical birth passage in Genesis 11, you will notice a slight variation in the phrasing. Consider Genesis 5:6–8 and 11:14–15, each of which is representative of its respective chapters:

Genesis 5:6–8
6 And Seth lived an hundred and five years, and begat Enos:
7 And Seth lived after he begat Enos eight hundred and seven years, and begat sons and daughters:
8 And all the days of Seth were nine hundred and twelve years: and he died.

Genesis 11:14–15
14 And Salah lived thirty years, and begat Eber:
15 And Salah lived after he begat Eber four hundred and three years, and begat sons and daughters.

The Genesis 5 text has a summary phrase adding up the number of years lived by each parent, whereas that phrase is missing from the Genesis 11 text. The same pattern occurs throughout both chronologies. This stylistic difference strongly suggests two separate sources were used for these chronologies. (It is also a small hint that both chronologies derived from earlier written sources instead of being made up out of whole cloth.

In any event, a decision has to be made as to which dates to use. Should the pre-Flood dates be made two years later? Should the post-Flood dates be made two years earlier? Or should there be a one-year compromise in both directions? My work follows the second course, placing Arphaxad's birth in Shem's one hundredth year, but using the Genesis 5 dating, which places the one hundredth year in 2105, the year of the Flood. Therefore, the dates in table 2.2 assume that Arphaxad was born in 2105 instead of 2103. In doing so, it must be remembered that all Genesis dates are subject to a two-year margin of error.

Other Birth and Death Dates

Although Genesis 11 only gives Abraham's birth date, 1815 B.C., Genesis 25:7 tells us that Abraham lived 175 years. Therefore, we can date his death to 1640. The chronology for Abraham's two son's, Isaac and Ishmael, as well as for Jacob and Joseph, also appears in Genesis chapters other than 5 and 11.

Genesis 21:5 places Isaac's birth in Abraham's one hundredth year, and Genesis 35:28 says that Isaac died at the age of 180. Calculating from Abraham's one hundredth year gives Isaac's birth and death dates as 1715 and 1535.[13]

Another player whom we will investigate in the course of our chronological cross-references is Ishmael, son of Abraham and older brother of Isaac. Genesis 16:16 says that he was born in Abraham's eighty-sixth year. This gives him a birth date of 1729.[14] Genesis 25:17 says that Ishmael lived for 137 years, which gives him a death date of 1592.

From Genesis 25:26 we know that Jacob was born in Isaac's sixtieth year, and from Genesis 47:28 we know that he died at the age of 147. Calculating from Isaac's sixtieth year, we can determine that Jacob was born in 1655 and died in 1508.[15]

Calculations for Joseph's birth and death are a little more complicated. Joseph had become prime minister of Egypt after interpreting
the pharaoh's unusual dream and predicting that there would be
seven good harvest years followed by seven years of famine. The
seven good years began with his appointment as prime minister,
which Genesis 41:46 places in Joseph's thirtieth year. Genesis 47:28
indicates that Jacob came to Egypt in his 130th year, and Genesis
45:6 indicates that was the second year of the famine. Because the
second year of famine occurred in Joseph's ninth year as prime minister, we can place his thirty-ninth year in Jacob's 130th year, giving
Joseph a birth date of 1564 and placing his appointment as prime
minister in 1534.[16] Genesis 50:26, the last verse of the Book of
Genesis, says Joseph lived 110 years, which dates his death to
1454.

The Sons of God

Genesis 6:1–3 preserves one of the more problematic biblical stories.
It tells of how God's anger at mankind, leading to his unleashing of
the Flood, was kindled by the actions of the Sons of God:

> And it came to pass, when man began to multiply on the face of
> the earth, and daughters were born unto them, That the sons of
> God saw the daughters of men that they were fair; and they
> took them wives of all which they chose. And the LORD said,
> My spirit shall not always strive with man, for that he is also
> flesh: yet his days shall be *an hundred and twenty years.* [Emphasis
> added]

This famous passage about the "sons of God" and the "daughters
of men" has long puzzled biblical scholars. Who were these sons of
God, and why did their actions trigger God's wish to destroy mankind?

The answer will be given in a later chapter. For now, note that the
triggering event occurred 120 years before the Flood. Above, we saw
that the Flood occurred in 2105, the same year that Methuselah
died. This dates the actions of the sons of God to 2225.

Table 2.3 summarizes all the birth and death dates calculated in
this chapter.

Table 2.3
The Birth-and-Death Chronology in Genesis

Generation	Birth Year	Death Year	Life Span
Adam	3761	2831	930
Seth	3631	2719	912
Enos	3526	2621	905
Cainan	3436	2526	910
Mahalaleel	3366	2471	895
Jared	3301	2339	962
Enoch	3139	2774	365
Methuselah	3074	2105	969
Lamech	2887	2110	777
Lamech(lxx)		2134	753
Noah	2705	1755	950
Sons of God	2225 (date of God's anger)		
Shem	2205	1605	600
(Noah's Flood,	2105)		
Arphaxad	2105	1667	438
Salah	2070	1637	433
Eber	2040	1576	464
Peleg	2006	1767	239
Reu	1976	1737	239
Serug	1944	1714	230
Nahor	1914	1766	148
Terah	1885	1680	205
Abraham	1815	1640	175
Ishmael	1729	1592	137
Isaac	1715	1535	180
Jacob	1655	1508	147
Joseph	1564	1454	110

Dates are B.C. Adam's birth is placed in 3761, the date of Creation in Jewish tradition. The life span for Lamech (lxx) comes from the Septuagint version.

3

The Throne of Horus

Modern Egyptologists divide Egypt's pharaonic history into thirty-one dynasties, beginning with the unification of Upper and Lower Egypt, at about 3100 B.C., and ending with the conquest of Egypt by Alexander the Great, at about 332 B.C. In order to better reflect Egypt's political and historical trends, these scholars prefer to group those dynasties according to the following convention:

Dynasties	*Collective Title*	*Time Frame* (B.C.)
I–II	Archaic Period	c. 3100–2700
III–VI	Old Kingdom	c. 2700–2100
VII–X	First Intermediate Period	c. 2200–2040
XI–XII	Middle Kingdom	c. 2134–1786
XIII–XVII	Second Intermediate Period	c. 1786–1576
XVIII–XX	New Kingdom	c. 1576–1087
XXI–XXXI	Late Dynastic Period	c. 1087–332

The dates given here represent only one particular set of estimates among several possible alternatives. Egyptologists still disagree over many issues concerning the correct dynastic chronology. The basic estimates, though, rarely differ by more than a couple of decades. Further below, and in the next four chapters, we will look at some of the issues involved, though our inquiries will end with the Nineteenth Dynasty.

The dynastic scheme above is not necessarily the one followed by the ancient Egyptians. It is traced to the writings of Manetho a third-century B.C. Egyptian priest, who, at the urging of King Ptolemy, the Greek ruler of Egypt, wrote a history of his native land. Still, the Egyptian archaeological record does indicate the existence

41

of a dynastic structure consistent with, if not identical to, the above arrangement.

Manetho's history was apparently quite popular and widely circulated. Regrettably, no original copy of his manuscript exists. What we do have are heavily edited and redacted extracts preserved by other writers.

Our three chief sources for Manetho are Josephus, the Jewish historian of the first century A.D., and two chronological summaries by the Christian historians Africanus (in the third century) and Eusebius (in the fourth century).

The Josephus passages contain mostly narrative text and deal primarily with the events of the Second Intermediate Period and the Eighteenth and Nineteenth Dynasties. Although the Josephus material spans the equivalent of several dynasties, he omits any reference to numbered dynasties or dynastic breaks. The only political division occurs between the Hyksos and the Thebans. (The Hyksos were a foreign group of rulers who conquered much of Egypt during the Second Intermediate Period and were expelled by the king of Thebes at the start of the Eighteenth Dynasty.)

On the other hand, the Africanus and Eusebius copies omit almost all the narrative details from Manetho's history, preserving only an occasional brief anecdote about one king or another. However, they do provide a chronological record of Egypt's dynasties beginning with the predynastic reigns by various gods and continuing through the thirty-one dynasties. In many instances they give the names of the kings and how long they ruled. Although both texts share the same dynastic framework, they often disagree about how long various kings ruled or how many kings belonged to a particular dynasty. The Africanus and Eusebius chronologies serve as the model for the dynastic scheme now in use by Egyptologists.

At this time we cannot know whether Manetho himself had such an arrangement or whether the numbered dynasties are the work of an intermediate redactor. The Josephus and Africanus-Eusebius versions conflict on this point. Still, attributing this scheme to Manetho is so deeply ingrained in the academic conscience, and relies on so many centuries of usage, that scholars continue to refer to this dynastic arrangement as the Manetho model.

Despite this consensus, many scholars still doubt whether certain dynasties even existed. Particularly troubling are the Seventh, Eighth, Ninth, Tenth, Fourteenth, and Sixteenth, all of which belong to either the First or Second Intermediate periods. Also the only evidence for a division between the First and Second Dynasties comes from the Manetho king list. No other record corroborates its existence.

Nevertheless, various archaeological finds, particularly other ancient king lists and monumental inscriptions, indicate that Manetho must have worked from genuine sources. Most of his unreliable material falls within the First and Second Intermediate Periods. These two eras were extremely chaotic, and the events of those eras are poorly documented. Even today Egyptologists can do little more than speculate about these two periods. For this reason, Egyptologists tend to forgive Manetho for those errors, arguing that his records must have been disorganized.

However, the discovery of several ancient king lists and numerous inscriptions with chronological information about how long a particular king ruled has enabled Egyptologists to supplement Manetho and put together a reasonably accurate chronological framework for Egyptian dynasties and kings. Consequently, the Manetho Model serves as the foundation of Egyptian dynastic chronology, but it is used cautiously, with scholars frequently amending and adapting it to fit archaeological evidence. The most important of these ancient king lists are:

1. *The Table of Abydos:* At Abydos, on the wall of the Temple of Sethos I, the Table of Abydos gives a series of seventy-six kings in chronological order, starting with the first ruler of the First Dynasty and ending with Sethos I of the Nineteenth Dynasty.[1] A mutilated copy of this list was also found in the Temple of Ramesses II. The more complete list arranges the kings in two rows, the lesser list in three rows.[2] The table omits dynasties seven through ten (the First Intermediate Period) and thirteen through seventeen (the Second Intermediate Period).[3]

2. *The Table of Sakkara:* Beginning with the sixth king of the First Dynasty, the Table of Sakkara preserves the cartouches of forty-seven (originally fifty-eight) kings, the last listed being Ramesses II.[4] Here, too, this table also omits dynasties seven through ten and thirteen through seventeen.[5]

3. The Table of Karnak: The Table of Karnak lists several kings, beginning with the first king of Dynasty I and continuing to Thutmose
III of the Eighteenth Dynasty.[6] It originally had sixty-one names,
forty-eight of which are legible in whole or in part, but the names are
not in chronological order.[7]

4. The Palermo Stone: Produced in the Fifth Dynasty, the Palermo
Stone provides one of the most interesting of ancient documents. In
its original form it contained a year-by-year record of the first five
dynasties.[8] Once a large slab of black diorite about seven feet long
and two feet wide, only fragments remain. The portions we do have
show one set of marks recording significant events for particular
years and another set referring to the levels of the Nile. Occasional
markings signify a change of reign.[9]

5. The Turin Papyrus (also known as the Turin Canon of Kings): After
Manetho, the Turin Canon is probably the most important of the
king lists. It comes to us on a papyrus prepared during the reign of
Ramesses II, but it is badly damaged and fragmented, with many
pieces missing. In its original undamaged state it contained a sequential list of over three hundred kings.[10] As in Manetho, the kings
are divided into subgroups approximately corresponding to dynasties, and the length of reign for each king has been recorded. Several
of the entries, though, are no longer legible. The Turin Canon lists
fifty-two kings for the first six dynasties, Manetho lists forty-nine,
and there are frequent disagreements between the Manetho and
Turin Canon chronologies.[11]

Even with Manetho, the other king lists, and numerous supple-
mental inscriptions on monuments, reconstructing Egypt's dynastic
history presents a formidable challenge. First, the various king lists
have missing portions, incomplete listings, and conflicting names
and sequences. Second, Manetho's list is the only one that continues
past the Nineteenth Dynasty. Third, Manetho's use of Greek names
for the Egyptian kings made it difficult to cross-reference his king
names with those found in other Egyptian king lists or writings.

Even if he had rendered the names in a more Egyptian manner,
cross-referencing would still be a difficult job. Not only are many
kings' names hard to distinguish from each other, several kings

shared the same names. In the Twelfth Dynasty, for instance, four kings were known as Amenemhe and three others were known as Senwosre. So, which of those several kings did an inscription refer to when mentioning one of those names?

Egyptian kings also had numerous titles and descriptions appended to their name, some of which they shared with other kings. Consider the following translation of the several names associated with Thutmose III. Those within the quotation marks are personal names adopted by the pharaoh; the names outside the quotation marks are epithets common to all pharaohs. Imagine the difficulty in trying to identify a particular pharaoh from an inscription containing only a portion of this full title.

> Life to the Horus "Strong Bull arisen in Thebes," the Two Ladies "Enduring of kingship like Re in heaven," the Horus of Gold, "Powerful of strength, Holy of appearances," the King of Upper and Lower Egypt "Menkheperre," the Son of Re "Dhutmose ruler of truth," beloved of Amen-Re who presides in Ipeteswe, may he live eternally.[12]

Memphis and the Foundation of Egypt

All traditions, including those of Manetho, the Turin Canon, and the tables of Abydos and Karnak, name Menes as the southerner who unified Egypt and founded the First Dynasty, but the archaeological record presents a somewhat different account. The drive to conquer Lower Egypt took place over more than one generation, and no one king can easily be identified as the sole conqueror. The events are vividly portrayed in a series of inscribed mace heads and other archaeological finds. At least three consecutive kings from the south, Scorpion (so-named because of his representation as a scorpion), Narmer, and Hor-Aha participated in the campaign, and on the available evidence any one of those three could have been Menes. None, however, can unequivocally be identified as Menes, nor can the founder of the dynasty be identified as the unifier of Egypt.

The most famous of the relevant artifacts is the Narmer Palette, a beautiful mace head depicting Narmer as king of both Upper and Lower Egypt. On one side, Narmer, wearing the white crown of Upper Egypt and holding a club in his hand, stands guard over a prisoner. Horus, the falcon god, surveys the scene. Narmer also appears on the reverse side, this time wearing the red crown of Lower Egypt. The scene includes two panthers with long intertwined necks, possibly signifying the union of the two territories, and a bull breaking through a fortification. If this were the only evidence, one would be inclined to credit Narmer with the completed conquest, but other finds, such as the one showing Scorpion, Narmer's predecessor, also wearing the crowns of both Upper and Lower Egypt, complicate the picture and leave us without a solution.

The struggle for control of Egypt may have started as a military effort, but the discovery of a tomb for a Queen Neith-Hotep suggests that the war ended with a royal marriage. Neith-Hotep, wife of Narmer and the mother of Hor-Aha, takes her name from the goddess Neith, a northern deity from the delta region of Sais. Because this queen's name indicates northern roots, many Egyptologists suspect that the two warring houses were united by marriage rather than conquest.

Whoever of the three pharaohs Menes was, he established his capital in the city of Hikuptah, a name meaning "Soul of the House of Ptah" (and which the later Greeks pronounced as Aigyptus, giving rise to the modern name of Egypt). Ptah was one of the most important deities in ancient Egypt, and the city, one of the nation's chief religious centers, was home to Ptah's cult. Egyptologists call the city Memphis, a Greek form of the Egyptian name Mn-Nfr, which was the name given to a nearby pyramid built in the Sixth Dynasty by the pharaoh Piopi I. Mn-Nfr translates as "[Piopi is] established and goodly."[13]

The Dynasty's founders were Horus worshipers, and from that time on, with some occasional interruptions, every pharaoh was thought to be a human form of the god Horus. When the pharaoh died he became identified with Osiris, father of Horus, and the new pharaoh became the new human form of Horus.

The designation of Memphis as Egypt's capital was equivalent to making it the seat of Horus's throne, and this endowed the city with special importance. Egyptians saw Memphis as the cradle of authority and viewed the line of kings ruling from Memphis as the only legitimate claimants to the throne. A challenge to the Memphis king was a challenge to Horus himself and could threaten the very stability of the nation.

The Memphite Kingdom

The line of kings ruling from Memphis lasted almost a millennium and encompassed either the first six, seven, or eight dynasties, depending upon which king list you follow. Each one presents a somewhat different perspective on the dynastic chronologies of the Sixth through Eleventh Dynasties.

Manetho's Sixth Dynasty names only six kings ruling for 203 years. He then provides some very bizarre descriptions of Seventh and Eighth Dynasties also ruling from Memphis. His Seventh Dynasty, for instance, consists of seventy kings ruling for seventy days,[14] while his Eighth Dynasty consists of twenty-seven kings reigning for 146 years, a length of time far too long for such a possible dynasty.[15] Unlike his descriptions of the first six dynasties, no king names are given for the Seventh and Eighth Dynasties.

Where Manetho has six kings ruling 203 years, the Turin Canon names twelve kings ruling 181 years. Unlike Manetho, the Turin Canon shows no additional Memphite Dynasties or Memphite kings after the Sixth Dynasty. Complicating the record, the Table of Sakkara ends the Sixth Dynasty after only four kings and then jumps to the middle of the Eleventh Dynasty, while the Table of Abydos lists twenty-two successive kings in the Sixth Dynasty without any dynastic break, and then it, too, jumps to the middle of the Eleventh Dynasty.

The above confusion stems from the collapse of authority in Memphis sometime during the Sixth Dynasty. Ambitious rivals with local power bases challenged Memphis for the right to rule over their territories. These concurrent pressures produced a wave of anarchy that spread rapidly across the land. A contemporaneous text gives an account of the corruption:

> The bowman is ready. The wrongdoer is everywhere. There is no man of yesterday. A man goes out to plough with his shield. A man smites his brother, his mother's son. Men sit in the bushes until the benighted traveler comes, in order to plunder his load. The robber is a possessor of riches. Boxes of ebony are broken up. Precious acacia-wood is cleft asunder.[16]

A scarcity of records from this time makes it difficult to determine exactly when the Sixth Dynasty came to an end, but a date between 2200 and 2100 B.C. is widely accepted.

Since the king lists show anywhere from four to twenty-two kings in the final line of Memphite rulers, Egyptologists tend to identify the Sixth Dynasty with the twelve kings indicated in the Turin Canon and arbitrarily assign the additional ten kings in the Abydos list to the Seventh and Eighth Dynasties. The consensus holds that these last ten kings had a collective reign of no more than about twenty-five years.

According to a widely accepted reconstruction of the Turin Canon by Alan Gardiner, one of the most respected of all Egyptologists, the Memphis kings of Dynasties One through Six ruled for 955 years, but he acknowledges that this record is not completely reliable.[17] In some cases, the duration of a king's reign as recorded in the Turin Canon conflicts with other chronological records. Also, Egyptologists cannot accurately date the first year of the First Dynasty or the last year of Dynasties Six, Seven, or Eight. Other disagreements concerning the length of each of the individual dynasties and the duration of rule for individual kings also leave the Turin Canon open to question.

At present, Egyptologists consider 955 years to be within a couple of decades of the true duration. In addition, to establish the true duration of the Memphite line we must add perhaps a quarter of a century to the Turin Canon total to account for the ten additional Memphite kings mentioned in the Table of Abydos.

The First Intermediate Period

The First Intermediate Period consists of dynasties seven through ten. We have already described some of the problems associated with Dynasties Seven and Eight. Dynasties Nine and Ten also present some difficulties.

Manetho claims that these two dynasties ruled from Herakleopolis. He assigned the Ninth Dynasty a total of nineteen kings ruling 409 years and the Tenth Dynasty also nineteen kings but ruling only 185 years. As with his Seventh and Eighth Dynasties, he omits, with one exception, all the king names for the two Herakleopolitan dynasties.

The one king named is Achtoes, and Manetho describes him as an especially cruel ruler. Tomb inscriptions and other sources do corroborate the existence of a House of Akhtoy in Herakleopolis during the First Intermediate Period. One such account describes the civil strife devastating the country:

> He cleared the sky, the entire land with him, the princes of Upper Egypt and the magnates of Heracleopolis, the region of the Mistress of the Land being come to repel fighting, the earth trembling . . . all people darting about the towns . . . ing, fear falling upon their limbs. The magistrates of the Great House are under the fear of, and the favourites under respect for, Heracleopolis.[18]

The Turin Canon also refers to a line of kings from Herakleopolis but indicates a combined total of only eighteen kings, almost all of whose names are illegible, but two of whom were named Akhtoy.[19] However, it indicates no more than one dynasty associated with this city. The Tables of Abydos and Sakkara totally omit any reference to a line of Herakleopolitan kings.

Because Manetho has two Herakleopolitan dynasties, each with nineteen kings, and the Turin Canon has one Herakleopolitan line with eighteen kings, Egyptologists are skeptical about Manetho's claim. Many suspect that Manetho somehow duplicated the Herakleopolitan line, making two dynasties where there should have been one. How long the Herakleopolitan kings ruled we cannot say with certainty, but certain correlations in the archaeological record suggest that the Herakleopolitan kings were on the throne when Theban princes established the Eleventh Dynasty, at about 2134 B.C. This would indicate that the Herakleopolitans ruled for at least a century, but how much more we do not know.

A related issue is whether or not the Memphite line of kings petered out before or after the start of a Herakleopolitan dynasty. We lack specific evidence showing any period of concurrent reigns. Some Egyptologists try to fit the Herakleopolitans in after the Sixth (or Eighth) Dynasty and before the Eleventh. The majority, however, believe that at least part of the Herakleopolitan line was concurrent with part of the Memphite line. In either event, the kings of Herakleopolis were obviously seen as illegitimate upstarts by the later chroniclers of the Egyptian king lists, which explains their absence from several of the lists as well as Manetho's remark about Achtoes's cruelty.

The Middle Kingdom

The House of Akhtoy eclipsed Memphis in power, gaining recognition in some of the later texts as the ruling dynasty. Meanwhile, another line of princes from Thebes, then a political backwater and later the southern capital and second most important city after Memphis, grew restless. This Theban family founded the Eleventh Dynasty, its first important ruler coming to the throne at about 2134 B.C. Not long thereafter it rivaled Herakleopolis as a center of power. About one century later (c. 2040), the Theban king Menthotpe II overwhelmed Herakleopolis and once again united Egypt under a single ruler.[20] Reunification marked the end of the First Intermediate Period and the beginning of the Middle Kingdom, which encompassed the Eleventh and Twelfth Dynasties.

Both the Table of Abydos and the Table of Sakkara begin the Eleventh Dynasty with Menthotpe II. The Turin Canon begins much earlier and gives the dynasty a duration of 143 years. The Manetho list omits any names for the kings in this dynasty and gives a duration of only forty-three years, far too short a period even if we begin with Menthotpe II, who by himself ruled for fifty-one years. This suggests that Manetho's forty-three years is actually a truncated version of the Turin Canon's 143 years, the one-hundred character being lost in transmission. If that were the case, then Manetho and the Turin Canon were in perfect agreement.

The ability of Thebes to unite the land and defeat the rebellious Herakleopolitans suggested to the Egyptians that Thebes was favored by the gods. In 1991 the Twelfth Dynasty supplanted the Eleventh. The first king, a Theban named Amenemhe I, was initially seen by some Egyptians as a usurper. But in later years he was looked upon quite favorably, and the Twelfth Dynasty became quite popular among later Theban kings, especially those in the Eighteenth Dynasty.

The Twelfth Dynasty gave way to the Theban Thirteenth Dynasty at about 1786 B.C. Gardiner notes that there seems to be little logic as to why the Egyptians thought the two dynasties should be politically separate, but, he adds, the Turin Canon, Manetho, and the

Sakkara list all record such a division.[21] The first kings of the Thirteenth Dynasty ruled for about ten years. Then followed a period of six years without a king. At about this time Egypt's dynastic history becomes terribly confused.

The above dates for the foundation of the Eleventh Dynasty, the defeat of the Herakleopolitans and the start and end of the Twelfth Dynasty, all assume the accuracy of the traditional majority view of Twelfth Dynasty chronology. In recent years two separate schools of thought have challenged this view, and although both still represent a minority opinion, support for their views has been growing. In this study I adhere to the traditional majority view.

The Second Intermediate Period

Early in the Thirteenth Dynasty, Theban influence remained strong, but rising pressures from the Asian immigrants residing in the northern delta caused a disruption in Theban power. When the Thirteenth Dynasty ended is a matter of speculation; we have no clear evidence on that point.

It was from this Asiatic base that the Hyksos kings arose and eventually came to dominate most, if not all, of Egypt. In the latter part of the eighteenth century B.C. they established a capital at Avaris and dedicated it to the god Set, whom they adopted as the Egyptian god most deserving of their worship. About fifty years later they captured Memphis and established their dominion over most of Egypt.

The capture of Memphis marked the start of the great Hyksos Fifteenth Dynasty, which lasted for about 108 years, according to the Turin Canon. At the end of that time the Thebans expelled the Hyksos and regained control over all of Egypt.

Egyptologists assign Dynasties Thirteen through Seventeen to the Second Intermediate Period, but except for the Great Hyksos Fifteenth Dynasty, it is hard to determine under what terms these existed, if in fact they existed at all. Despite the unreliability of Manetho's history of this era, Egyptologists generally follow his assignment of five dynasties to the Hyksos period.

The prevailing view holds that Dynasties Thirteen and Seventeen ruled from Thebes, holding some authority in Upper Egypt throughout the entire Hyksos era; the Fourteenth Dynasty, based in the northern city of Xois, may have been either a Hyksos dynasty or a local regional power obedient to the Hyksos; the Fifteenth Dynasty was certainly the major Hyksos dynasty; and the Sixteenth Dynasty, if it existed—a very debatable proposition—was probably Hyksos.

No clear chronological line separates the Thirteenth from the Seventeenth Dynasty. Some Egyptologists have even suggested that these two dynastic divisions might be further subdivided into a larger number of dynasties. This is especially true with regard to the last few kings of what is traditionally identified as the Seventeenth Dynasty. Some scholars suspect that these kings formed a political entity separate from their immediate predecessors.

The Theban king who launched the war to drive out the Hyksos was named Kamose. His brother Ahmose successfully finished the job, once again reuniting Egypt and cementing Theban influence in political and theological affairs. Although Ahmose clearly belongs to an earlier dynastic line, his success in reuniting Egypt caused Egyptians to identify him as the inaugurator of the Eighteenth Dynasty. Thebes remained the center of political power for over five hundred years.

The New Kingdom

The Eighteenth Dynasty, centered in Thebes, was the most glorious in all Egyptian history. It established a mighty empire that reached further than at any other time in the nation's history. It produced magnificent works of art and architecture, and its kings are among the most famous in all of ancient history. It is the time of the Thutmoses, great military strategists, and Tutankhamen, the boy king whose grand tomb treasures continue to fascinate us, and it is the age of Akhenaten, the religious heretic who stands at the center of this study. This dynasty lasted approximately 250 years and ended about 1315 B.C.

The last king of the Eighteenth Dynasty was Horemheb. During his last year or so he appointed Ramesses I as his coregent—a general with a northern base. Upon Horemheb's death, Ramesses I became sole ruler of Egypt and shortly thereafter appointed his son Sethos I as coregent.

Egyptologists generally mark the end of the Eighteenth Dynasty with the death of Horemheb, but this convention demonstrates the problems associated with defining when dynasties begin and end. If Horemheb and Ramesses I were coregents, why should the former belong to one dynasty and the latter to another?

Horemheb, like Ramesses I, had no royal blood. He was the first pharaoh after Akhenaten to represent a clean break with Akhenaten's family line. Furthermore, it was he who began the attack against remnants of the Akhenaten cult. Logic suggests that Horemheb should be taken as the starting point for the Nineteenth Dynasty.

In any event, the resolution of that problem need not affect our analysis. We are primarily concerned with time frames. Akhenaten served for seventeen years; his immediate successors were Smenkhkare, Tutankhamen, Aye, Horemheb, Ramesses I, Sethos I, and Ramesses II. Evidence from inscriptions indicates high-year marks for Akhenaten's successors as three, nine, four, twenty-seven,[22] two, eleven, and sixty-seven, respectively. (High-year marks, it should be noted, establish only minimum lengths of reign, not maximums. New evidence could always surface.)

From the beginning of Akhenaten's reign to the end of Horemheb's is then approximately fifty-seven to fifty-nine years. (Ramesses I had a one-year coregency with Horemheb, and Smenkhkare had anywhere from zero to three years of coregency with Akhenaten.) This is somewhat corroborated by an independent inscription from the reign of Ramesses II that refers to a lawsuit in the fifty-ninth year of Horemheb. Many Egyptologists understand this reference to mean that Ramesses II meant to incorporate the reigns of Akhenaten and his successors within that of Horemheb.[23]

Dating the Dynasties

Reconstructing Egyptian chronology and ascertaining the starting dates, durations, and order of Egyptian kings and dynasties was not an easy task. The Egyptians did not date events according to fixed years. Instead, they noted in which year of a pharaoh's reign an event occurred and used that as the reference point. Unless you knew how long each pharaoh served and in what sequence the pharaohs ruled, or used some independent corroboration such as correspondence from a foreign ruler, it is almost impossible to assign specific dates to the start and end of a pharaoh's reign.

The various king lists, our primary sources of information, are essential, but due to either original mistakes or subsequent damage they are insufficient. The missing portions are especially vexing with respect to the First and Second Intermediate periods, making it quite difficult to figure out how much time elapsed between the Old Kingdom and the Middle Kingdom, and then between the Middle Kingdom and the New Kingdom. Only the Turin Canon and Manetho provided any substantial chronological information, but not only was Manetho at odds with the Turin Canon, the different Manetho texts also contradict each other.

For example, the Africanus version of Manetho assigns 184 years to the Fourteenth Dynasty, while a copy of the Eusebius version has 484 years.[24] The Turin Canon, in the portion concerned with the Second Intermediate Period, is badly damaged and may have originally listed as many as 180 kings in six columns, but only about sixty names are readable, and only about twenty of those have been corroborated by independent records.[25]

Inconsistency within the king lists concerning the names, sequences, and durations of the kings, as well as their number within a dynasty, presents additional handicaps. In some cases entire dynasties were omitted. And of these lists only Manetho's continues past the Nineteenth Dynasty, making it difficult to know how great a breach existed between the earlier dynasties and the better-documented dynasties of later classical times.

A related issue is whether any of the dynasties existed concurrently with others. This is particularly important in the First and Second Intermediate periods. According to Manetho's redactors, the Second Intermediate Period consisted of five consecutive dynasties and lasted over 1,000 years. Now, however, we know that some of the dynasties ruled concurrently and that the entire period couldn't have lasted more than about two centuries. Inscriptions on monuments and papyri resolve many conflicts, but troublesome gaps in the historical record still remain.

The Sothic Cycle

At first it seemed that there was no way to reconcile all the records and bring order out of the chaos. Fortunately, a quirk in Egypt's civil calendar led to a solution. The solar year lasts 365¼ days, but the

Egyptian civil calendar, based on a 365-day year, did not allow for the extra quarter day, as we do with the quadrennial leap year. So every year the civil calendar fell another quarter day out of line with the true solar year (a full day every four years, a full month every 120 years). As a result, the civil calendar could not tell farmers when the seasons began and when the Nile flood would begin its annual inundation. An old papyrus states the problem quite poetically:

> Winter is come in the summer, the months are reversed, the hours in confusion.[26]

Because Egyptian agriculture depended upon the Nile flood, farmers needed to know when the river would overflow its banks. Since the civil calendar couldn't be used for that purpose, they had to come up with an alternative way to mark the start of the flood cycle. Fortunately, the priests noticed a correlation between the heliacal rising of the star Sothis and the onset of the Nile flood.[27]

This sighting depended upon both the height of the star above the horizon and the latitude of the observer. In different areas of Egypt sightings could be as much as a day apart, but this was still close enough to permit farmers to make the appropriate arrangements, and the heliacal rising of Sothis came to be celebrated as New Year's Day.

While this solved the immediate problem for the Egyptians, their interest in natural patterns and cycles led them to take one additional step, which provides the key to the chronological puzzle. The Egyptians thought it important that there be harmony between the solar cycle and the Nile flood. Because the civil calendar fell out of synch by one quarter of a day every year, they realized that it should take 1,460 solar years for the civil calendar to lose 365 days.[28] This meant that every 1,460 solar years the New Year on the civil calendar and the heliacal rising of Sothis would coincide, creating harmony between the Nile and the sun. This occurrence was a matter of great religious moment, and from time to time events were recorded as having occurred on a particular date within the 1,460-year period.

This 1,460-year Sothic cycle, also known as the Sothic Year, mimicked the civil calendar. Egyptians divided the Sothic Year into the same pattern of days and months as found in the civil calendar, giving Sothic days (4-year periods) and Sothic months (120-year periods) the same names as those in the civil calendar. This Sothic calendar offered Egyptologists the means to build a skeletal structure for Egyptian chronology.

First, however, they needed to know on what date a Sothic cycle started. Then they had to find some archaeological records linking events in Egypt to specific dates within the Sothic Year. Once they had a Sothic Year date it could be converted into an absolute year by determining how many Sothic days passed from the start of the cycle to the indicated date. Since each Sothic day equaled four years, the calculation would be rather simple.

Unfortunately, historians know of only one reference to the start of a Sothic cycle. The Roman historian Censorinus noted the coincidence of a Sothic New Year and a civil New Year in A.D. 139, during the reign of the Roman emperor Antoninus Pius, a claim that is corroborated by the issuance in Alexandria of a coin commemorating the event.[29] Although the evidence for Censorinus's dating is sparse, Egyptologists have seized upon it as the foundation from which they could establish not only the chronology of ancient Egypt but, by cross-referencing the extensive Egyptian records of Mediterranean and Middle Eastern contacts, much of the chronology of those other areas as well. By counting backwards in 1,460-year cycles, starting with A.D. 139, Egyptologists determined that Sothic cycles would have started in 2781 and 1321 B.C.[30] These dates, however, assumed that the length of a Sothic cycle was always 1,460 years. This assumption was wrong.

The time between the consecutive heliacal risings of Sothis depends on the length of time in which the center of the sun passes from the elliptic meridian of Sothis and returns to that position. If the position of Sothis were fixed this event would take 365.25636 days, what astronomers call the sidereal year, and the Sothic cycle would be 1,460 years long. But Sothis is not fixed in position. It has its own period of motion, which means that a Sothic cycle could vary by as much as ten years.[31]

Theodor Oppolzer first calculated the true length of the Sothic year in 1884. In 1904 Eduard Meyer used those calculations to obtain starting dates for the Sothic cycles before A.D. 139,[32] determining that Sothic cycles began in 2773 and 1317 B.C.[33]

A more recent set of studies, conducted in 1969, found that the cycle preceding A.D. 139 lasted 1,453 years and the one before that

1,456 years, providing alternative starting dates of 1314 and 2770 B.C.[34] Egyptologists still disagree over which set of dates to use, but since the various dates proposed for the start of the Sothic cycle differ by only a few years over several millennia, the overall impact on the chronological framework is not significant.[35] The more difficult problem was obtaining archaeological links to the Sothic cycle.

Sothic Dating for the Eighteenth Dynasty

After much searching, Egyptologists found three important inscriptions connecting three separate kings to a Sothic cycle. One referred to the year 1469 B.C., which fell in an unspecified year of the reign of Thutmose III, another to the ninth year of Amenhotep I, and the last to the seventh year of Senwosre III. Thutmose III and Amenhotep I were from the Eighteenth Dynasty. Senwosre III ruled during the Twelfth Dynasty. This gave us links to the New and Middle Kingdoms.

Next Egyptologists had to determine how many Sothic cycles intervened between A.D. 139 and the Eighteenth Dynasty and the Twelfth Dynasty. If only one complete cycle existed between the Eighteenth Dynasty and A.D. 139, then the dynasty came to power sometime in the sixteenth century B.C. If two cycles occurred, then the Eighteenth Dynasty began about 3000 B.C. Too much historical and contextual data exists to allow for the latter date, and the Eighteenth Dynasty must have started sometime in the sixteenth century.

The time frame established, a date for the ninth year of Amenhotep I could be determined. Initial calculations showed a date of 1536, but soon after a new debate broke out. Did the observation of the heliacal rising of Sothis occur in Thebes or Memphis?[36] The initial calculation assumed Thebes. If Memphis were the location the date had to be adjusted to 1542, and perhaps as early as 1544.[37] Scholars remain divided on the matter, and, as a result, some date the ninth year of Amenhotep I between 1542 and 1544, and others to 1536.

Amenhotep I was the second king of the Eighteenth Dynasty. Allowing for some disagreement over how long his predecessor served and whether there was a coregency between them, the two alternative Sothic dates establish a starting date for the Eighteenth Dynasty somewhere between 1560 and 1577. The 1560 date assumes a twenty-two-year reign for Ahmose (his highest known year mark), a six-year coregency between Ahmose and Amenhotep I, and a Sothic date of 1517 for the ninth year of Amenhotep I. The 1577 date assumes a twenty-five-year reign for Ahmose (the Manetho figure), no coregency, and 1544 as the ninth year of Amenhotep I. Solutions put forth by prominent Egyptologists include Gardiner's 1575, Wente's 1570, and Redford's 1569.

The Sothic reference to an unspecified year in the reign of Thutmose III presented a different problem. In addition to the Sothic reference for Thutmose III, Egyptologists also had correlation's to Egypt's lunar calendar. The lunar calendar, which established the dates of religious festivals, consisted of a twenty-five-year cycle, the number of years it would take for the lunar and civil calendars to coincide. As a result, religious festivals fell on the same civil calendar date every twenty-five years.

The Thutmose references to the lunar calendar allowed for two possible dates upon which that king could have ascended to the throne, 1504 or 1490.[38] Since Thutmose III ruled for fifty-four years and the Sothic date of 1469 B.C. was not connected to any specific year within his reign, both 1504 and 1490 were plausible solutions. Egyptologists still disagree over which starting date to choose.

Sothic Dating and the Nineteenth Dynasty

Determining an end date for the Eighteenth Dynasty and, therefore, the death year of Horemheb affect our analysis of the events surrounding the Exodus and the identity of the pharaoh. This requires that we examine some fixed dates within the Nineteenth Dynasty and a possible connection to the start of a Sothic cycle.

Records indicate a lunar calendar correlation with the fifty-second year of Ramesses II, but the data is somewhat ambiguous. Egyptologists generally agree that this correlation indicates one of three possible starting dates for Ramesses II—1304, 1290, or 1279. Which one to choose causes much debate among scholars. Wente and Van Siclen III, two prominent Egyptologists who have studied the data, suggest that no perfect solution to this problem exists because all three choices assume that the person recording the lunar date made an observational error.[39] One type of error, they say, "could easily be caused by unfavorable atmospheric conditions, when cloudiness, haze, or smoke from village fires might obscure the visibility of a final lunar crescent with the result that New Moon day would be declared one day in advance of actual conjunction."[40] The 1304 and 1279 dates assume just such an error.[41] Advocates of the 1290 date propose that the observers thought they saw a final crescent when none was actually present.[42]

Assuming that a trained observer might, due to blockage, fail to see a crescent rather than mistakenly see one when it wasn't there, most Egyptologists prefer either 1304 or 1279 as the starting date. The twenty-five-year gap between these possibilities leaves a wide margin for error in our effort to pinpoint exactly who was on the throne during the Exodus. Fortunately, we have some other data that can help narrow the options.

Particularly important is the existence of a letter from the Hittite king Hattusili III to the Babylonian king Kadasman-Enlil II seeking a treaty to counteract troubles with Egypt. Since Hattusili III had also signed a treaty with Ramesses II, the question of whether the letter to the Babylonian king was written before or after the Ramesses treaty has some effect on the dating of Ramesses II. Again, Egyptologists are deeply divided on the matter. They argue that if the letter came first it suggests a date of 1290 for the ascension of Ramesses II, and if written after it favors a date of 1304.[43]

Wente and Van Siclen III, who favor 1279, acknowledge that on the basis of the most recent studies of Near Eastern chronology, the evidence supports 1304. But they point to a possible ten-year error in Near Eastern chronology, which could lower the possible date enough to accommodate their 1279 hypothesis.[44] In defense of their position, they cite the author of one such study to the effect that "There is not a single shred of positive evidence in favor of either alternative."[45] Such a claim does not prove that Wente and Van Siclen III are correct, merely that this is possible.

Further evidence in support of the 1304 date for Ramesses II comes from the reign of his predecessor, Sethos I. The highest known year marker for Sethos I is eleven, indicating a minimum term of ten years plus a fraction, and there is an interesting issue concerning the date of his ascension.[46] Referring to the period of the Sothic cycle, Theon, an Alexandrian mathematician, said it started "from Menophres."[47]

Many Egyptologists believe *Menophres* to be a slightly corrupted form of the epithet Mry-n-Pth, which means "beloved of Ptah."[48] This epithet normally appears at the beginning of Sethos I's second cartouche, indicating that the Sothic Year may have started in his reign.[49] Other inscriptions show that this pharaoh identified himself as the inaugurator of a new period, referring to the first and second year of his reign as the Repetition of Births, a term that could easily be identified with the start of the Sothic cycle.[50]

In our examination of the Sothic cycle we saw that at one time it was thought to have started in 1318 B.C. For that reason many Egyptologists dated Sethos I's reign to that year, and it is the date used by the *Cambridge Ancient History*.[51] Such a solution requires that Ramesses II began in 1304 and that Sethos I ruled approximately fourteen years instead of the ten to eleven years supported by the high-year marker. Since many Egyptologists supported one of the later dates, 1290 or 1279 for Ramesses II, they were inclined to dismiss the connection between Sethos I and the Sothic cycle.

As we saw earlier, though, later studies indicated that the Sothic cycle began in 1314, not 1318. If we add Sethos I's ten to eleven years to the proposed 1304 starting date, we arrive at 1314 or 1315 as a starting date, and there is no reason to assume any extra years beyond the eleven indicated by the high-year marker. So if Ramesses II did take the throne in 1304, then linking the start of Sethos I's reign with the start of a Sothic cycle is probably correct. Such a coincidence is hard to resist.

Sothic Dating for the Twelfth Dynasty

Egyptologists also needed to know how long a gap existed between the Twelfth and Eighteenth Dynasties. In between was the Second Intermediate Period, that poorly documented era of political and social chaos. If no Sothic cycle intervened between these two dynasties then the seventh year of Senwosre III had to occur sometime between 1872 and 1877 B.C.[52] If there were an intervening cycle, then the date in question had to be around 3300 B.C. Such an early date seemed unlikely, but the historical record didn't present the same clear historical context as existed for the Eighteenth Dynasty.

The king lists were of little help. Three lacked any references to the Thirteenth through the Seventeenth Dynasties. One, the Table of Karnak, had only a partial list and it wasn't in chronological order. The Turin Canon and Manetho both had chronological information, but, as noted above, they did not provide sufficient reliable information on the Second Intermediate Period.

Further, despite the conflicts in the Manetho numbers, both Africanus and Eusebius indicated that the Second Intermediate Period lasted over 1,000 years, which, even if close to correct, would put the Middle and New kingdoms in separate Sothic cycles. Flinders Petrie, one of the earliest and greatest of Egyptologists, thought, at least in part based on the Manetho numbers, that the Twelfth Dynasty must have occurred in the previous Sothic cycle, creating an approximate break of 1,800 years between the Twelfth and Eighteenth dynasties.[53]

Such an interval has no support in the archaeological record, and the absence of such evidence is the chief argument against the claim. Today, Egyptologists accept that the Twelfth Dynasty and the early Eighteenth Dynasty belong to the same Sothic cycle, yielding a Sothic date of somewhere between 1872 and 1877 B.C. for the seventh year of Senwosre III, with the vast majority of scholars favoring 1872.[54]

Based on this Sothic date, most Egyptologists date the start of the Twelfth Dynasty to 1991 B.C. Then, on the basis of the Turin Canon's claim that the Eleventh Dynasty lasted 143 years, they date the start of the Eleventh Dynasty to 2134 B.C. As to the Twelfth Dynasty itself, a good deal of information about the sequence and dates for the various rulers enables Egyptologists to establish a fairly reliable chronology for its kings. (As noted above, there are at least two minority schools of thought that argue for a different chronology of the Twelfth Dynasty, both of which would lead to a later starting date. Despite some growing support for these views, the majority still accept the traditional chronology.) This dating for the Twelfth Dynasty reduces the Second Intermediate Period to approximately 200 to 250 years.

Of the five dynasties routinely assigned to the Second Intermediate Period, Egyptologists, based on Manetho, associate Dynasties Thirteen and Seventeen with the Theban kings, Dynasties Fifteen and Sixteen with the Hyksos, and Dynasty Fourteen to another line of kings, either native or Hyksos, and perhaps contemporary with the

Thirteenth Dynasty. Opinion is divided about whether the Theban dynasties were truly independent of the Hyksos kings. The lack of any archaeological evidence for a line of kings belonging to a Hyksos Sixteenth Dynasty generates healthy skepticism as to whether it ever existed. Doubts also exist as to whether the Fourteenth Dynasty represented a true dynasty or simply constituted a local line of princes with no real power in the shadow of the Hyksos.

With the three main Sothic dates now well accepted, it could confidently be claimed that the seventh year of Senwosre III occurred between 1872 and 1877 B.C., the ninth year of Amenhotep I between either 1542 and 1544 or in 1536, and some portion of the reign of Thutmose III in 1469 with possible starting dates of either 1504 or 1490. Historians now commanded three beachheads from which they could launch their campaign against chronological confusion, three solid dates from which they could count the number of years between the known dates and other chronologically connected events in the reigns of other kings. Many gaps still existed, along with much disagreement, but a reasonably reliable framework for Egypt's dynastic history had been established.

Before You Read Chapters 4–7

Chapters 4–7 describe what I believe to be one of the most important discoveries ever made in biblical studies. The evidence proves that the Genesis birth-and-death chronology derives from Egyptian king lists and coincides precisely with what Egyptologists refer to as the "high chronology," i.e., a starting date of 1991 B.C. for the Twelfth Dynasty and 1576 to 1574 B.C. for the Eighteenth Dynasty. The Genesis chronology provides accurate starting years for every datable dynasty between the First and the Eighteenth, accurate starting dates for the reigns of several important kings, the start of a Sothic Cycle, and year dates for the occurrence of several major political events, such as the Second and Third unification, the foundation of Avaris by the Hyksos, and the defeat of the Hyksos by Thebes.

Not only does this enable us to resolve most of the chronological debates concerning second millennium chronology for Near Eastern and Mediterranean societies, it provides us with a powerful tool that permits us to place various biblical claims relevant to dating the Exodus in their proper historical and political context.

To appreciate how accurately the Genesis chronology tracks Egyptian dynastic history, consider these examples based on the "high chronology."

Genesis Event	Date	Egyptian Event	Date
Lamech born	2134	Dyn. XI starts	2134
Eber born	2040	Second Unification	2040
Terah dies	1680	Dyn. XV starts	1680
Eber dies	1576	Dyn. XVIII starts	1576–1574
Joseph born	1564	Hyksos defeated	1564
End of 7 Lean Years	1521	Transition from Thutmose I to Thutmose II	1521–1520

In addition, after making a slight adjustment due to the double-counting of coregencies, Genesis has four consecutive birth dates that coincide with the exact starting year for the first four kings of the Twelfth Dynasty.

For Dynasties Eleven through Eighteen Egyptologists can only determine accurate starting dates for five of them, and Genesis has the matching date for four of those, along with accurate starting dates for several Twelfth Dynasty kings. As to the one missing dynastic date, chapter 5 explains why Genesis had a different date.

Unfortunately, even though the evidence is heavily redacted from a longer and more expansive study (see pages 280–82), one cannot lay it out in a dramatic and pulse-pounding narrative. The material consists of much dry data, numerous bits of obscure archaeological references, Egyptological jargon, numerous king lists with confusing, repetitive, and hard-to-remember royal names, summaries of conflicts among Egyptologists, and numerous arithmetical calculations. While the slow and difficult review of that evidence would be highly rewarding on an intellectual level, some readers might prefer to skip over these chapters and return to them after they have read the balance of the book.

For those choosing to skip over the material, it is only necessary to know that given the corroboration by Genesis of Egypt's "high chronology," together with some additional evidence from Egyptian records, we can set forth an accurate chronology for the Eighteenth and early Nineteenth Dynasties. That chronology is set forth in table 7.1 (page 118). With that information, you can proceed to chapter 8, where we determine the date of the Exodus as well as identify the Pharaoh of the Oppression and the Pharaoh of the Exodus.

4

Enoch and Sothis: A Solar Clue

Shifting our attention from Egyptian chronology back to the Genesis chronology, consider Genesis 5. It contains chronological information on the first eleven generations of mankind born before Noah's Flood. Table 2.1 in chapter 2 summarizes what it says, showing each generation's birth and death date along with its life span.

There is something curious about that list. While each generation lived exceedingly long lives, mostly close to or in excess of nine hundred years, Enoch lived only 365 years, less than half as long as the next shortest life.[1] Genesis also singles him out for special mention. It says that "he walked with God." Because a solar year has 365 days, many biblical commentators have suggested that Enoch's life span signifies some sort of solar reference.

E. A. Speiser, author of the Anchor Bible commentary on Genesis, notes the difficulty presented by the Enoch problem:

> Thus Enoch's total of years corresponds to the 365 days in the solar year, and is surely related in some way to the notice of his unprecedented treatment by God, with whom Enoch "walked" . . . A numerical puzzle of an entirely different sort helps to deepen the already profound mystery of Enoch. As the seventh in the line of antediluvian patriarchs, Enoch parallels the Mesopotamian Enmeduranna, who is the seventh king before the Flood according to the best textual evidence. . . . What is more, Enmeduranna's capital city was the ancient center of the sun god of Sippur, which could explain the solar number of 365 that is reserved for Enoch. . . . Yet the slight similarity in names is apparently coincidental.[2]

In the above quote, Speiser refers to the Mesopotamian king lists, which also feature numerous long-lived kings in the period before

the Mesopotamian flood. However, those kings had life spans rang-
ing from 18,600 to 65,000 years, way in excess of those in the Genesis
chronology.

Mesopotamians also believed in a worldwide flood, and the king
lists described above show either nine or ten kings prior to the del-
uge. Because Noah was the tenth generation in Genesis, scholars
generally agree that the Genesis and Mesopotamian flood myths
derive from common sources. But nothing in the Genesis account
requires that its flood myth was written down earlier than the Babylonian captivity, in the sixth century B.C.

While Speiser suggests a possible connection between the 365 solar year reference attached to Enoch and a Mesopotamian city where
a sun god was worshiped, the comparison is wanting. The Mesopotamians did not use a 365-day solar calendar; they used a lunar
calendar of 354 days. (There is some evidence of a Mesopotamian
360-day calendar that existed alongside the regular lunar calendar,
but this was still not a 365-day calendar.[3] The 360-day calendar may
also have been connected to the Mesopotamian numerical system,
which used units of 60 instead of units of 10.)

If Enoch's life span symbolizes the 365-day solar year, why does it
appear in Genesis? Hebrews and all their major non-Egyptian neighbors used a lunar calendar of 354 days, with an extra month periodi-
cally added to keep the lunar calendar in close harmony with the
seasons.[4] The solar calendar belonged mainly to the Egyptians. The
Genesis chronology provides an important clue.

The Sothic Cycle

Enoch died in 2774 B.C. In our examination of the Sothic cycle, we
saw that one cycle began in either 2773 or 2770. Since Enoch's death
coincides with the end of a Sothic cycle according to one set of calculations, it is tempting to simply claim that the Sothic cycle started in
2773 and that Enoch's death marks the end of the previous cycle. On
the other hand, if the Sothic cycle started in 2770, it would seem that
there is no link between it and Enoch's death in 2774.

Both arguments would be wrong, failing to take into account that
as far as the Egyptians knew the Sothic cycle always lasted 1,460
years. They lacked sufficient mathematical and astronomical skills to

accurately measure the Sothic cycle, and, as did the earliest Egyptologists, simply assumed that every four years they lost one day, and that after 1,460 years (365 × 4) the cycle would begin again. Of course, this would leave them with an occasional rude shock at the beginning of a new Sothic cycle, when the heliacal rising of Sothis didn't quite coincide with the start of New Year's Day on the civil calendar. Nevertheless, they would make the appropriate adjustment.

Since recent calculations indicate the start of a Sothic cycle in 1314 B.C., we will use that as our reference point. An Egyptian scribe writing around 1314 would simply assume that the previous cycle started 1,460 years earlier than the 1314 cycle (even though the correct length would only be 1,456 years), yielding the equivalent date of 2774 B.C.—the year Enoch died. If the scribe were preparing a king list and wanted to show when the Sothic cycle started, he would count back 1,460 years and place his marker at whatever event happened in that year—2774 in this case. He would be wrong as to when the cycle actually started, but there would be no way for him to know that, even if there was a record to contradict his finding.

For the sake of argument, assume that his own records showed that the Sothic cycle must have started in the second year of a given pharaoh, but that a separate record showed that the Sothic cycle started in the pharaoh's sixth year. This would occur if the Sothic cycle lasted only 1,456 years. The scribe, unable to conceive of a cycle lasting other than 1,460 years, would either assume that there is a missing record of four years or an error in the source documents.

If the original Genesis chronographer intended the death of Enoch in 2774 to signify the start of a Sothic cycle, then the subsequent cycle should have started in 1314 B.C., 1,460 years later. But does Enoch's death signify the start of a Sothic cycle?

Common sense suggests that a person raised and educated in the Egyptian royal court, as Moses is alleged to have been, would have used Egyptian conventions and practices. And he would have used a Sothic cycle to tie the king list to a particular point in time.

Enoch's life span and date of birth certainly suggest that this patriarch served as a marker for the start of a Sothic cycle, but without more evidence such a conclusion remains only a theory. Still, such a suggestion warrants further investigation into the connection between the Genesis birth-and-death chronology and events in Egyptian history. The next three chapters will explore those relationships and show that the Genesis chronology derives from Egyptian dynastic chronology.

5

Eber and Thebes

When Menthotpe II defeated Herakleopolis and unified Egypt under a single king, Thebes replaced Memphis as the center of political authority. The impact of his achievement on the Egyptian mind can be seen in a temple inscription dating to the Nineteenth Dynasty. In it, the names of Menes, Nebhepetre (Menthotpe II), and Ahmose are linked together, "obviously," says William C. Hayes in the *Cambridge Ancient History*, "as the founders of the Old, Middle, and New Kingdoms."[1]

The bringing together of these three names suggests that the Egyptians of the Nineteenth Dynasty saw the nation's history as divided into three epochs, each initiated by a pharaoh who united the country after a period of discord. First came the period of Memphite rule, initiated by Menes at the start of the First Dynasty and which ended in the chaos of the First Intermediate Period. Next followed the period of Theban rule brought about by Menthotpe II during the Eleventh Dynasty and later subordinated to the Hyksos invaders for almost two hundred years. When Ahmose defeated the Hyksos a second Theban era came into existence, dating from the start of the Eighteenth Dynasty.

Because of the many difficulties in reconstructing the chronological history of Egypt's first two dynasties, Egyptologists cannot set a firm date for the rise of Menes. They commonly place the beginning of the pharaoh's reign at 3100 B.C., give or take 150 years. As to the defeat of Herakleopolis by Menthotpe II, most Egyptologists would accept 2040 B.C. as its date (assuming the validity of the traditional Twelfth Dynasty chronology). And for the start of the Eighteenth Dynasty, for reasons stated in chapter 3, its founding date falls between 1577 and 1542 B.C.

Now consider the Genesis birth and death dates for Eber—2040 and 1576. Astonishingly, they appear to mark two of the three most important dates in Egyptian dynastic history, each denoting the start of a united Egypt under Theban rule. The 2040 birth date coincides exactly with the accepted date for Menthotpe II's conquest. The 1576 death date falls within the very narrow time frame allowed for the start of the Eighteenth Dynasty.

Unfortunately, the lack of a precise starting date for Ahmose's reign leaves the connection between Eber and the Theban conquest dates less than perfect. Given the many Genesis birth and death dates over such a long period of time, it would not be surprising if at least two or three weren't coincidentally close to some historical events in Egypt, either a dynastic foundation date or other important happening. But we need a good deal more correlation before we can establish a connection between the Genesis and Egyptian chronologies.

Table 5.1 shows all the Genesis 11 birth and death dates that fall during Eber's life span—a period of 464 years. His death is the final event in the Genesis 11 chronology. Notice several features of this listing, the importance of which will be explained later.

To begin with, Eber was born first and died last, forming a chronological frame around all the other patriarchs and terminating the Genesis 11 chronology at about the start of the Eighteenth Dynasty. Second, all the births occur during the Middle Kingdom while all the deaths fall in the Second Intermediate Period, suggesting a logical chronological pattern to the births and deaths. Third, Peleg and Nahor are the only two patriarchs who died before their fathers. Fourth, Peleg and Nahor also died at about the same time, 1767 and 1766 B.C., respectively.

In the following pages it will be argued that: All the birth dates following Eber's were intended to coincide with the starting dates for kings of the Twelfth Dynasty, and all the death dates were intended to coincide with either dynastic starting dates during the Second Intermediate Period or with other important political events within that era.

The Twelfth Dynasty

Table 5.2, from Gardiner's *Egypt of the Pharaohs*, shows the traditional chronology of the Twelfth Dynasty.[2] The list of kings has two unusual features. One is the repeated use of the same name by several kings,

Table 5.1
Genesis 11 Birth and Death Dates
During Eber's Life Span

Patriarch	Birth	Death
Eber	2040	1576
Peleg	2006	1767
Reu	1976	1737
Serug	1944	1714
Nahor	1914	1766
Terah	1885	1680
Abram	1815	1640

Dates are B.C.

four of whom adopted the name Amenemhe and three others who used the name Senwosre. The other is the large number of coregencies in this dynasty. Five of the eight rulers share a portion of their reigns with their successors.

Table 5.3 presents an outline of the coregencies. For each king it shows: the number of years shared with his predecessor; the number of years ruled independently of a coregent; and the number of years shared with his successor as coregent. We will return to this data later when we compare the Genesis dates to the Egyptian dates. For now, note that the coregencies add up to nineteen years.

Coregencies create something of an anomaly in Egyptian theology. If the sitting pharaoh represented the god Horus, which of the coregents filled that role? Although coregencies were not unknown prior to the Twelfth Dynasty, they appear to have been extremely rare. The sudden appearance of so many coregencies in one dynasty is a radical departure from tradition. This phenomenon, coupled with the repeated use of names, appears to have caused ancient Egyptian chronographers to make some errors in compiling their king lists, errors which appear to have been replicated in the Genesis chronology regarding the Twelfth Dynasty.

Egyptian king lists provide two chronological histories of the Twelfth Dynasty, one in the Turin Canon and the other in Manetho. Before comparing the Genesis chronology with the Egyptian, let's look at how these lists described this dynasty.

Table 5.2
Standard Chronology of the Twelfth Dynasty

King	Date of Rule	Highest Year Mark	Length of Coregency With Successor
Amenemhe I	1991–1962	30	10
Senwosre I	1971–1928	44	2
Amenemhe II	1929–1895	35	3
Senwosre II	1897–1877	6	2
Senwosre III	1878–1843	33	
Amenemhe III	1842–1797	45	2
Amenemhe IV	1798–1790	6	
Sobeknofru	1789–1786		
Total Years			19

Adapted from Gardiner, *Egypt of the Pharaohs*, 439. Dates are B.C.

Table 5.3
Outline of Twelfth Dynasty Coregencies

King	Coregency With Predecessor	Independent Reign Without Coregents	Coregency With Successors
Amenemhe I		20	10
Senwosre I	10	32	2
Amenemhe II	2	30	3
Senwosre II	3	16	2
Senwosre III	2	34	
Amenemhe III		44	2
Amenemhe IV	2	7	
Sobeknofru		4	
Total Years		187	19

The Turin Canon

For lengths of reigns in the Twelfth Dynasty, the Turin Canon has four complete entries and four damaged entries.[3] The four readable entries are as follows:

Senwosre I	45 years
Senwosre II	19 years
Amenemhe IV	9 years, 3 months, 27 days
Sebeknofru	3 years, 10 months, 24 days

The Turin Canon also says that the dynasty had a total duration of 213 years, 1 month, and 16 days. This is approximately seven years longer than the actual total for the Twelfth Dynasty and indicates some confusion about the treatment of coregencies.

Senwosre I, Senwosre II, and Amenemhe IV each shared portions of their reign with a coregent, but the Turin Canon does not indicate which portions of which reigns were served by coregents. Senwosre I shared ten years with his predecessor and two years with his successor. Senwosre II shared three years with his predecessor and two years with his successor. Amenemhe IV shared two years with his predecessor.

While both of Senwosre I's coregencies are included in the length of his reign, only one of the two coregencies for Senwosre II is included in his reign. The one coregency of Amenemhe IV appears to be included in his length of reign.

This suggests that the Turin Canon author either shortened other reigns to account for some of the additional coregencies or may have mistakenly recorded the lengths of reign for some of the other kings. Unfortunately, it is these other reigns that have damaged entries, which prevents us from knowing how the dating problems were handled.

The following example illustrates the problem. The Turin Canon total for the first king of the dynasty, Amenemhe I, only preserves a "9"[4]—a portion of the total number of years served. But the king served at least into his thirtieth year, which indicates that if the entry weren't damaged, it would have read either "19" or "29." If "19" were the original entry, it would mean that the Turin Canon shortened Amenemhe I's reign by ten years to account for the coregency. If the correct entry were "29," then no adjustment would have occurred and the dynastic total would have been off by an additional ten years.

In any event, we see that as early as the Nineteenth Dynasty, Egyptian scribes had trouble accounting for coregencies and recording an accurate dynastic duration.

Manetho

Manetho's Twelfth Dynasty introduces us to a large number of additional errors, the detailed examination of which is beyond the scope of this work. To begin with, the two versions of Manetho, Africanus and Eusebius, have different information. Although both agree on the chronology of the first five kings, the two lists radically differ with regard to the balance of the dynasty.

Africanus lists two additional kings with a total reign of twelve years, and gives the dynasty a total of 176 years.[5] Eusebius describes an unidentified number of successors ruling for forty-two years and gives an unusually long dynastic total of 245 years, forty-seven years longer than the sum of all the durations listed and thirty-nine years longer than the actual length of the dynasty.[6]

For purposes of our analysis, I want to focus only on Manetho's first five kings. He gives the following sequence and durations:

Ammenemes	16 years
Sesonchosis	46 years
Ammanemes	38 years
Sesostris	48 years
Lachares	8 years

The Manetho list presents a few problems. It gives the first king a reign of sixteen years instead of twenty or thirty (depending on whether the coregency is included), and the second king (corresponding to Senwosre I) a reign of forty-six years. The second reign coincides quite well with the forty-five years in the Turin Canon and would appear to include all of the years served as coregent. But the first two reigns added together total sixty-two years, the exact number for the first two reigns if you exclude the coregency at the end of the second reign.

This suggests that four years belonging to the first king were mistakenly assigned to the reign of the second. If we reassign those four years, then Manetho's second king ruled only forty-two years, which coincides exactly with the true length of that king's reign prior to the start of his coregency with the third king. This would require that the coregency between Senwosre I and his successor (Amenemhe II) be included in the reign of Amenemhe II, and as we are about to see, that is the case.

According to Manetho, the third king, who should correspond to Amenemhe II, had a reign of thirty-eight years. But the true length of that reign, including the coregencies at the beginning and end, should be no more than thirty-five years, leaving ample time for the initial coregency to be included in the total but giving this pharaoh at least three more years than he should be allowed. Those years appear to have been erroneously transferred from Manetho's fourth king, Sesostris.

Many commentators believe that Manetho's Sesostris incorporates the reigns of both Senwosre II and Senwosre III (the fourth and fifth kings). In support of this conclusion, consider the following: In the traditional chronology, the first five kings to the end of Senwosre III ruled a total of 149 years (1991–1843 B.C.), whereas the first four kings in Manetho reigned a total of 148 years.

This means that the reigns of Manetho's first four kings have exactly the right length for the first five Egyptian kings in the dynasty. (The one-year difference can be easily accounted for by a rounding error with the last year of reign.) Therefore, if Manetho's third king had a reign that is three years too long, those years must have been transferred from somewhere else. By coincidence, we see that Manetho's fourth reign is three years too short.

Manetho's fourth king, combining Senwosre II and Senwosre III, ruled forty-eight years. Senwosre II's independent reign started in 1894 and Senwosre III's ended in 1843, resulting in a total reign of fifty-two years. Four years are missing, one of which was due to the rounding error. That leaves three years unaccounted for. Logic suggests they must have been assigned to the fourth king's predecessor, who has three years too many.

This erroneous transfer of three years most probably occurred because of ambiguities in some earlier source document concerning the three-year coregency. A scribe probably wrote that Senwosre II shared three years with Amenemhe II and the later editor may not have realized that the three shared years were already incorporated into the given length of reign for Amenemhe II. Consequently, the editor mistakenly transferred three additional years from Senwosre II's independent reign to Amenemhe II.

This brings us to Manetho's fifth king, Lachares, who served eight years. Lachares ought to correspond to the sixth king, Amenemhe III, who served for forty-five years. The Manetho reign is far too short, and at this point the two Manetho versions break apart. Africanus has two additional kings serving twelve years; Eusebius has an unidentified number of kings serving forty-two years.

From Manetho, then, we have confusion over coregencies, the combining of reigns, two instances in which years belonging to one reign were mistakenly transferred to another, and a breakdown after Senwosre III.

The Twelfth Dynasty in Genesis

We now turn to the births following Eber (See table 5.1.) The evidence below will show that those dates coincides with the starting dates for several kings of the Twelfth Dynasty, beginning with Amenemhe I and ending with the start of Amenemhe IV.

Table 5.4 shows the proposed correlations. It aligns the six Genesis birth dates with the starting dates for six Twelfth Dynasty kings (showing both their first years on the throne and, where coregencies occurred, their first years of independent reign). It also shows the differences in the number of years between the Genesis and Egyptian dates.

The most obvious problem with this comparison is that none of the Genesis dates coincides with any of the Egyptian dates. However, if you look at the differentials between the two sets of dates, in most instances you will see a cluster of either seventeen or fifteen years of difference.

Table 5.5 shows a filtered version of table 5.4, aligning the Genesis dates with a specific year for each of the corresponding kings, either the king's first year on the throne or the first year of independent reign after a coregency. Here we see a clearer pattern. With the exception of the fifth reign, we see a declining differential between the two sets of dates, first nineteen years, then seventeen, then fifteen. The analysis below shows that these declining differentials all result from errors in the source documents used by the Genesis author.

These errors, I believe, were of the following nature: First and most important, one of the source documents contained an erroneous line of summation. In a manner similar to the Turin Canon, an earlier editor added up the total lengths of reign for each king, and, without allowing for coregencies, used that total as the dynastic length. This resulted in extending the duration of the dynasty by nineteen years. The Genesis author, not knowing about the erroneous summation line, assumed that these nineteen years belonged to additional unidentified kings who ruled in the final years of the dynasty. This caused the Genesis author to move the start of Amenemhe IV's reign back nineteen years, which would have also moved all the preceding reigns back by the same number.

In addition to that error, the source documents contained some additional mistakes. In several instances the lengths of reign for certain kings were recorded, but only the independent portions of the reign were entered into the document. On two occasions, this

Table 5.4
Proposed Correspondence Between
Genesis Birth Dates and Twelfth Dynasty Kings

Egyptian King	First Throne Year	First Independent Year	Genesis Patriarch	Birth Date	Years Apart
Amenemhe I	1991	1991	Peleg	2006	15/15
Senwosre I	1971	1961	Reu	1976	5/15
Amenemhe II	1929	1927	Serug	1944	15/17
Senwosre II	1897	1894	Nahor	1914	17/20
Senwosre III	1878	1876	Terah	1885	7/9
Amenemhe III	1842	1842			
Amenemhe IV	1798	1796	Abram	1815	17/19

* There are two ruling dates for each king. The first is the year he took the throne, the second is the year he started his independent reign. "Years Apart" refers to the difference between the Genesis birth date and the ruling date. The number to the left of the slash represents the difference between the throne date and the Genesis birth date. The number on the right side of the slash represents the difference between the Genesis birth date and the independent reign date. All dates are B.C.

Table 5.5
Proposed Alignment Between
Genesis Birth Dates and Twelfth Dynasty Kings

Egyptian King	Starting Year*	Genesis Patriarch	Birth Date	Years Apart
Amenemhe I	1991	Peleg	2006	15
Senwosre I	1961	Reu	1976	15
Amenemhe II	1927	Serug	1944	17
Senwosre II	1897	Nahor	1914	17
Senwosre III	1876	Terah	1885	9
Amenemhe III	1842			
Amenemhe IV	1796	Abram	1815	19

* With the exception of Senwosre II, whose starting date begins with a coregency, all the proposed alignments of the patriarchal birth dates with the Egyptian king dates begin with the first year of independent reign. Dates are B.C.

omission caused two, two-year coregencies to be dropped from the chronology. The first occasion in which this occurred happened when the two-year coregency between Amenemhe III and Amenemhe IV was overlooked. Only the independent portions of the two reigns were recorded. This caused the Genesis dates for Amenemhe III and all his predecessors to be moved forward two years, reducing the differential from nineteen years to seventeen.

The second occasion occurred with the reigns of Senwosre I and Amenemhe II. Again, only the independent portions of these two reigns were recorded, and the two-year coregency was omitted from the total. This caused the dates for Amenemhe I and Senwosre I to be moved forward another two years, reducing the differential from seventeen years to fifteen.

A different error seems to have occurred with the correlation between Terah and Senwosre III, but we shall discuss the nature of that mistake later.

Peleg, Reu, and Serug

The first three Genesis births after Eber belong to Peleg, Reu, and Serug. The following chart shows the birth date for each and the number of years until the next birth, in sequence.

Peleg 2006 30 years
Reu 1976 32 years
Serug 1944 30 years
Nahor 1914

Compare these three durations with the lengths of reign for the first three kings in the Twelfth Dynasty. Amenemhe I, the first king, ruled for thirty years. His successor, Senwosre I, shared a ten-year coregency and then ruled independently for thirty-two years, at which point he began a coregency with his successor. The third king, Amenemhe II, ruled for a total of about thirty-five years, only thirty of which were as an independent ruler without coregencies.

Note the solid correlations here:

Twelfth Dynasty Durations		*Genesis Durations*	
Amenemhe I	30 years	Peleg	30 years
Senwosre I	32 years	Reu	32 years
Amenemhe II	30 years	Serug	30 years

There is one small inconsistency. The last two durations include only the years of independent reign, whereas the first duration overlaps the coregency. This discrepancy can be explained by the fact that New Kingdom Thebans held Amenemhe I, founder of the dynasty, in great esteem. Some scribes may have chosen to ignore the coregency and credited him with the entire duration of his reign.

We also have a small error here that affected the Genesis chronology. Since only the independent portions of the second and third reigns were marked off by Genesis births, the two-year coregency between those reigns was omitted. This caused the dates of the first and second reigns to be moved forward by two years and clearly shows how at least one of the chronological errors in Genesis came about.

Overall, these three precise correlations between Genesis birth dates and Twelfth Dynasty lengths of reign present striking evidence connecting the two chronologies. It seems unlikely that such a set of coincidences can be explained by random chance, especially when you add the fact that the previous birth in the sequence—Eber's—corresponds to the date of Egypt's second unification.

Overall Duration

The Genesis birth dates, according to the proposed correlations, encompass the period from the start of Amenemhe I to the start of Amenemhe IV. In the traditional Twelfth Dynasty chronology that period ran from 1991 B.C. to either 1798 (for the start of his coregency) or 1796 (for the start of his independent reign). This indicates a total duration of either 193 or 195 years.

The Genesis period starts at 2006 B.C. and ends at 1815, a period of 191 years. This is either two or four years shorter than the true total. However, as we saw above, at least two of those years were lost from the reign of Senwosre I. And, as we shall see in a moment, there is a second two-year period that appears to have been subtracted from the reign of Amenemhe IV.

Since we have already shown that two years are missing from the total number of years ruled by the first three kings, let's turn our attention to the second three kings. The above analysis showed that the Genesis chronology for the third king ended at the start of the coregency with his successor, Senwosre II. Since this king came to the throne in 1897 B.C., we will take that date as our starting point.

The end of the sixth king's reign can be dated to either the start of the coregency with Amenemhe IV in 1798 or the end of the coregency in 1796, which gives a total duration for the three kings of either 99 or 101 years.

The corresponding Genesis duration begins with Nahor's birth in 1914 and ends with Abram's birth in 1815, a period of 99 years. This raises the question of whether the date of Abram's birth was meant to coincide with the start of Amenemhe IV's coregency or the start of his independent reign. If the former, then we have a perfect correlation; if the latter, then we have a correlation problem indicating that the two-year coregency was lost from Amenemhe IV's reign.

Our underlying assumption about the displacement of the Genesis chronology holds that it was due to a nineteen-year insertion based on the total number of years of coregency. This caused the start of Amenemhe IV's reign to be pushed back nineteen years. Subtracting nineteen years from Abram's birth date puts us at 1796 B.C., the year in which his independent reign began. However, the corresponding 99-year period in the Twelfth Dynasty chronology, ends with the beginning of the coregency. Two years are missing.

Logic suggests that the two missing years fall between the start of the coregency and the start of his independent reign. This would have caused all the subsequent reigns in Genesis to be moved forward two years.

A Perfect Alignment

This brings us back to table 5.5, which shows the proposed alignments and time differentials. Beginning with Amenemhe IV, we have a nineteen-year displacement, moving his starting date back to 1815 B.C. But omission of his coregency caused all the earlier reigns to have their starting dates moved forward by two years, reducing the differential from nineteen years to seventeen. Table 5.5 reflects this result, showing that the birth dates for Serug and Nahor, corresponding to the start of the reigns of Amenemhe II and Senwosre II, both fall seventeen years before the starting dates of the corresponding kings.

We also saw that the Genesis chronology lost the two-year coregency between Senwosre I and Amenemhe II, causing another two-year forward movement in the reigns of Amenemhe I and Senwosre I, reducing the differential from seventeen to fifteen years. That, too, shows up in table 5.5, where we see that those two reigns fall exactly fifteen years earlier than the actual starting date.

This means that five of the six Genesis dates, allowing for the corrections, correspond exactly to the starting dates for five Twelfth Dynasty kings. Such a coincidence can not be dismissed as random chance. The probability of such a set of correlations happening by accident is far too overwhelming.

This clearly shows that this portion of the Genesis chronology derives from Egyptian dynastic history, and that the Genesis author worked from reasonably accurate Egyptian records in putting this history together. Such evidence also reinforces the argument that Eber's death date of 1576 B.C. defines the start of the Eighteenth Dynasty.

Nahor, Terah, and the Combined Reigns

Cross-referencing Genesis birth dates with the Twelfth Dynasty chronology provides clear and convincing evidence that five of the last six birth dates in Genesis 11 correlate with the starting dates for five kings in that dynasty. This leaves us with one unexplained departure from this pattern. The fifth birth date, 1885 B.C., belongs to Terah. Using the formula above, this reign does not align with any of the Twelfth Dynasty starting dates.

The closest Egyptian date we have is for the start of Senwosre III, either in 1878 or 1876 B.C. Following the arrangement set forth in table 5.5, the corresponding Genesis date should fall seventeen years earlier, either in 1995 or 1993 B.C. Obviously we have an error. The dividing line between Senwosre II and Senwosre III has been moved forward eight or ten years too many.

We have already seen that the period between Nahor's and Abram's births correctly corresponds to the three kings falling within that time frame. This means that the only logical explanation for this error is that someone mistakenly took eight or ten years belonging to Senwosre III and attached them to the reign of Senwosre II. This error is not unlike that in Manetho's Twelfth Dynasty, where he twice transferred years belonging to one king to another. In this case, the error may have come about because the two kings had the same name and an editor was confused as to which of the two the years belonged to. Whether the Genesis author made the error or it appeared in the source documents we cannot know.

The Second Intermediate Period

Of the five dynasties (Thirteen to Seventeen) making up the Second Intermediate Period, the date and duration of only one appears to be defined in the archaeological record. The Turin Canon refers to "[total chieftains] of a foreign country, six, they made 108 years."[7] Since Manetho's Fifteenth Dynasty consists of just six Hyksos kings, Egyptologists generally accept that Manetho's six Hyksos kings correspond to the Turin Canon's six kings, ruling 108 years, and identify this dynasty as the Great Hyksos, or Fifteenth, Dynasty.

Egyptologists believe that the Great Hyksos Dynasty is the one defeated by Ahmose at the start of the Eighteenth Dynasty. Since this defeat came in the fourth or fifth year of Ahmose's reign, Egyptologists usually add about 104 or 105 years to the start of the Eighteenth Dynasty to get a founding date of about 1680 B.C. for the Fifteenth Dynasty.

Terah and the Fifteenth Dynasty

Eber's death in 1576 B.C. corresponds to one of the acceptable dates for the start of the Eighteenth Dynasty. Looking at the Genesis 11 death sequence, we see that Terah died in 1680, the date consistent with the foundation of the Fifteenth Dynasty. Once again, then, we seem to have two perfect correlations, Terah in 1680 with the start of the Fifteenth Dynasty and Eber in 1576 with the start of the Eighteenth Dynasty.

These correlations assume that Eber's death date of 1576 accurately reflects the starting date of the Eighteenth Dynasty. By itself, without further evidence or context, our conclusion might be somewhat speculative. But once again we are faced with a highly unlikely juxtaposition of dates.

The Genesis sequence of two consecutive dates, 1680 for Terah and 1576 for Eber, corresponding to the dates of two consecutive dynasties (at least according to one mainstream theory about the start of the Eighteenth Dynasty), is certainly an unusual coincidence. When you couple this with Eber's birth date coinciding with the second unification of Egypt, and five of the next six birth dates immediately following Eber coinciding with the dates for five kings in the Twelfth Dynasty, it seems an inescapable conclusion that Eber's birth and death define the dates for Egypt's second and third unifications, and that the dates in between correspond to key events in the Middle Kingdom and Second Intermediate Period.

Peleg and the "Division"

In the Genesis 11 death sequence we saw that Peleg and Nahor died at about the same time, 1767 and 1766 B.C., respectively. We also saw that Nahor died before his father, disrupting the chronological sequence of births and deaths in which fathers and sons died in the orders of their births. Nahor's son, Terah, died in 1680 B.C., the year marking the start of the Hyksos's Fifteenth Dynasty.

If the Genesis dates describe dynastic and monarchical divisions, then these two death dates, 1767 and 1766, should mark the beginning of separate concurrent dynasties. The idea of a dynastic split associated with Peleg calls to mind an unusual Genesis passage about this patriarch: "in his days was the earth divided."[8]

The origin of this name and the associated description has puzzled biblical scholars. Speiser suggests that it derives from a Hebrew word *nipleg*, meaning "divided" or "broken up."[9] J. H. Hertz, another noted biblical scholar, suggests an alternative explanation, proposing that the name derives from the Assyrian *palgu*, meaning "canals," and that the division of the earth refers to the introduction of a system of canals into Babylonia.[10]

This last explanation, though highly imaginative, seems singularly out of context with the biblical story. The passage in question appears in the chapter known as the Family of Nations, which explains the rise of the different nations after the Flood. There is nothing in that text to even remotely suggest that it has anything to do with the introduction of a canal system into Babylonia.

Speiser, on the other hand, may have correctly determined the Hebrew etymology of Peleg, but such discovery tells us nothing about why he was identified with the division of the earth. The biblical explanation for his name is particularly vexing in that Genesis 10 describes the evolution of nations (a division of the earth if you will), and as only one of many descendants mentioned in that context, Peleg should be identified with one of the nations, not with the concept of dividing the nations.

Since Peleg's death date falls in the Second Intermediate Period, and together with Nahor's death date suggests the existence of two concurrent dynasties, perhaps we have arrived at the true origin of Peleg's description. From the Egyptian viewpoint, the division of the world signified a split between the Hyksos and Theban kingdoms.

The rise of the Hyksos's power would have begun a few decades before they established Avaris as their capital. This would place their early stages at about the time of Peleg's death. They may not have reached full strength at this point, but they may certainly have developed enough of a local base to declare independence from Thebes. In this regard, some information from the Turin Canon may be helpful. According to that document, following the close of the Twelfth Dynasty there were two kings who ruled for ten years, and then came a period of six years in which there was no king.[11] Subtracting these sixteen years from the 1786 end date of the Twelfth Dynasty gives us a date of 1770 B.C., only three years before Peleg's death. A kingless period among ambitious rivals is exactly the kind of political vacuum that could generate competing claims for the throne, or at least allow rival kings to set up an independent territory.

Bearing the above in mind, I want to briefly call your attention to a controversial archaeological find. Richard A. Parker, the Egyptologist responsible for putting together the traditional Twelfth Dynasty chronology, subsequently acknowledged the existence of an inscription for Amenemhe IV, seventh king of the dynasty, which indicates that this king served thirteen years instead of the nine given in the traditional chronology (and in the Turin Canon). While some Egyptologists argue that the inscription refers not to Amenemhe IV but to Amenemhe III, who served well over thirteen years, if it does belong to Amenemhe IV then the kingless period ended four years later, in 1766 B.C., right at the time of Peleg's and Nahor's deaths. That the kingless period ended in 1766 rests on the acceptance of a thirteen-year reign for Amenemhe IV. But from the evidence it is not clear that the inscription in question belongs to this pharaoh. Unlike our earlier correlations, this one remains tentative, subject to future validation.

However, even if the kingless period doesn't end exactly at 1766, it is clear that the deaths of Peleg and Nahor fall at a time consistent with the rise of the Hyksos. These two patriarchs may signify the date of the first political division between the Theban and Hyksos kings, and for this reason Peleg may have been identified with a "division of the world."

One additional clue may indicate that we are on the right trail when we define the deaths of Peleg and Nahor with the split between Thebes and the Hyksos. If you look at the sequence of deaths in table 5.1, you will notice that Nahor's death and the sequence of births is out of order. While it makes sense to have a birth and death define an era, why should such a carefully worked out chronology have Nahor die out of order? Why don't all the patriarchs die in the order of their births?

The answer, I believe, is that the Genesis chronographer wanted to have a chronological clue separating the Hyksos and Theban dynasties. If you look at table 5.1, you will see that Nahor's immediate successor is Terah, who defines the start of the Great Hyksos Fifteenth Dynasty. This suggests that Nahor signifies the start of an earlier Hyksos dynasty, while Peleg and his two immediate successors signify periods of Theban rule.

Ishmael and Avaris

The Hyksos kings worshiped the Egyptian god Set as their chief deity, and one of the most important political events in Hyksos history was the dedication of the city of Avaris to this god. According to Ramesses II, his father, Sethos I (Set), came in the four hundredth year of the god Set to do him honor.[12] Egyptologists interpret Ramesses's remark to mean that four hundred years after the dedication of the city of Avaris, Sethos I came to pay honor to his namesake god.

Sethos's act occurred in an undefined year in the reign of Horemheb. This pharaoh appears to have ruled about twenty-seven years, but his starting date depends upon which theory is followed for the beginning of the reign of Ramesses II—1304, 1290, or 1279. Gardiner, who dates Ramesses II to 1290 and Horemheb from 1335 to 1308, suggests that Sethos's act occurred around 1330, and therefore dates the founding of Avaris to 1730 B.C.[13] This would be about fifty years before his chosen date for the founding of the Great Hyksos Dynasty.

In the Egyptian chronology followed in our study, Ramesses II came to the throne in 1304 B.C. and Horemheb ruled from 1341 to 1315. Since Sethos's celebration of Set could have occurred anytime during Horemheb's reign, a date of 1330 is consistent with our chronology, but we still don't know if that was the date of the celebration.

In the Genesis chronology, Ishmael, the son of Abraham, was born in 1729, virtually the same date for the founding of Avaris suggested by Gardiner (although, admittedly, this date was not based on hard evidence). What makes this coincidence especially interesting is that in a later chapter, when we consider the mythical origins of Abraham's family, Ishmael will be identified with the god Set.

There is another important chronological coincidence involving Ishmael's birth date. In Manetho's very confused chronology of the Second Intermediate Period, the Africanus version indicates that the Seventeenth Dynasty lasted 151 years but that it consisted of both Theban and Hyksos kings.[14] If we count back 151 years from the founding of the Eighteenth Dynasty (1576), we arrive at a date of 1727 B.C., virtually the same as Ishmael's birth date, for the start of Manetho's Seventeenth Dynasty. This suggests that in Manetho the event signifying the start of the Seventeenth Dynasty was the foundation of Avaris as the Hyksos capital, an event that demonstrated how militarily weak the Theban kingdom had become.

The Thirteenth Dynasty

Egyptologists date the start of the Thirteenth Dynasty to the end of the Twelfth Dynasty, (1786 or 1782 B.C.). We have no corresponding Genesis date. No births or deaths occur between the birth of Abram in 1815 B.C. or the death of Peleg in 1767. The reason may have to do with the early death dates of 1766 and 1767 for Nahor and Peleg, dates which fall only sixteen to twenty years after the end of the Twelfth Dynasty.

While Egyptologists tend to assign the Thirteenth Dynasty a substantial length of time, perhaps over 150 years, we have no compelling evidence supporting that view. If we have correctly identified the reason for the given death dates for Nahor and Peleg, it may be that the Genesis chronographer considered the time period between the end of the Twelfth Dynasty and the rise of the Hyksos at about 1767 too short a period for a separate dynasty, especially since it included six years without a king. Under such circumstances he may have thought that this short period belonged to the tail end of the Twelfth Dynasty.

The Fourteenth and Sixteenth Dynasties

Opinion remains divided among Egyptologists as to whether the Fourteenth and Sixteenth Dynasties ever existed. In any event, we have no archaeological data from which reasonable dynastic starting dates could be established, which prevents us from determining whether or not Genesis has corresponding dates.

Manetho, however, gives the Fourteenth Dynasty a duration of 184 years. While we can't verify the validity of that claim, we should note that this dynasty would have ended no later than the start of the Eighteenth Dynasty, and probably at least a few years earlier. If we can agree that 1576 B.C. dates the start of the Eighteenth Dynasty, then, following Manetho's figure, the Fourteenth Dynasty should have started no later than 1760, and perhaps a few years earlier, bringing us very close (perhaps right on target) to the 1766 death date for Nahor. This would identify Nahor with the start of the Fourteenth Dynasty.

Reu and Serug

Reu and Serug died in 1737 and 1714 B.C., respectively. The confused and incomplete record of the Second Intermediate Period prevents us from assigning these dates to specific events. I can only suggest that they probably represent some sort of shift in Theban political power. Most of the Theban kings in this period served for brief periods, perhaps only a year or two, indicating instability in the lines of succession. On these two Genesis dates a new Theban family may have seized the reins of power. However, it is worth noting that Serug's death in 1714 coincides with the birth of Isaac in 1715, a date and event which play key roles in our attempt to date the Exodus.

Summary

In this chapter we examined several Genesis birth and death dates and cross-referenced them to events in Egyptian monarchical history. The evidence shows an astonishingly high number of correlations, too numerous to be explained by random chance.

The period in question began with the birth of Eber in 2040 B.C. and ended with his death in 1576. In between there were six births and six deaths. The six births all occurred during the Middle Kingdom, and the six deaths all fell during the Second Intermediate Period, suggesting a logical chronological pattern.

Egyptologists generally accept Eber's birth date of 2040 as the date of Egypt's second unification. Eber's death date of 1576 falls into the narrow range of acceptable dates for Egypt's third unification.

The analysis compared the six Genesis birth dates to the starting dates (of either the first year on the throne or first year after a coregency) for several kings in the Twelfth Dynasty. After allowing for a fixed displacement of nineteen years, based on double-counting the nineteen years of coregency, we saw that five of the six birth dates aligned with five starting dates of Twelfth Dynasty kings. (In two cases, the Genesis total erroneously omitted a two-year coregency from its calculations.) The sixth birth date was off by a couple of years, but given that the total duration for the six births coincided with the total duration for the corresponding kings, it was evident that this error resulted from some confusion over whether these years belonged to Senwosre II or Senwosre III, an error probably caused by the identity of names.

For the Second Intermediate Period, we have insufficient archaeological evidence for a detailed examination of Egyptian starting dates. The one solid indication that we have from this period is for the Fifteenth Dynasty, which lasted about 108 years and ended about four or five years into the Eighteenth Dynasty. Assuming Eber's death date of 1576 is an accurate dating of the Eighteenth Dynasty, the Fifteenth Dynasty would have started at about 1680, the date of Terah's death. (Gardiner has respective dates of 1680 and 1575.)

Genesis also had two earlier death dates that occurred at about the same time, Peleg in 1767 and Nahor in 1766, both falling either a couple of years after or just at the end of a six-year kingless period. In the Bible, Peleg is identified with a division of the world, and his death date is consistent with the rise of a Hyksos power base independent of Thebes, suggesting that these two birth dates define the first split between Thebes and the Hyksos. Lack of sufficient evidence, however, prevents us from making an exact correlation.

We also observed that Ishmael's birth of 1729 B.C. was consistent with estimates of the foundation date of Avaris as a Hyksos capital. Gardiner gives an estimated date of 1730, and Manetho's Seventeenth Dynasty chronology implies that this Theban dynasty began at about 1727, indicating a connection between the foundation of Avaris and a dynastic division in Thebes. Again, we lack sufficient evidence to prove the point one way or the other.

While the lack of archaeological records prevents us from accurately cross-referencing all Genesis and Egyptian dates, in those cases where we can make comparisons the correlations appear to be near perfect. All the births can be connected to the Middle Kingdom, particularly to kings of the Twelfth Dynasty, and two deaths can be linked to the Fifteenth and Eighteenth Dynasties.

The next two chapters examine other time periods in Genesis and show several more correlations with Egypt's dynastic history.

6

Methuselah and Memphis

The Memphite Kingdom

The Memphite Kingdom began with the foundation of the First Dynasty by King Menes and ended sometime after the start of the Sixth Dynasty, as anarchy and chaos spread throughout the land. This ensuing period of upheaval, known as the First Intermediate Period, continued for almost a century after the foundation of the Eleventh Dynasty, until Menthotpe II reunited Egypt under Theban rule. The confusion surrounding the collapse of authority in Memphis affected several king lists, each of which presents a different perspective on events.

Manetho's Sixth Dynasty names six kings ruling for 198 years. He follows this with a Seventh and Eighth Dynasty from Memphis, a Ninth and Tenth Dynasty from Herakleopolis, each containing nineteen kings, and an Eleventh Dynasty lasting only forty-three years.

A very different view comes from the Turin Canon. Its Sixth Dynasty lists twelve kings with a collective reign of only 181 years, no Seventh or Eighth Dynasty, one group of eighteen Herakleopolitan kings, and an Eleventh Dynasty with several kings ruling for a total of 143 years.

In the Table of Abydos the Sixth Dynasty consists of twenty-two kings, but no lengths of reign are provided. It gives no indication of a Seventh or Eighth Memphite Dynasty, nor does it mention any Herakleopolitan kings. In addition, the Abydos list skips over the first few kings of the Eleventh Dynasty, jumping from the last Memphite king to Menthotpe II.

Except for the number of kings listed in the Sixth Dynasty, the Table of Sakkara closely follows the arrangement in the Table of Abydos. It names only four kings from Memphis and then it, too,

90

jumps to Menthotpe II. As with the Abydos list, no Herakleopolitan kings are mentioned.

One of the chronological puzzles challenging Egyptologists is whether the Memphite line of kings ended long before, just before, or during the Eleventh Dynasty. Unfortunately, we have no chronological anchor tying any specific Memphite king to an absolute chronological date. Similarly, we do not know if the Memphite line ended before or during the rise of the Herakleopolitan kings.

Because of the lack of evidence for dynastic sequences in the First Intermediate Period, Egyptologists have a variety of opinions about the correct dynastic chronology for this period. Some terminate the Memphites before either the Herakleopolitans or Thebans came to power; others place an overlap between the Memphites and Herakleopolitans but end the Memphites before the rise of the Thebans. Still others have the Memphites overlapping both the Herakleopolitans and Thebans.

One widely accepted solution identifies the Sixth Dynasty with the Turin Canon's twelve kings and assigns the ten additional kings in the Abydos list to Manetho's Seventh and Eighth Dynasties. But this solution doesn't solve the question of when the Memphite line ended.

At the other end of the Memphite continuum, Egyptologists also can't set a precise date for the start of the Memphite line. Due to a wide range of opinions about how long the first two dynasties lasted, the consensus holds that Menes founded the First Dynasty at about 3100 B.C., give or take 150 years.[1]

As to the duration of the Memphite line, Gardiner's widely accepted reconstruction of the Turin Canon chronology indicates that the first six Memphite dynasties lasted 955 years. Although archaeological evidence contradicts a number of entries in the Turin Canon and many of the other entries are either damaged or lost, many Egyptologists still consider 955 years a reasonable estimate of how long the Memphite line lasted, but they accept that the correct number of years may be off by a few decades in either direction. To this total we must also add some twenty or thirty years to account for the ten additional kings included in the Abydos list but missing from the Turin Canon roster. Keeping these factors in mind, Egyptologists generally accept that the Memphite line probably came to an end sometime between 2200 and 2100 B.C., give or take a few years.

Turning to the Genesis chronology, only two dates fall within the acceptable time frame for the foundation of the First Dynasty—Methuselah in 3074 B.C. and Enoch in 3139. While both dates are consistent with the evidence, we have already suggested that Enoch's birth had to do with establishing a 365-year life span that ended with the start of the Sothic cycle. This leaves Methuselah with the only viable Genesis date consistent with the founding of the First Dynasty.

Methuselah lived 969 years, putting his death in 2105 B.C. A period of 969 years coincides well with estimates of how long the Memphite kingdom lasted, and a date of 2105 falls into the acceptable framework. Just as Eber's birth and death framed the first Theban kingdom, we shall now see that Methuselah's birth and death framed the Memphite kingdom.

Table 6.1 shows all the Genesis 5 deaths that fall during Methuselah's lifetime, along with the proposed correlations to Egyptian dynasties. The last column shows Gardiner's suggested dates for those dynasties. Note several interesting features about this comparison.

Perhaps the one date that stands out most prominently is the death date for Lamech (lxx), 2134 B.C., which exactly coincides with the accepted date for the start of the Eleventh Dynasty. Gardiner has also suggested conjectural dates of 2620 and 2340 for the start of the Fourth and Sixth Dynasties. These dates at first appear to coincide almost exactly with the Genesis death dates of 2621 for Enos and 2339 for Jared, but in these cases the apparent correlations are an accident.

In the first place, Gardiner's Sixth Dynasty chronology consists of the 181 years in the Turin Canon plus the approximately twenty-five years assigned to the ten additional kings in the Abydos list, ending the Memphite line at the start of the Eleventh Dynasty. The proposed Genesis chronology provides for a much longer period of time for the Sixth Dynasty, ending some twenty-nine years after the start of the Eleventh Dynasty.

Also, if you look at the indicated Genesis date for the Fifth Dynasty (table 6.1) you will see that it provides for a longer Fourth Dynasty and a shorter Fifth Dynasty than Gardiner recognizes. Since Genesis provides for a longer Fourth and Sixth Dynasty, and a shorter Fifth Dynasty than Gardiner, to claim a chronological match between the dates for his Memphite kingdom and the proposed Genesis dates wouldn't be acceptable. Nevertheless, as we examine the evidence below we will see that the Genesis dates are consistent with the archaeological evidence.

The chief problem in comparing Genesis dates in the Memphite period with proposed Egyptian dates is that we do not have the kind of chronological anchors for this era that the Sothic dates give us for the Twelfth and Eighteenth Dynasties. Therefore we can't set any precise target dates for the Memphite dynasties. We do, though, have enough material in the Turin Canon and the archaeological record to establish parameters for how long each of these dynasties lasted. Therefore, for purposes of examining the relationship between the Genesis dates and the Memphite dynasties, our primary emphasis will be on the issue of dynastic length rather than specific dates.

The Archaic Period: The First and Second Dynasties

One of the most difficult chronological problems facing Egyptologists concerns the lengths of the First and Second Dynasties. Outside of Manetho, there is no evidence for a dynastic division between these two groups of kings. Because of a lack of reliable chronological evi-

Table 6.1
Comparison of Genesis Death Dates During Methuselah's Lifetime and Egyptian Dynastic Chronology

Genesis Event	Date	Egyptian Event	Gardiner Date*
Methuselah born	3074	First Dynasty	3250–2950
Adam died	2831	Second Dynasty	?
Enoch died	2774	Sothic date	
Seth died	2719	Third Dynasty	2700
Enos died	2621	Fourth Dynasty	2620
Cainan died	2526		
Mahalaleel died	2471	Fifth Dynasty	2480
Jared died	2339	Sixth Dynasty	2340
Lamech(lxx) died	2134	Eleventh Dynasty	2134
Methuselah died	2105	Last Memphis king	

* Gardiner dates are from *Egypt of the Pharaohs*, 433–436.

dence, scholars often group these dynasties together and refer to them as the Archaic Period.

The Turin Canon appears to have about sixteen to eighteen kings assigned to this period, but the lengths of reign for all but the last four are lost.[2] The Palermo Stone, although badly damaged, indicates a total of 450 years for these two dynasties, but Gardiner warns, "we must again stress the improbable nature of the 450 years which the Palermo Stone seems to demand for the two dynasties combined."[3]

According to the Africanus version of Manetho, the First Dynasty lasted either 253 or 263 years, (the summation line disagreeing with the actual sum for the individual reigns), and the Second Dynasty lasted 302 years, for a total of 555 or 565 years. Eusebius has several small variations from Africanus and assigns the First Dynasty either 252 or 258 years, (his summation line also disagreeing with the actual sum of the individual reigns), and 297 years for the Second Dynasty, yielding a two-dynasty total of either 549 or 555 years. (Note that each version of Manetho has one set of figures that add up to 555 years.) Most Egyptologists would probably consider Manetho's First Dynasty figures to be within the ballpark but would place his Second Dynasty figures way out of the accepted range.

The lack of evidence results in a wide range of opinions concerning the duration of these two dynasties. In the *Cambridge Ancient History,* William C. Hayes provides a survey of the following views: 544 years (Borchardt, 1917 and 1935 B.C.), 520 to 543 (Sethe, 1905 B.C.), 519 (Weigall, 1925 B.C.), 453 (Meyer, 1904 B.C.), 444 (Parker, 1957 B.C.), 420 (Breasted, 1921 B.C.), 419 (Meyer, 1925 B.C.), 400 (Frankfurt, 1948 B.C.), 373 (Sewell, 1942 B.C.), 310 (Hall, 1924 B.C.), and 295 (Helck, 1956 B.C.).[4] He then suggests a compromise figure of about 415 years.[5]

In my analysis of the Genesis chronology I propose a starting date for the First Dynasty of 3074 B.C. (the birth of Methuselah), a starting date for the Second Dynasty of 2831 (the death of Adam), and a starting date for the Third Dynasty of 2719 (the death of Seth). This gives the First Dynasty a length of 243 years and the Second Dynasty a length of 112 years, for a combined length of 355 years.

For purposes of this study we can only observe the following:

1. The Genesis total of 355 years falls near the low end of the above range of estimates but within the mainstream of Egyptological opinion.

2. The Genesis total of 243 years for the First Dynasty is very close to the Manetho sums, which range from 252 to 263 years, and is in line with what Egyptologists would accept for the First Dynasty.

3. The Genesis total of 112 years for the Second Dynasty falls short of what most Egyptologists would accept for this period.

The Third Dynasty

Three major issues divide archaeologists in their reconstruction of Third Dynasty chronology. First, who was its first pharaoh, Nebka or Djoser? Second, how long did Nebka rule? Third, how long did Djoser rule?

The chief source of information about this dynasty's chronology is the Turin Canon. It places Nebka immediately before Djoser, attributing a reign of nineteen years to each, but nowhere does it explicitly state when the Third Dynasty begins.[6] It does, however, draw special attention to Djoser's name by the unusual use of red ink to write his name, suggesting that this pharaoh was highly respected among later Egyptians.[7] (His grandest achievement was the construction of the Step Pyramid of Sakkara, Egypt's first monumental tomb.) After Djoser, the Turin Canon enumerates three more pharaohs before reaching the Fourth Dynasty, and assigns them respective reigns of six, six, and twenty-four years.[8]

Nebka also precedes Djoser in the Abydos list, but the Sakkara list omits him altogether.[9] Both lists show four kings between Djoser and the end of the Third Dynasty, but there are discrepancies in the names given.[10] Another document, the Westcar Papyrus, reverses the order and places Djoser before Nebka.[11]

If the Third Dynasty begins with Djoser, the Turin Canon allots the dynasty fifty-five years; if with Nebka, seventy-four years. This latter duration is accepted by Hayes in the *Cambridge Ancient History*,[12] but W. Stevenson Smith, also writing for the *Cambridge Ancient History*, says:

There is far from complete agreement concerning the length of this dynasty. In spite of the fact already mentioned that the lengths of the five kings listed in the Turin Canon add up to seventy-four years, it is difficult not to believe that *at least a hundred years should be allowed* for a period so important for the political and cultural experimentation which reached its culmination in the Fourth Dynasty. [Emphasis added.]

One reason for not accepting the Turin Canon's seventy-four years for these five kings (counting Nebka) is the widespread belief among Egyptologists that Djoser's reign must have stretched far beyond the nineteen years allotted in the Turin Canon. That is Gardiner's view also. He writes:

> The nineteen years allotted to Djoser seem an absurdly short time for the completion of so stupendous a monument as his. The twenty-nine years given by Manetho might be accepted the more readily were it not that his Dynasty III counts nine kings, all of them except Tosorthros (Djoser) with unidentifiable names and having 214 years as the total of their reigns.[13]

Smith, also supporting a longer reign by Djoser, argues:

> If Sanakhte is really the Horus-name of Nebka, and if he was also the king who began the construction of the building later incorporated into the Step Pyramid of his younger brother Djoser, it is difficult not to doubt the figure of nineteen years given to each in the Turin Canon. The remarkable architectural achievement of Djoser and Imhotep [Djoser's architect] as well as the lasting memory which they left in the minds of later Egyptians, would seem to imply a longer reign for Djoser than Sanakhte, at least in the present state of our knowledge of the latter's monuments which seem very scanty.[14]

That the Third Dynasty should last about one hundred years, if we include Nebka, coincides quite well with the ninety-eight-year period indicated by the Genesis chronology. But there is an interesting side issue. Did Nebka actually rule nineteen or fourteen years?

Noah and Djoser

The Turin Canon says Nebka ruled nineteen years, but according to Smith, the Palermo Stone connects the year after an "eighth biennial count" (of cattle) with the last year of Nebka's reign.[15] Since the biennial counts usually occurred in each odd numbered year of a pharaoh's reign, beginning with year one, this would ordinarily refer to Nebka's sixteenth year. But, Smith observes, another fragment of the stone indicates that the first and second count occurred in consecutive years, indicating only fourteen or fifteen complete years of service.[16] If the third count occurred in the third year, returning to the pattern of cattle counts in odd-numbered years, the duration would be fourteen years.

If Nebka only ruled about fourteen years, then counting from Seth's death date of 2719 B.C., Djoser's reign would have begun in 2705. Coincidentally, that is the year in which Noah was born. This would suggest that the Genesis author began the Third Dynasty with Nebka, but, as in the Turin Canon, chose to single out Djoser for special attention.

The Fourth Dynasty

Gardiner estimates that the dynasty lasted 140 years, while the *Cambridge Ancient History* claims 119 years. The Genesis chronology indicates 150 years.

The Turin Canon lists eight or nine kings for this dynasty, preserving lengths of reign for six, those six adding up to seventy-nine years. One of those reigns, eighteen years for Mycerinus, is a damaged entry and may have been twenty-eight years. One of the missing reigns belongs to the long-ruling Chephren, for whom we have a high-year mark of at least twenty-five years. This suggests a minimum dynastic duration of either 104 or 114 years, depending upon the length of Mycerinus's reign.

Additionally, there is some ambiguous evidence about the length of reign for Snofru, the first king in this dynasty. The Turin Canon gives him a reign of twenty-four years but Manetho says twenty-nine. An inscription makes reference to a "Seventeenth Occasion of the Count" in his reign, which would ordinarily indicate he reached the thirty-third year of rule.[17] But other inscriptions indicate that no census was taken in the year after the "Sixth Occasion" and that the "Seventh" and "Eighth" came in consecutive years.[18] Whether the census was resumed after that on an annual or biennial basis is not known.

The Sixth Occasion brings us up to the eleventh year. Then came a year without a census, followed by two consecutive censuses, which takes us to year fourteen. If the remaining nine censuses were done annually, the total would be about twenty-two or twenty-three years. If only the seventh and eighth counts were done annually, the total would be thirty or thirty-one years. The former calculation favors the Turin Canon, the latter Manetho.

Since departure from the biennial counts was rare, it is likely that the traditional practice was restored rather quickly, favoring Manetho's twenty-nine years over the Turin Canon's twenty-four. This gives the Fourth Dynasty a minimum length of either 109 or 119 years, plus the duration of the two missing reigns. The *Cambridge Ancient History* sum of 119 years is based on the above figures, assuming twenty-eight years for Mycerinus, and a very brief period for the two missing reigns.

Gardiner appears to accept an eighteen-year period for Mycerinus, which makes his 140-year duration approximately thirty-one years longer than the estimated minimum.[19] In his *Egypt of the Pharaohs,* he doesn't explain where these extra years come from, but his calculation appears to be consistent with the argument below for a thirty-one-year duration of the two missing reigns.

The Genesis figure exceeds the *Cambridge Ancient History* by thirty-one years, implicitly suggesting that Genesis has a twenty-eight-year reign for Mycerinus plus Gardiner's additional thirty-one years. The area of conflict has to do with the unknown length of a gap between two Fourth Dynasty pharaohs, Chephren and Mycerinus. The consensus holds that this gap, if it existed at all, was quite brief and has no impact on the overall length of the dynasty. But archaeological records and other evidence suggest that ancient Egyptians had a different view of the events in this period. The evidence below shows that this gap of unknown length lasted thirty-one years.

Between Chephren and Mycerinus

The Turin Canon provides for either eight or nine kings in the Fourth Dynasty, preserving the names of five and the lengths of reign for six.[20] The document places at least one name between Chephren and Mycerinus, but there may have been two.[21] Unfortunately, the document is so damaged in the area where the second name should appear that it cannot be stated with certainty that a second name was present.

That there was a ninth king in the Turin Canon listing, however, is supported by the Table of Sakkara, which does list nine kings for this dynasty. Unfortunately, the two lists disagree on the sequence. The Sakkara list has no break between Chephren and Mycerinus.[22] Instead, there are four names given after Mycerinus, all unreadable because of damage.[23]

On the Abydos list there are only six names, the first five in agreement with the Sakkara list and allowing for no break between Chephren and Mycerinus, but the sixth is unknown on any of the other lists.[24] On all of these lists, Chephren is the fourth king.

In addition to the king lists, there is a rock inscription in the Wady Hammamat, dating to the Middle Kingdom, which has a row of cartouches containing the names Cheops, Redjedef, Chephren, Hordedef, and Baufre.[25] The first three correspond to the second, third, and fourth names on all three of the above king lists, but the last two are unknown on any of the other lists. Since they follow immediately after Chephren, they fall logically between Chephren and Mycerinus, where the Turin Canon has the two-king gap.

Although not on the other king lists, Hordedef and Baufre were well-known members of the Fourth Dynasty royal family. Hordedef was even the object of later cult worship.[26] A musician in an Eleventh Dynasty court sang, "I have heard the sayings of Imhotep and Hordedef with whose words men so often speak."[27]

Most Egyptologists believe that if Hordedef and Baufre were the kings who belong in the Turin Canon gap between Chephren and Mycerinus, then the lengths of their reigns were very brief. The primary basis for this view is the lack of archaeological evidence about the reigns of these two kings. In that regard, we must note certain archaeological problems.

It was not uncommon for ancient Egyptian monarchs to destroy monumental evidence relating to hated rivals or predecessors. The most obvious example consists of Horemheb's treatment of Akhenaten's monuments and inscriptions. There are many other such instances in Egyptian history. Such was also true in the Fourth Dynasty. Smith points out that Hordedef's tomb was subjected to malicious damage, a clear indication that shortly after his reign he was looked on with disfavor by some later member of the dynasty.[28] Chephren, Baufre, Hordedef, and Redjedef (the third king of the dynasty) were all brothers, sons of Cheops.[29] Smith remarks that inscriptions attributed to the granddaughter of Cheops indicate that dissension split the royal family after Cheops died.[30]

He adds that Redjedef had long been viewed as a usurper, and, that by virtue of parentage, Hordedef may have had a better claim to the throne.[31] Clearly, some sort of royal feud was evident and it is likely that all of Cheops's sons were in constant conspiracy against each other.

That Hordedef's successors looked upon him (and probably Baufre too) with disfavor, even going so far as to desecrate his tomb, explains why there is so little evidence about the kings serving between Chephren and Mycerinus: The evidence was destroyed. Under these circumstances, the lack of evidence regarding the lengths of these reigns cannot be used to prove, authoritatively, that they must have been brief.

Bicheris and Thampthis

In Manetho's account of the Fourth Dynasty, which contains many problems, he lists two kings named Bicheris and Thampthis, serving twenty-two and nine years, respectively (a total of thirty-one). We don't know who these two names refer to, but Smith, commenting on the two-king gap in the Turin Canon, suggests that Manetho's Bicheris and Thampthis, not identified with any other kings in the record, may be the two missing kings.[32] If so, this creates a possible correspondence between Manetho's Bicheris and Thampthis, and the earlier reference to Hordedef and Baufre.

Hordedef and Baufre

Redford, in his very valuable study of ancient Egyptian king lists, states that later Egyptians viewed Hordedef and Baufre as kings. He points out that during the Middle Kingdom great literary interest was shown in Cheops (second king of this dynasty) and his sons, and that legends about them began to grow. "Part of this interest," he says, "entailed the assumption, *quite natural for those times,* that each of the sons had been king and reigned in succession to Khufu [Cheops]. Three of them in fact had done so, and why not the rest?"[33] [Emphasis added.]

He then cites the Wady Hammamat inscription as evidence that Twelfth Dynasty kings viewed Hordedef and Baufre as kings. According to Redford, this view of the Fourth Dynasty continued into the New Kingdom's Nineteenth Dynasty, the time in which the Genesis chronographer most likely began his work. Redford writes:

By the Nineteenth Dynasty this falsification of the Fourth Dynasty succession had achieved canonicity. TC [Turin Canon] and the Sakkara list undoubtedly embody this distortion, the former ending with Shepsekaf, Hordedef, and Baufre in that order, the latter perhaps adding a fourth at the end, the enigmatic *Vorlage of Thampthis.* The tradition to which Manetho fell heir is precisely this one.[34]

At present, Egyptologists do not count Manetho's twenty-two years for Bicheris and nine for Thampthis in their chronology of the Fourth Dynasty. Inserting them into the gap between Chephren and Mycerinus, however, increases the *Cambridge Ancient History*'s estimate of 119 years for the Fourth Dynasty to 150 years, the same as suggested by Genesis.

Corroboration From Herodotus

Herodotus, the Greek historian of the fifth century B.C., provides important corroboration for the 150-year period suggested by the Genesis chronology. In his history of Egypt, he talks about the kings of this dynasty, making Mycerinus the direct successor to Chephren and claiming that Chephren ruled for fifty-six years.[35] The highest known year marker for Chephren, however, is twenty-five years, which is the period of time Egyptologists usually assign to this pharaoh.[36]

If we subtract that twenty-five years from Herodotus's fifty-six, we have the thirty-one years that may belong between Chephren and Mycerinus. This suggests that in some ancient Egyptian traditions Hordedef and Baufre ruled for about thirty-one years combined, and those reigns were subsequently incorporated into the reign of Chephren, much in the manner, perhaps, that the reigns of Akhenaten and his successors were incorporated into the reign of Horemheb.

Herodotus also tells a story about King Mycerinus that indicates that the kings of the Fourth Dynasty had ruled for 150 years. According to his account, an oracle predicted that Mycerinus would live only six more years and die in the seventh. The king was astonished to learn that he would lead such a short life, especially since he had reversed the cruel and oppressive policies of the long-lived Cheops and Chephren. Why then, he asked, should he have such a short life?

In answer to this, Herodotus writes, "there was another message from the oracle, which declared that his life was being shortened precisely because he had not done what he ought to have done: for *it was fated that Egypt should suffer for a hundred and fifty years*—a thing which his two predecessors, unlike himself, understood very well."[37] [Emphasis added.]

So, in Herodotus we have an unexplained thirty-one-year insert between Chephren and Mycerinus, and an oracle suggesting that the Fourth Dynasty kings were associated with a period of 150 years. Since his information came from Egyptian priests, we can reasonably assume that Herodotus's history accurately reflects ancient Egyptian traditions about the chronology of the Fourth Dynasty.

Cainan's Death

Readers may be curious about the unexplained death date for Cainan, which falls into the middle of the Fourth Dynasty. In a more detailed study of Egyptian chronology, far too lengthy to be included here and to be published at a later date, I show that Cainan's death date falls exactly on the dividing line between Hordedef and Baufre (Manetho's Bicheris and Thampthis), dividing the dynasty into two political subgroups.

The Fifth Dynasty

While Gardiner estimates that the Fifth Dynasty ruled for 140 years, Egyptological opinion currently leans toward an even longer Fifth Dynasty.[38] The *Cambridge Ancient History,* for instance, gives this dynasty a duration of 149 years, while Genesis suggests that it lasted only 132 years.

This entire discrepancy between the Genesis figure and current opinion is due almost completely to a dispute over the reign of one king—Nyuserre. The entry for the length of his reign in the Turin Canon is damaged and indicates only a number in excess of ten.[39] The way in which Egyptians wrote numbers would require that the missing entry be eleven, plus some multiple of ten.

Gardiner takes this reign as eleven years,[40] the *Cambridge Ancient History* as thirty-one.[41] Obviously, if eleven were the correct number, as Gardiner suggests, the *Cambridge Ancient History* figure would be reduced to 129, almost exactly what the Genesis chronology requires. The Genesis date, therefore, would fall between Gardiner and *Cambridge*. A closer look at the chronological data for this dynasty will enable us to make a stronger case for the Genesis point of view.

According to the Turin Canon, nine kings reigned during the Fifth Dynasty. The lengths of reign for six have been preserved, and a seventh (Nyuserre) has been partially preserved. The kings (with their lengths of reign from the Turin Canon in parentheses) are: Userkaf (7), Sahure (12), Neferirkare (unknown), Shepsekare (7), Khanefere (unknown), Nyuserre (at least 11), Menkauhor (8), Djedkare (28), and Unas (30).[42]

The six reigns for which complete durations are entered add up to ninety-two years. Nyuserre's eleven-year minimum increases the total to 103 years. This leaves us with two missing reigns, Neferirkare and Khanefere, and one partial reign, Nyuserre, to account for.

Inscriptions from the archaeological record provide us with some additional chronological material that supplements and amends the Turin Canon. For the missing reign of Neferirkare, we have an entry on the Palermo Stone that credits him with reaching a "Year after the Fifth Occasion."[43] This permits us to add at least ten years to the Turin Canon subtotal.

From other sources we know that Sahure reached a "Year after the Seventh Occasion" and Djedkare reached a "Year of the Twentieth Occasion," indicating that these two kings served at least fourteen and thirty-nine years, respectively.[44] Therefore, for Sahure's reign we must add two years to the Turin Canon total and eleven years for Djedkare's reign. With the other ten years for Neferirkare added in, the new subtotal is at least 126 years.

The only reign for which no information exists is Khanefere. On the basis of this king's achievements (or lack thereof) the experts believe it is unlikely that he served more than seven years.[45] Therefore, counting only eleven years for Nyuserre, and recognizing that at least one reign is a pure guess, this gives the Fifth Dynasty a minimum dynastic total of somewhere between 127 and about 133 years.

As in both the Third and Fourth Dynasties, a key piece of chronological evidence is missing. In each case, definitive evidence for the length of reign of a particular king is missing. Once again, we can only claim that the dynastic time period in Genesis corresponds to what we know about the archaeological evidence.

The Sixth and Eleventh Dynasties

The Theban Eleventh Dynasty, based on the Turin Canon claim that it lasted 143 years, is traditionally dated to 2134 B.C. As we have already seen, Lamech (lxx) died in the same year. The Genesis chronology, assuming that Methuselah's death date corresponds to the end of the Memphite line of kings, shows a twenty-nine-year overlap between the last kings of Memphis and the first kings of Thebes. Unfortunately, the archaeological record is silent about the correctness of such an arrangement.

A reexamination of the various king lists may help solve the problem. As already noted, the Turin Canon, Manetho, the Table of Abydos, and the Table of Sakkara each present a different picture of what occurred. The reason for these discrepancies, I believe, has to do with theological and political disputes among various cult centers.

The chief theological problem of the First Intermediate Period occurred when Horus, the god who ruled Egypt in the human form of a pharaoh, stopped ruling from Memphis and started ruling in Thebes. If part of the Sixth Dynasty overlapped part of the Eleventh Dynasty, this could be a rather thorny theological question. Obviously, the priests of Memphis and Thebes would disagree. But how would priests in other cult centers see the issue? Obviously their political and theological relationships to Memphis and Thebes would influence their judgments.

The Turin Canon, the Table of Sakkara, and the Table of Abydos each suggest a different viewpoint. The Sakkara list mentions only four Memphite kings, ignores the Herakleopolitans, and then jumps to Menthotpe II, skipping over several Theban kings in the Eleventh Dynasty. The Table of Abydos lists twenty-two Memphite kings, and it, too, skips over the Herakleopolitans and those Theban kings preceding Menthotpe II. The Turin Canon names twelve Memphite kings, includes some Herakleopolitans, and includes the entire Eleventh Dynasty. Can these lists be reconciled?

Reading between the lines, I think we can set matters straight. The omission of the Herakleopolitans and the first Thebans from the Sakkara and Abydos lists suggests that the authors of those lists did not consider those kings legitimate rulers. Only when Menthotpe II reunited Egypt did Thebes gain authority.

The long list of twenty-two Memphite rulers in the Abydos list indicates a Memphite loyalist holding out to the bitter end. The short list of four kings in the Sakkara list indicates that something happened during the reign of the fourth king to shake his faith in Memphite rule. What could that event have been?

The Herakleopolitans must have staked out their own territorial claims and undermined the authority of Memphis. For the Sakkara scribe, this was enough to terminate authority in Memphis but not enough for him to accept authority elsewhere.

In the Turin Canon we have the most direct Theban viewpoint: It starts the Eleventh Dynasty at the earliest possible time and also recognizes the existence of the Herakleopolitans.

The inclusion of a Herakleopolitan dynasty serves as Theban propaganda. It is a theological reminder that Memphis couldn't stop these upstarts but Thebes could. Therefore, the rise of the Theban hierarchy must have been a sign that the gods favored Thebes over Memphis.

Arrangements in various lists suggest the following scenario: Sometime during the reign of the fourth king of the Sixth Dynasty the Herakleopolitans successfully undermined Memphite authority. (This fourth king, Phiops, apparently ruled for over ninety years.) During the reign of the twelfth king of the Memphite Sixth Dynasty the Theban Eleventh Dynasty was founded. The Memphites fielded an additional ten kings against Thebes but the line finally petered out. Subsequently, Thebes defeated Herakleopolis and united Egypt.

This seems to be the scenario followed by Genesis. As we have seen, Lamech (lxx) died in 2134 B.C., the date for the founding of the Eleventh Dynasty, and Methuselah died in 2105, indicating a brief overlap between Memphis and Thebes.

But there is something unusual about Lamech's death. He is the first patriarch to predecease his father, a fact which seems to single him out for special attention, for all the Genesis dates for the Memphite dynasties belong to patriarchs who die in the order in which they were born.

Lamech's out-of-order death suggests that his death date refers to an event that had less authority than the start of a Memphis dynasty, and that the rise of the Eleventh Dynasty had to be recognized but that it did not have full legitimacy until the conquest of Menthotpe II, which was signified by the birth of Eber.

Duration of the Sixth Dynasty

Gardiner dates the Sixth Dynasty to 2340 B.C., virtually the same date as Genesis, 2339, but the two alternatives derive from different viewpoints about Memphis chronology. Gardiner has apparently chosen to end the Memphite line of kings with the start of the Theban Eleventh Dynasty. His span of 206 years from the start of the Sixth Dynasty to the start of the Eleventh is based on the 181 years in the Turin Canon and the approximately twenty-five years arbitrarily assigned to the ten additional kings in the Abydos list.

The evidence relating to the Genesis chronology suggests that the last ten Memphite kings ruled twenty-nine years and began at the start of the Eleventh Dynasty, leaving a total of 205 years for the Memphis kings preceding the Eleventh Dynasty. Gardiner, therefore, has a total Memphite line of 206 years, while Genesis has 234 years.

A similar disparity exists between Manetho and the Turin Canon. The former has 198 years for the first six kings while the Turin Canon has 181 years for the first twelve kings. For the six kings in the Turin Canon not included in Manetho, only four reigns, totaling about nine years, are preserved. The two missing reigns are generally thought to have been very brief. This means that for the six kings in both Manetho and the Turin Canon there is a chronological discrepancy of about twenty-seven to thirty years.

If we add the 198 years for the six kings in Manetho to the twelve-plus years for the remaining six kings in the Turin Canon, we arrive at a total of about 210 years, which is fairly close to the 205 years indicated by the Genesis chronology. The question to be asked, therefore, is which chronology of the Sixth Dynasty is more accurate, Manetho or the Turin Canon? The evidence, I suggest, favors Manetho.

There are numerous problems in reconciling Manetho and the Turin Canon with the archaeological record, and we cannot focus on all those issues at this time. We can, however, examine one of the most important issues, one which accounts for almost the entire difference between Manetho and the Turin Canon. The problem concerns the chronology of two consecutive pharaohs.

In Manetho they are named Phius and Methusuphis, with respective reigns of fifty-three and seven years. In the Turin Canon they are named Piopi and Merenre, the former having a reign of twenty years and the latter having a damaged entry of at least fourteen years, with Egyptologists arguing over whether the restored value should be fourteen or forty-four.

For Piopi, inscriptions have been found indicating that he reached a twenty-first and twenty-fifth "Occasion of the Count,"[46] documenting a reign of at least forty-nine years, which coincides quite well with Manetho's fifty-three years, but which is at great variance with the Turin Canon's claim of twenty years. It is this differential between the Turin Canon and the documented record that is at the root of the problem. If this were the only evidence, we can say that the Turin Canon is off by about thirty years, accounting for virtually all of the difference between it and Manetho. But there are other issues.

Piopi's successor, Merenre, appears to have ruled independently of any coregency for only a short period. Evidence suggests coregencies both at the beginning and end of his reign.[47] In order to account for the short period of time assigned to Piopi in the Turin Canon, many Egyptologists argue that there was a very long coregency between Piopi and Merenre, and that the restored figure for Merenre's reign should be forty-four years.

According to this view, Egyptologists argue that the Turin Canon assigns the period of coregency to Merenre's reign, thereby cutting short the time allotted to Piopi. Continuing this line of argument, it is also alleged that Manetho made the alternative choice, assigning the period of coregency to Piopi and cutting short the reign of Merenre.

If this view is correct, then Manetho's combined reign of sixty years for these two kings coincides rather closely with the Turin Canon's amended total of sixty-four years for the same two kings. However, there is no evidence that Merenre had any such long reign. At best, two inscriptions, one mentioning a year after the "Fifth Occasion" and the other mentioning a year of the "Fifth Occasion," document no more than a ten-year independent reign.[48]

Unfortunately, there are gaps in the chronological record. Under some circumstances, it is conceivable that the damaged entry for Merenre could read "44," which would require that Manetho have two significant errors in his lengths of reign for two kings. He has thirty years for his first king and twelve years for his last. The archaeological record only shows a high-year mark of twelve for the first king and there is no evidence regarding the reign of his last king. Since Manetho has reasonably accurate reigns for the other four kings in this dynasty, it is difficult to accept that he is way off on the other two. Nevertheless, it is possible.

Once again, we are stymied by the lack of definitive information about the reigns of particular kings. However, if we take Manetho's 198 years for his six kings and add the nine to twelve years for the six additional kings mentioned in the Turin Canon, we get 207 to 210 years. The corresponding Genesis duration is 205 years. If we reduce Manetho's fifty-three-year reign for Piopi to the forty-nine documented in the archaeological record, Manetho and Genesis appear to be in perfect chronological accord.

The Seventh and Eighth Dynasties

The only evidence for the existence of the Seventh and Eighth dynasties comes from Manetho. It is the general practice to identify these two dynasties with the ten additional Memphite kings mentioned in the Table of Abydos and allot them about a quarter of a century.

Space limitations prevent me from providing a full treatment of the problems associated with these two dynasties. For purposes of our present examination we will accept the present convention of giving them a collective duration of about twenty-five years and note that the Genesis chronology indicates a twenty-nine-year period for these ten kings, beginning with the start of the Eleventh Dynasty in 2134 and ending in 2105 with the death of Methuselah.

Herakleopolis and the Sons of God

Genesis 6:1–3 contains a puzzling passage. It tells us that God had become angry because the "Sons of God" married the "Daughters of Man." This event triggered God's determination to wipe out mankind with a flood. "And the LORD said, My spirit shall not always strive with man, for that he also is flesh: *yet his days shall be an hundred and twenty years.*" [Emphasis added.]

Who the "Sons of God" were remains a biblical mystery. And why their marriage to the "Daughters of Man" would so anger God that he wanted to destroy mankind is another mystery. Perhaps Egyptian history holds a solution.

The Flood occurred in the year that Methuselah died, 2105 B.C. The above warning occurred 120 years before the Flood, or in 2225. Is there any event in 2225 B.C. that may shed some light on this matter?

Manetho describes two Herakleopolitan dynasties, each with nineteen kings, but with the exception of a King Achtoes, no names are given. The first of these dynasties ruled for 409 years, the second for 185 years. The Turin Canon lists only one group of eighteen Herakleopolitan kings. For this reason many Egyptologists believe that Manetho's two Herakleopolitan dynasties may be duplicates.

The Herakleopolitan period came to an end in 2040 B.C., when Menthotpe II reunited Egypt, but we don't know how long it lasted. Estimates vary from about one hundred to two hundred years, but there is no hard evidence.

Manetho's second Herakleopolitan group lasted 185 years. Counting back from 2040 we arrive at 2225, the very year that the "Sons of God" married the "Daughters of Man." Not only do we have a coincidence of dates for the start of the Ninth (or Tenth) Dynasty and the "marriage," we also have a coincidence between the end of the 120-year warning and the end of the Memphite line of kings in Genesis.

In the biblical story, the "Sons of God" would originally have been the sons of the Memphis pharaoh, the god Horus. The "Daughters of Man" would have been the daughters of a Herakleopolitan king, the false Horus—a man. The biblical story suggests that a marriage occurred between members of the Memphis court and the Herakleopolis court, one that led to a dispute over which line of princes—Herakleopolitans or Memphites—would ascend to the throne of Horus. It would have been this marriage that gave the Herakleopolitans a veneer of legitimacy to their claim for the Egyptian throne.

7

Joseph and the Eighteenth Dynasty

All major theories about the date of the Exodus place it somewhere between the start of the Eighteenth Dynasty and the end of the reign of Nineteenth Dynasty pharaoh Ramesses II. Therefore, in order to date the Exodus and set it in its proper historical context, we should first establish an accurate chronology for this time period.

As you may recall from chapter 3, for the Eighteenth and Nineteenth Dynasties there are three astronomically fixed dates in question, but Egyptologists disagree as to what these dates should be. At issue are: the correct Sothic date for the ninth year of Amenhotep I, second pharaoh of the Eighteenth Dynasty (either between 1544 and 1542 or 1536 B.C.); the starting date for Thutmose III (either 1504 or 1490); and the starting date of Ramesses II, third pharaoh of the Nineteenth Dynasty (either 1304, 1290, or 1279).

The first two kings of the Eighteenth Dynasty are Ahmose and Amenhotep I. For the ninth year of Amenhotep I we have (in chapter 5) accepted the high range Sothic date of 1544 to 1542 B.C., giving him a starting date between 1552 to 1550. Ahmose has a high-year mark of twenty-two years,[1] but Manetho gives him twenty-five years.[2] Most Egyptologists are inclined to follow Manetho's figure. If Ahmose came to the throne in 1576 (Eber's death date) we can date the start of Amenhotep I to 1551. The latter has a high-year mark of twenty-one, yielding an end date for Amenhotep I's reign of about 1530 B.C., which we will return to further on.[3]

The starting dates for Thutmose III and Ramesses II, however, are still up in the air. Setting a date for Amenhotep I does not resolve the debate. Gardiner, for instance, who supports a 1575 starting date for Ahmose (consistent with our 1576 date) chooses 1490 for Thutmose III and 1290 for Ramesses II.[4] Wente and Van Siclen III, on the other hand, support the earlier 1504 date for Thutmose III and the later 1279 for Ramesses II.[5]

In chapter 3 we have already noted some of the arguments over the different dates for Ramesses II. In that regard, I just want to recall that Wente and Van Siclen III, who argue for the 1279 date, acknowledge that the most recent studies of Near Eastern chronology support a date of 1304 B.C.

If 1304 is the correct starting date (and it is the one adopted in this study) then it corroborates some evidence that Sethos I, the immediate predecessor to Ramesses II, came to the throne at the start of the Sothic cycle beginning in 1314 B.C. Sethos I had a high-year mark of eleven, indicating a reign of ten years or more. This places his first year in the same year as the beginning of the Sothic cycle.

Working backwards from Sethos I, we can establish dates from Akhenaten to the end of the Eighteenth Dynasty. There are six kings in this sequence: Akhenaten, Smenkhkare, Tutankhamen, Ay, Horemheb, and Ramesses I, Ramesses I forming a bridge between the Eighteenth and Nineteenth Dynasties. He served no more than about two years, part as coregent with Horemheb and part as coregent with Sethos I.[6] Therefore his dates would fall at about 1315 to 1314 B.C.

Horemheb has a high-year mark of twenty-seven, but the inscription comes from graffiti, not an official record.[7] Nevertheless, it is widely accepted among Egyptologists and gives a starting date for Horemheb of 1342 and an end date of 1316 or 1315, overlapping in part with Ramesses I.

Horemheb's two immediate predecessors were Ay and Tutankhamen. The former had a high-year mark of four, and the latter a high-year mark of nine. We also know both died in the year corresponding to the high-year mark. This places Ay from 1346 to 1343 B.C. and Tutankhamen from 1355 to 1347.

The dates for Tutankhamen coincide with some additional evidence from two documents relating to Near Eastern chronology, which reinforces the decision to choose 1304 as the starting date for Ramesses II. The first document is a Hittite text indicating that a solar eclipse occurred in the tenth year of the Hittite king Mursili II.[8] Middle Eastern scholars generally accept that this eclipse occurred in March of 1335,[9] placing the ascension of Mursili II in 1344 B.C.

For the other document we turn to a remarkable letter written by the widow of Tutankhamen, in which the Egyptian queen asked the Hittite king Suppiluliuma I to send her a Hittite prince for marriage.[10] Since Suppiluliuma preceded Mursili II, the latter's ascension had to be at least a year or two after Tutankhamen's death.[11] This means that Tutankhamen could have died no later than about 1346 B.C., which is consistent with the 1347 date established above. It also requires either a starting date of 1304 for Ramesses II or the addition of another fourteen to twenty-five years for the reigns of Horemheb and Sethos I, a highly unlikely proposition.

Preceding Tutankhamen were Akhenaten and Smenkhkare. Akhenaten ruled for seventeen years and Smenkhkare, Akhenaten's chosen successor, for three, but for some or all of those years he may have served as coregent. This places Akhenaten's starting date somewhere between 1375 and 1372 B.C.

In summary, we have the following chronology for the kings from Akhenaten to Ramesses II:

King	Starting Date	Ending Date
Akhenaten	1375 to 1372	1358 to 1356
Smenkhkare	1358	1356
Tutankhamen	1355	1347
Ay	1346	1343
Horemheb	1342	1315
Ramesses I	1315	1313
Sethos I	1314	1305
Ramesses II	1304	1237

The above chronology leaves us with one major decision: Did Thutmose III come to the throne in 1504 or 1490? To help us resolve this question, we return to the Genesis chronology.

The Genesis chronology ends with the death of Joseph in 1454. Coincidentally, whichever choice we make, Joseph's death falls within the reign of Thutmose III. This is particularly important because the Bible tells us that the persecution of the Hebrews began in the reign of a pharaoh "who knew not Joseph," that is, some time after Joseph's death.[12] As we shall see in the next chapter, this provides important clues concerning the date of the Exodus and the circumstances under which it occurred. Therefore, it is important to know if Joseph's biblical chronology is reliable or a disembodied addition to the biblical text.

About Joseph

Joseph is arguably the most important character in the Book of Genesis. Because of him the Israelites moved to Egypt and through him the covenant with God passed to the nation of Israel. His death marks the final event in the Book of Genesis.

Although he was the eleventh of Jacob's twelve sons, he was the first-born of Rachel, Jacob's beloved wife, and Joseph rapidly became Jacob's favorite son. At an early age he demonstrated a facility for dream interpretation, an indication that he had a close connection with God. A somewhat precocious and rather obnoxious child, at an early age he interpreted a number of dreams to mean that he would become the family leader and that all would bow down before him, even (to their disappointment and shock) Jacob and Rachel.

His brothers grew to hate him and his grandiose prophecies. They plotted to kill him but at the last minute the idea repelled even them. Instead, they sold him into slavery. To explain his disappearance to his father, they soaked Joseph's famous multicolored robe in blood and told their father that his favorite son had been devoured by an evil beast.

The slave traders carried Joseph to Egypt and sold him to Potipher, a high official in the Egyptian court. Joseph served Potipher well, running the household and managing his affairs, and Potipher prospered. Unfortunately, Potipher's wife took a liking to Joseph and tried to seduce him. Joseph, loyal to his master, rejected her enticements and angered her. To get even, she told her husband that Joseph had tried to force himself on her. Potipher couldn't quite believe this about his trusted servant but couldn't allow his wife to be thought of as a liar. So he had Joseph imprisoned.

While in prison, Joseph continued to demonstrate his ability to interpret dreams and his reputation spread to the pharaoh, who was deeply disturbed by some of the visions in his sleep, the meanings of which defied his own counselors. As a last desperate measure, the pharaoh sent for Joseph and conveyed the dreams to him. In his first dream:

[Pharaoh] stood by the river: And, behold, there came up out of
the river seven well favoured kine and fatfleshed; and they fed
in a meadow. And, behold, seven other kine came up after them
out of the river, ill favoured and leanfleshed; and stood by the
other kine upon the brink of the river. And the ill favoured and
leanfleshed kine did eat up the seven well favoured and fat
kine.[13]

And in his second dream:

[S]even ears of corn came up upon one stalk, rank and good.
And, behold, seven thin ears and blasted with the east wind
sprung up after them. And the seven thin ears devoured the
seven rank and full ears.[14]

Joseph listened carefully to what the pharaoh had to say and then
explained the meaning of the dreams to him: Egypt was about to
enter into a seven-year period of great prosperity. However, these
seven "fat" years would be followed by seven "lean" years in which
famine would spread throughout the land. That the two dreams followed so closely upon each other, he said, indicated that this time
was close at hand. Joseph then gave the pharaoh the following advice:

Now therefore let Pharaoh look out a man discreet and wise,
and set him over the land of Egypt. Let Pharaoh do this, and let
him appoint officers over the land, and take up the fifth part of
the land of Egypt in the seven plenteous years. And let them
gather all the food of those good years that come, and lay up
corn under the hand of Pharaoh, and let them keep food in the
cities. And that food shall be for store to the land against the
seven years of famine, which shall be in the land of Egypt; that
the land perish not through the famine.[15]

The pharaoh, thoroughly impressed with Joseph's performance
and advice, appointed him to the post of prime minister. Joseph
served with distinction, and in accordance with his prophesy, Egypt
experienced seven wonderful years of prosperity and the famine arrived in the eighth year, on cue. The famine devastated Egypt but
the pharaoh, by following Joseph's advice, had vast grain storages.

This enabled him to sell grain to the people, and eventually the pharaoh used the grain to buy up all the land of Egypt.

The famine had a second consequence. It reached into Canaan, the land where Jacob and his children dwelled. Needing grain, Jacob sent his children to Egypt to buy some provisions. When they arrived at the pharaoh's court, Joseph immediately recognized them, but they did not recognize him. Seeing an opportunity to explore their ethical and moral status, Joseph subjected them to a number of dramatic tests, generating fear and tension both among his brothers and his father. Finally, Joseph revealed his identity, made peace with his brothers, and invited his family to live in Egypt, where the pharaoh gave them a land of their own.

Genesis ends with Joseph's death. The story resumes in the Book of Exodus with the enslavement of Israel. By way of transition, we are told that the Israelites had become a rich and powerful people and that the pharaoh feared them. The identity of this pharaoh is not given. We are told only that he "knew not Joseph."

Many scholars consider the biblical account of Joseph and his brothers to be among the most beautiful and poignant in all of literature. The rich detail and strong emphasis on human psychology and ethical traits leads many to believe that Joseph was a historical figure and played an important role in Israel's early origins. In this regard, it's worth noting that Joseph, with a life span of 110 years, is perhaps the only person in the Genesis chronology whose number of years falls within a believable, albeit rare, human life span.

Suspecting the possibility that the portrayal of Joseph may be based on real events, biblical scholars and Egyptologists have tried to place him in the context of Egyptian political history. Of those who consider Joseph to be truly historical, the overwhelming view is that he must have served one of the Hyksos kings, for only in such an administration could a non-Egyptian such as Joseph have risen to such a position of power. It would also explain why there is no record of such a powerful person in the large number of administrational records that exist for the Eighteenth and Nineteenth Dynasties.

The chief problem with such a view about Joseph and the administration that he served is that it doesn't coincide with the Genesis chronology. Joseph was born in 1564 B.C. and became prime minister on his thirtieth birthday, in 1534.[16] No matter which of the acceptable theories about the starting date of the Eighteenth Dynasty one adopts, all such theories place 1534 B.C. after the expulsion of the

Hyksos kings. It is not possible under the Genesis chronology for Joseph to have served a Hyksos king. Given the evidence of the preceding chapters, which clearly shows that the Genesis chronology must have been based on Egyptian dynastic history, Joseph, if he existed, must have served in the Eighteenth Dynasty, and if he did, we ought to have some evidence of his existence, unless, of course, the story of his political influence is highly exaggerated.

Another problem with accepting Joseph as a historical figure is that key dates in his chronology continue the Genesis pattern of aligning the Genesis chronology with Egyptian dynastic chronology. If, as we show below, Joseph's chronology serves as an extension of the Genesis chronological markers, it is unlikely that the chronology applies to a genuine person.

Joseph died in 1454 B.C. He became Prime Minister in 1534 at the age of thirty. His ascendancy marks the start of the seven fat years and seven lean years, giving an end date of 1521 B.C. Do these dates—1564, 1534, 1521, and 1454—have any significance in Egyptian dynastic history? Let's take a closer look.

Joseph's Birth and the Hyksos

In the previous chapters, we established that the Genesis chronology coincides with Egyptian dynastic history and that Eber's death date in 1576 defines the start of the Eighteenth Dynasty, when King Ahmose of Thebes came to the throne. When Ahmose came to power the Theban kings were at war with the Great Hyksos dynasty. We also saw that according to the Turin Canon, the Great Hyksos Dynasty lasted 108 years, and if the Hyksos were expelled from Egypt in the fourth year of Ahmose's reign, as many Egyptologists believe, they came to power in 1680, the same year that Terah died.

Although the Hyksos were driven from Egypt in the fourth year of Ahmose's reign, they were not driven from the political scene. They continued to challenge the Theban kings, but some years later, at Sharuhen, a town in southwest Palestine where the Hyksos maintained a fortress, they were decisively beaten and thereafter ceased to pose a major threat for Egypt.

Information about this battle comes from an ancient document known as the Rhynd Mathematical Papyrus, which was a copy of an earlier document belonging to a Hyksos king, and to which had been appended information about the fight at Sharuhen. According to the appended account, Ahmose I, in his eleventh year, moved against the Hyksos at Sharuhen. Hans Goedicke, a prominent Egyptologist who has studied the text, maintains that "11" is an error and should have read "10."[17] That prior to this battle the Hyksos continued as a force to be reckoned with can be seen from the fact that it took about three years to defeat them, at Sharuhen.[18]

If Ahmose came to the throne in 1576 B.C., and in his tenth or eleventh year of reign launched a battle against the Hyksos that lasted about three years, then the Confrontation ended about 1564 or 1563 B.C., when Joseph was born. Not only did Joseph not serve a Hyksos king, this evidence suggests that his birth marks the date of their final defeat.

Joseph's Death and Thutmose III

In chapter 3 we observed that Egyptologists were divided as to which of two dates marked the start of the reign of Thutmose III, 1504 or 1490. Wente and Van Siclen III note that a number of recent studies show that the better solution is 1504.[19] Since we know from inscriptions that this pharaoh ruled for fifty-three years, ten months and twenty-six days,[20] if he came to the throne in 1504 then his final year was about 1451, close to Joseph's death date of 1454 but not the same year.

However, there is some question as to whether this pharaoh's successor, Amenhotep II, served as a coregent towards the end of Thutmose's reign. Again, opinion is divided, but several Egyptologists, such as Redford,[21] Wente, and Van Siclen III[22] say that there was a coregency, and date its beginning to 1453 B.C. This places Joseph's death date in the last year of Thutmose III's independent reign, providing an exact correlation between the Genesis date and the start of the reign of Amenhotep II.

Thutmose III was perhaps the most powerful ruler ever to sit on Egypt's throne. Under his reign, Egypt's territorial control extended farther than at any other time in Egypt's history. Therefore, Joseph's birth and death dates serve to mark one of the most important eras in Egypt's history, from the final defeat of the Hyksos in 1564 to the end of the reign of Egypt's most powerful monarch. And once again there is a precise correlation between the Genesis and Egyptian dates.

The connection between the death of Joseph and the final years of Thutmose III gives the Bible an ironic plot structure. The Book of Genesis ends with Egypt at the height of its power. The story continues in the Book of Exodus with the humbling of that most powerful nation by the God of Moses.

Table 7.1
Proposed Chronology of the
Eighteenth Dynasty and Early Nineteenth Dynasty

Eighteenth Dynasty

Ahmose	1576–1551
Amenhotep I	1551–1531
Thutmose I	1534–1521
Thutmose II	1520–1504
Hatshepsut	1504–1483
Thutmose III	1504–1451
Amenhotep II	1453–1432
Thutmose IV	1431–1412
Amenhotep III	1411–1375
Akhenaten	1374–1358
Smenkhkare	1358–1356
Tutankhamen	1355–1347
Ay	1346–1343
Horemheb	1342–1315

Nineteenth Dynasty

Ramesses I	1315–1313
Sethos I	1314–1305
Ramesses II	1304–1238
Merneptah	1237–1228

Joseph and Thutmose I

If Joseph didn't serve under a Hyksos king, then who was the pharaoh who elevated him to his high rank? Joseph became prime minister at the age of thirty, and with his appointment began the period of seven fat years followed by seven lean years. On the basis of biblical chronology, we can date those years to between 1534 and 1521 B.C.

Genesis never explicitly says that the same pharaoh ruled during all fourteen years, but it is implied. And since the Genesis chronology is built around the sequence of births and deaths, it is not necessary to show that this fourteen year period falls within the reign of a single king. Still, it would be a neat solution if it can be shown that the fourteen years define the reign of a single king.

The four Eighteenth Dynasty kings who preceded Thutmose III were, in order, Ahmose, Amenhotep I, Thutmose I, and Thutmose II. Since we already have a fixed Sothic date of 1544 to 1542 B.C. for the ninth year of Amenhotep I, we can use his reign as an anchor for the chronology up to Thutmose III. Based on the Sothic date, Amenhotep I came to the throne between 1552 and 1550 B.C. (1551 by our analysis above). His highest known year mark is twenty-one,[23] bringing his final year to about 1532 to 1530 (most likely 1531, again based on our above analysis). This places him on the throne during the early portion of Joseph's fourteen-year period.

Amenhotep I's successor was Thutmose I. His highest known year mark is either four or nine, there being some disagreement among Egyptologists over the correct interpretation of the relevant inscription. But Thutmose I was a great military leader who accomplished much in his reign. Few Egyptologists believe that four years are enough to encompass his achievements. Many believe that even nine years are insufficient. How many years scholars assign to Thutmose I depends upon how they resolve other gaps and inconsistencies in the record. Gardiner, for instance, gives this pharaoh eighteen years.[24]

If Thutmose I served about nine or ten years, which most Egyptologists would accept, then his last year would be approximately 1521 B.C., coinciding with the end of the seven lean years. In and of itself, this provides a remarkably good fit to the Genesis chronology, terminating the fourteen-year period with the end of Thutmose I, although dividing the fourteen years between Thutmose I and his predecessor, Amenhotep I.

However, if in addition to those nine or ten years, Thutmose I also ruled for about four years as coregent with Amenhotep I, then he would have been the pharaoh for the entire fourteen-year period. Since a high-year mark determines only the minimum length of reign, not the maximum, a longer reign is not out of the question.

However, there is some dispute as to whether or not such a coregency existed.

Wente and Van Siclen III, for instance, state unhesitantly that there was no coregency.[25] William C. Hayes, on the other hand, writing in the *Cambridge Ancient History*, takes a contrary view. He suggests that the presence of both the figures and names of Amenhotep I and Thutmose I on a chapel at Karnak indicates the existence of a short coregency.[26]

One other piece of evidence should be noted. Manetho also provided a chronology of the Eighteenth Dynasty, although, as preserved in Josephus, it is badly garbled. Because of an enormous number of problems with that chronology, a full discussion is beyond the scope of this work. But, for the pharaoh whom he names as Chebron and who appears to correspond to Thutmose I, he assigns a reign of thirteen years.[27] Since such a reign allows for a partial fourteenth year, it strongly suggests that Thutmose I ruled for the entire fourteen-year period of the Joseph prophesy and shared a brief coregency with Amenhotep I.

Although we cannot prove at this time whether or not the coregency existed, in either case the fourteen-year period ends with the final year of Thutmose I and encompasses his entire reign, once again reinforcing the correspondence between the Genesis chronology and Egyptian dynastic history.

Since the fourteen years expires with the end of Thutmose I's reign, it also marks the start of the reign of Thutmose II. The above chronology allows for a period of sixteen to eighteen years for this pharaoh (1521 or 1520 to 1505 or 1504), depending upon how much of the partial years at the beginning and end of his reign were counted. How long he ruled, though, is uncertain.

At the center of the dispute is a lost copy of an inscription prepared by George Daressy, a prominent Egyptologist. Daressy's copy of the inscription indicated a high-year mark of eighteen for Thutmose II, but, unfortunately, his papers have been lost. Wente and Van Siclen III, though admitting that the inscription cannot easily be dismissed, add that Daressy was not noted for epigraphic accuracy and may have miscopied "14" as "18," a mistake which may have arisen from damage to the broken stele from which the inscription was copied.[28]

Either choice fits our data. A high-year date of eighteen implies only completion of a seventeenth year, and the time frame in question, 1521 or 1520 to 1505 or 1504, allows for the entire period to fit in without a coregency. But even if a very brief coregency is necessary, evidence supports such a possibility. Some inscriptions have Thutmose III saying he was "promised the rulership of the Two Lands . . . *at the side of*" his father, Thutmose II.[29] [Emphasis added.] For a number of Egyptologists this proves the existence of a brief coregency, although, as in most issues of Egyptian chronology, other scholars again disagree.

Implications of the Joseph Chronology

Joseph's birth date coincides with the final defeat of the Hyksos. The start of the seven "fat" years very probably defines the start of the reign of Thutmose I. The end of the seven lean years coincides with the end of the reign of Thutmose I and the beginning of the reign of Thutmose II. Joseph's death date marks the end of the independent reign of Thutmose III and the start of the reign of Amenhotep II. Genesis ends with Joseph's final year, thematically placing Egypt at the height of its power and foreshadowing that country's subsequent fall from grace.

Such a close alignment with Egyptian chronology demonstrates that the Joseph chronology belongs to the earlier Genesis birth-and-death chronology, which argues against the authenticity of Joseph as a historical figure. Joseph, like the other patriarchal leaders, belongs to the realm of myth, and later chapters will explore some of the mythological sources that contributed to the patriarchal stories. First, however, we need to date the Exodus and set the event in its proper historical context. The Joseph chronology provides some important clues.

Since, as I have demonstrated, the birth-and-death chronology derives from Egyptian chronology and dynastic king lists, the author of Genesis, presumably Moses, must have had close and intimate contact with Egyptian records and libraries. Such a writer, so familiar with Egyptian history, would have to have been familiar with when and if the Exodus occurred. Since he was familiar with events before 1454 B.C., the Exodus must have occurred at a later date. But when?

In Genesis there is some evidence for the date of the Exodus, and it places the event after 1454, but the evidence is problematic. Not only do the relevant passages contain ambiguities, they are contradicted by passages from other parts of the Bible. Nevertheless, now that we know Genesis provides an accurate chronological guide to events in Egyptian dynastic history, we have a powerful tool to enable us to resolve many of these contradictions and place evidence for the Exodus in its proper political and historical context.

Table 7.1 shows the proposed chronology for the Eighteenth and early Nineteenth Dynasties as set forth in this chapter.

8

Dating the Exodus

Historians generally cite three major difficulties in dating the Exodus. First, some biblical passages concerning its date contradict others. Second, the archaeological record does not corroborate the biblical account. Third, scholars see no satisfactory historical context in which such an enormous logistical undertaking could have occurred. Consequently, most of what biblical scholars say about the date of the Exodus relies upon educated guesses that attempt to balance the above factors in the least inconsistent manner.

Despite the lack of solid evidence about the Exodus date, scholars all agree that the monotheistic revolution of Pharaoh Akhenaten and the religious teachings of Moses have no common origin. They always choose dates with an eye toward eliminating any possible contact between these two extraordinary thinkers. Given the unchallenged belief that Israel's roots lie outside of Egypt, we shouldn't be surprised by such an attitude.

Yet, here we have seen that the Genesis birth-and-death chronology draws upon Egyptian king lists and provides a historically accurate account of Egyptian dynastic starting dates. This discovery provides us with a powerful tool for placing biblical events in historical context. By applying what we have learned about Genesis, we can place biblical events in their proper chronological context and meet the demands imposed by the archaeological record.

That process will enable us to date the Exodus, examine the conditions that brought Israel into existence, identify the pharaoh of the bondage and the pharaoh of the Exodus, and understand why Egypt actively suppressed all record of this momentous occasion. The analysis will prove that Moses and Akhenaten worked together to change the nature of Egyptian religion, and that Israel originated in the aftermath of Egypt's bitter reaction to Akhenaten's monotheistic revolution.

The Permissible Time Frame

According to Exodus 1, after Jacob and his family moved to Egypt at the invitation of Joseph, the Israelites became "fruitful, and increased abundantly, and multiplied, and waxed exceeding mighty; and the land was filled with them." And there came to rule over Egypt a pharaoh, "which knew not Joseph." This pharaoh feared the Israelites and, to halt their growing power, he "set over them taskmasters to afflict them with their burdens. And they built for Pharaoh treasure cities, Pithom and Raamses."

During the period of enslavement, Moses was born. Hidden away at first, his mother set him afloat upon an ark and sent him down the Nile, praying that God would take care of him. The pharaoh's daughter discovered the child and raised him as her own in the royal household. As an adult, Moses interfered with the punishment of a Hebrew slave and killed an Egyptian guard, then fled from Egypt for his safety. The Bible does not say how old he was at the time, but rabbinical tradition says he was forty.[1]

Eventually, Moses returned to Egypt, confronted the pharaoh, and liberated the Hebrews. The Bible doesn't explicitly say how old Moses was when Israel left Egypt but, since Deuteronomy says that after the Exodus he wandered for forty years[2] and that he died at the age of 120,[3] we can easily conclude that the Exodus occurred in his eightieth year.

According to our chronological reconstruction, Joseph's death occurred at the onset of the coregency between Thutmose III and Amenhotep II. When the text says the pharaoh "knew not Joseph," it implies that the monarch who came to the throne must not have been alive during Joseph's lifetime. That eliminates Amenhotep II as the pharaoh in question, since he was alive during the latter part of Joseph's generation. The period of persecution, therefore, could have started no earlier than the reign of Thutmose IV, successor to Amenhotep II.

Amenhotep II had a high-year mark of twenty-three.[4] Since there is no evidence of a coregency between him and his successor, Thutmose IV couldn't have come to the throne earlier than about 1430 B.C. If the Exodus took place in the eightieth year of Moses, then it couldn't have occurred any earlier than 1350, which, according to our chronological reconstruction, falls during the reign of Tutankhamen.

At the closest end of the time line we have the Merneptah "Victory" or "Israel" stele, which requires that the Exodus preceded Merneptah's reign. In our reconstruction, Ramesses II came to the throne in 1304, which places the start of Merneptah's reign at about 1237. This leaves a period of about 113 years during which the Exodus might have occurred (1350 to 1237 B.C.), and limits the period of oppression to no more than 193 years. The only possible pharaohs who could have been on the throne at the time of the Exodus were, in order of service, Tutankhamen, Aye, Horemheb, Ramesses I, Sethos I, and Ramesses II.

Raamses and Pithom

For most scholars, the reference in Exodus to the Hebrew slaves working on the Egyptian cities of Raamses and Pithom provides the chief evidence of the identity of the pharaoh of the Exodus. Historians generally agree that these two cities correspond to the Egyptian cities of Pi-Ramesses and Pi-Tum. The history of Pi-Tum is not well known, but it was in existence at least in the time of Merneptah and presumably much earlier.[5] Pi-Ramesses, however, received that name during the reign of Ramesses II.

Since this city was named by Ramesses II, scholars argue that this proves Ramesses II must have been the pharaoh of the Exodus. If the author of the phrase referring to the city of Raamses participated in the Exodus, then the event must have happened in the reign of Ramesses II. His is the only reign before Merneptah in which that city had that name, and as already noted, Merneptah had to have come to the throne after the Exodus.

Despite the wide support for this argument, it is flawed. The city of Raamses existed prior to Ramesses II but under a different name. Most Egyptologists believe that it was originally the city of Avaris, the Hyksos capitol dedicated to Set, a deity that was particularly important to Ramesses II and his son Sethos I (Set).[6]

Under these circumstances, the reference to the city of Raamses could be anachronistic, written after the Exodus by a scribe using the name existing at the time of writing rather than the one used at the time of the event. There are many such anachronistic references in the Bible. For example, in Genesis, when Canaanite kings captured Abraham's brother Lot, the patriarch raised an army "and pursued them unto Dan." But that territory wasn't known as Dan at the time. It only received that name after the Exodus, presumably when the tribe of Dan moved into the area.

In this regard, we should also note that if the Exodus happened shortly before Ramesses II took the throne, as argued below, the author of the passage could have participated in the Exodus when the city of Raamses had its former name and been alive when the city changed names, and he might have used the new name when writing his history in later years.

In addition, when we study the Egyptian version of the Exodus story (in chapter 10), written by Manetho and preserved by Josephus, we will learn that Moses and his followers were confined to the city of Avaris, the very city that most Egyptologists identify with Raamses.

The Solomon Date

1 Kings 6:1 says, "And it came to pass in the four hundred and eightieth year after the children of Israel were come out of Egypt, in the fourth year of Solomon's reign over Israel . . . he began to build the house of the Lord." Judges 11:26 adds that Jephthah, a judge of Israel prior to the period of kings, performed his office three hundred years after the Exodus.

Unfortunately, no archaeological evidence contemporaneous with the time of Solomon proves that this king ever existed. Nevertheless, historians generally agree that he became king between 970 and 950 B.C., (approximately) even though biblical chronology dates the fourth year of his reign to 1017.[7]

If 950 were the date of Solomon's first year, adding 480 years to the fourth year of his reign gives an Exodus date of about 1426. Allowing for a little "wiggle room" due to the uncertainty of the actual starting date, we arrive at about the start of Thutmose IV's reign. But, as indicated above, this date could at best be only the beginning of the period of persecution, not the date of the Exodus. Using the earlier starting dates for Solomon would be even more objectionable.

Since this 480-year period places the Exodus close to Thutmose

III, Amenhotep II, or Thutmose IV, most scholars find the 480-year claim implausible. Instead, they argue, 1 Chronicles 6 shows twelve generations from the Exodus to Solomon. This, they maintain, indicates that 480 years was not meant literally but rather symbolized the time elapsed by twelve generations. But, the argument continues, forty years are too long for a generation, and a more realistic twenty-five years should be substituted, making the total time span three hundred years and dating the Exodus between 1270 and 1250 B.C., right where the majority would like it.

The problem with this theory is that that there is no biblical reference to a generation lasting forty years, twenty-five years, or any other number. The proponents of this position decided how many years prior to Solomon they wanted to date the Exodus and divided the total by twelve. This approach proves nothing about the date of the Exodus; the argument only means that advocates of this view would like the Exodus to fall in the reign of Ramesses II, and despite the absence of proof the proponents simply declare it so.

The Sojourn Date

Exodus 12:40–41 says, "the sojourning of the children of Israel, who dwelt in Egypt, was four hundred and thirty years. And it came to pass at the end of the four hundred and thirty years, even the self-same day it came to pass, that all the hosts of the Lord went out from the land of Egypt."

Read literally, the phrase "children of Israel" refers to the House of Jacob and implies that the sojourn began sometime during Jacob's lifetime. Since Jacob and his family didn't move to Egypt until 1525 B.C., Joseph's thirty-ninth year, the passage implies that the sojourn began in that year. Others could reasonably argue that since Joseph was one of the children of Israel the sojourn could have begun with his arrival in Egypt in his seventeenth year, 1547.

Counting 430 years from either of those dates indicates an Exodus in either 1117 or 1095 B.C. Neither date is acceptable. Not only do they conflict with the Merneptah "Israel" stele, which gives a latest possible date of 1237 for the Exodus, they require that we eliminate the entire period of Judges and jump straight from the Exodus to the Hebrew monarchy.

The 430-year sojourn also runs into problems with some other biblical data. The generations from Jacob to Moses are: Jacob, Levi, Kohath, Amram, and Moses. Levi lived 137 years,[8] Kohath 133 years,[9] and Amram 137 years.[10] In addition, according to Genesis 46:11, Levi and Kohath came into Egypt with Jacob.[11] This means that the sojourn can't encompass more than part of the life span of Kohath, all of Amram, and eighty years for Moses. Assuming that: Kohath arrived in Egypt as an infant; Amram's birth happened in Kohath's last year; and Moses's birth occurred in Amram's last year; the maximum period for the sojourn would be 350 years, not 430.

In addition, a sojourn of 430 years conflicts with the biblical allegation of four hundred years of slavery. The sojourn began in either Joseph's seventeenth or thirty-ninth year, and the period of slavery began after the death of Joseph. Since Joseph lived to the age of 110, there must be a gap of at least seventy-one years between the sojourn and the onset of bondage.

This means that if the sojourn lasted 430 years, the bondage could have lasted no more than about 360 years, not the four hundred years indicated elsewhere. Alternatively, if the bondage lasted four hundred years, the sojourn must have lasted at least 471 years.

As early as the Hellenistic and Roman periods, Jewish scholars recognized a problem with this 430-year sojourn and began to reinterpret it. The traditional belief developed that the sojourn dated not from the arrival of Jacob in Egypt but to the arrival of Abraham in Canaan, which, incidentally, is the very same year Abraham also sojourned in Egypt.

Josephus, for example, a member of a priestly family with access to the sacred books of the Jewish people as well as a historian, wrote that the Exodus occurred "430 years after the coming of our forefather Abraham to Canaan, Jacob's migration having taken place 215 years later."[12] In other words, there were 215 years from Abraham's arrival in Canaan (and also in Egypt) to Jacob's arrival in Egypt, and 215 years from Jacob's arrival in Egypt to the Exodus.

This idea did not originate with Josephus. It appears even earlier in the writings of Demetrius, a Hellenistic Jew who preceded Josephus and attempted to write a complete and detailed chronological history of ancient Israel. He, too, noted that there were 215 years from Abraham's arrival in Canaan to Jacob's arrival in Egypt.[13] Then, citing figures for the ages of Kohath and Amram when they became fathers, he demonstrated that there were 215 years from

Jacob's arrival in Egypt to the Exodus.[14] Unfortunately, his evidence contradicts the Bible. In his account, Kohath was born the year Jacob died (after seventeen years in Egypt.)[15] Genesis 46:11, however, says that Kohath was among the children of Israel who arrived with Jacob in Egypt.

While the Genesis chronology clearly shows that 215 years elapsed between the arrival of Abraham in Canaan and the arrival of Jacob in Egypt,[16] where did the 215 years in Egypt come from? Other than this late rabbinical interpretation that the sojourn began with Abraham instead of Jacob, there is no evidence in the Bible for a 215-year Egyptian sojourn. And, as the Demetrius evidence discloses, these late scholarly interpretations relied on extrabiblical data that contradicted the biblical text.

However, even if we accept the idea of a 430-year sojourn beginning with Abraham, that view also contradicts the claim that there was a four-hundred-year period of bondage.[17] If the maximum period of time during which Israel remained in Egypt was 215 years, and 71 of those years occurred during Joseph's lifetime, the maximum period of slavery could only be about 145 years.

That the Hellenistic Jews remained confused about the sojourn chronology is evidenced by Josephus. While in one instance he accepts the idea that Israel was in Egypt for only 215 years, he elsewhere embraces the claim that there were four hundred years of bondage in Egypt. Both propositions can't be true.

Another problem with starting the sojourn when Abraham arrived in Canaan is that the text identifies the sojourn with the "children of Israel," a term that refers to the children of Jacob, all of whom were born well after Abraham died. However, if we recognize that by the time of the biblical redaction the term "children of Israel" had become an idiomatic expression for the Hebrew nation, the phrase could have been maladroitly used to describe the Hebrew nation at the time of Abraham, who was considered its father.

Since Abraham arrived in Canaan in his seventy-fifth year, we can date that event to 1740 B.C. So, if the sojourn lasted 430 years from that date, the Exodus would have taken place in 1310. Interestingly, that date falls only five years later than the Exodus date proposed in the arguments below, and is consistent with the Atenist theory set out in the beginning of this work. Whether the 1310 date can be trusted will have to wait until we look at additional evidence.

The Bondage Date

The most important piece of evidence concerning the Exodus date comes from Genesis 15:13–16, which sets forth God's prophesy to Abraham: "Know of a surety that thy seed shall be a stranger in a land that is not theirs, and shall serve them, and *they shall afflict them four hundred years*. And also that nation, whom they shall serve, will I judge: and afterward shall they come out with great substance. And thou shalt go to thy fathers in peace; thou shalt be buried in a good old age. *But in the fourth generation they shall come hither again;* for the iniquity of the Amorites is not yet full." [Emphasis added.]

Biblical scholars almost unanimously accept that this prophesy refers to the Egyptian enslavement of the Hebrews following Joseph's death. They identify the strange land as Egypt and interpret the prophesy to mean that the Exodus will come after four hundred years of bondage, when the power of the Amorites in Canaan has peaked.

This passage presents many problems. To begin with, despite the claim of four hundred years of bondage, we have already seen that, based on the Genesis chronology and the Merneptah stele, the period of slavery had to be less than 113 years. Also, since we have already indicated that the bondage could have started no earlier than about 1430 B.C., a four-hundred-year period would give a thoroughly unacceptable Exodus date of 1030 B.C. or later, during the Hebrew monarchy.

From the discussion above, we should also recall that a claim of four hundred years of bondage conflicts with the other biblical claim of a four-hundred-and-thirty-year sojourn.

In addition, in one place the prophesy talks of a *departure* (from the strange land) after four hundred years, and elsewhere of a *return* (to a homeland) in the fourth generation, as if both events were one and the same and the four generations lasted four hundred years.

Speiser notes that the Hebrew word translated as "generation" has a primary meaning of "time span," and that "generation" is only a secondary interpretation. The context, he argues, doesn't permit the reader to know which sense of the word to use.[18] Speiser attempts to discredit this passage for the purpose of dating the Exodus,[19] But his argument strikes me as off the mark.

If the primary meaning of *generation* describes an undefined period of time, as in *age* or *duration*, why refer to four such periods? It makes no sense. Unless there is some definable boundary between each period, the number four is superfluous. As long as the time period is undefined, four periods and one mean the same. The enumeration of a specific number of such periods clearly implies that the secondary meaning of generation is intended.

In their attempt to reconcile the four generations with four hundred years, biblical scholars observe that Moses is in the fourth generation after Jacob, (Jacob, Levi, Kohath, Amram, and Moses). Unfortunately, the text indicates that his return is *in* the fourth generation, which would be Amram, not *after* the fourth generation, which would be Moses. Not only that, the prophesy seems to suggest that the return will be to Canaan, and Moses died before the Hebrews entered Canaan, failing to fulfill the prophesy even if we extend it to the fifth generation.

Also, as we have already shown, the genealogy from Jacob to Moses allows for a maximum of only 350 years in Egypt, and that's only if you accept both the very long life spans of Kohath and Amram and that they fathered their children only in their last years.

Still another difficulty concerns the need for the Israelites to wait for the iniquities of the Amorites to end. Why should that be necessary? A god mighty enough to bring Egypt to its knees, the most powerful nation in the known world, shouldn't have much difficulty subduing the fading remnants of the Amorites in Canaan.

Understanding the Prophesy

The prophesy describes two events: four hundred years of affliction in a strange land and a return to a homeland after four generations. Biblical scholars have always assumed that the return was from Egypt to Canaan after a period of four hundred years of slavery in the strange land of Egypt. Given the present form of the text, it's not easy to disagree with such an interpretation. Nevertheless, I would like to suggest an alternative:

1. The departure after four hundred years and the return in four generations describe two separate and distinct events.

2. The strange land was Canaan, not Egypt.

3. The affliction in the "strange land" refers to what the Hyksos kings from Canaan did to the people of Egypt.

4. The return in four generations referred to the return of a Theban ruler in Lower Egypt after the expulsion of the Hyksos.

5. The four generations were Abraham, Isaac, Jacob, and Joseph.

6. The iniquities of the Amorites refers to Hyksos domination in Egypt.

7. The reference to four hundred years of affliction mistakenly combines two separate and distinct afflictions, one referring to what the Hyksos kings from Canaan did to the people of Egypt, the other to what the Egyptians did to the followers of Akhenaten.

8. The four hundred years of Abraham's seed began with the birth of Abraham's son Isaac, in 1715 B.C.

9. The Exodus occurred four hundred years after Isaac was born, in 1315 B.C.

Implicit in this scheme is that the biblical redactors made a major error in transcription. I believe that by the time the Bible achieved its final form, sometime well after the Babylonian captivity in 587 B.C., the Hebrew scribes, immersed first in Babylonian and then Persian culture, lost close touch with their Egyptian roots. They had come to identify Egypt only with the oppression that triggered their departure and had come to believe that they were primarily a Semitic-speaking, Canaanite-Mesopotamian people who had lived only for a short time in Egypt. This led to a misunderstanding of older texts and resulted in erroneous accounts of what happened.

In the case of the Abraham prophesy, the redactors saw two predictions about Abraham's family, both involving affliction and both involving movement to another territory. They mistakenly thought that both predictions described the same event and concatenated the two visions into a single prophesy. The key to reconstructing it is to recognize that originally, like the Genesis chronology, it was written from a native Egyptian perspective and describes events happening in Egypt.

The Strange Land

The prophesy says that Abraham's seed will be strangers in a land that is not theirs. Since the prophesy says that Abraham's seed will suffer affliction in that land, biblical scholars routinely identify it as

Egypt. Genesis and Exodus, however, continuously refer to Canaan as the land where they are strangers.

In Genesis 17:8, where God makes his covenant with Abraham, he says "I will give unto thee, and to thy seed after thee, the *land wherein thou art a stranger, all the land of Canaan,* for an everlasting possession." And, in Genesis 37:1 the text reads, "And Jacob dwelt in the *land wherein his father* (i.e., Isaac, son of Abraham) *was a stranger, in the land of Canaan."* Also, in Genesis 28:4, Isaac says to Jacob, "And give thee the blessing of Abraham, to thee, and to thy seed with thee; that thou mayest inherit *the land wherein thou art a stranger."* [Emphasis added.] And about Jacob and his brother Esau, in Canaan, we are told in Genesis 36:7, "For their riches were more than that they might dwell together; and *the land wherein they were strangers* could not bear them because of their cattle. And in Exodus 6:4, about Abraham, Isaac, and Jacob, God says to Moses, "And I have also established my covenant with them, *to give them the land of Canaan,* the land of their pilgrimage, *wherein they were strangers."* [Emphasis added.] Over and over, then, we are told that Canaan was the land where the patriarchs were strangers. It is as if the author has gone out of his way to emphasize the point.

On no occasion in Genesis or Exodus (other than in the proposed interpretation of the prophesy) does the text refer to Egypt as a land where the Hebrews are strangers. Egypt is usually referred to as the "land of bondage," which is as it should be. According to Genesis, Jacob came to Egypt with less than seventy descendants from his loins.[20] When Israel left Egypt there were allegedly 600,000 Hebrew males.[21] Prior to the Exodus, the only land ever really known by the Hebrews was Egypt. It was the only land where the children of Israel were *not* strangers.

If Canaan is the strange land, as the Bible clearly indicates in all other relevant passages, then the affliction suffered must have something to do with Canaan, not Egypt. At the same time, if Canaan is the strange land then it is not the land of return. How can this be?

Abraham's Sojourn in Egypt

According to the Bible, In Abraham's seventy-fifth year God directed him to leave Mesopotamia and move to Canaan. In the very year of his arrival the land suffered a famine and he had to move to Egypt. His seventy-fifth year fell in 1740 B.C.

Coming from Canaan, Abraham's arrival point in Egypt would have been the delta in Lower Egypt. By about 1740 this territory had already experienced a rapid expansion in Hyksos power. Only a few years later, the Hyksos controlled much of the northern territory and boldly established their capital in Avaris.

Egyptian literature describes the period of Hyksos domination as one of great horror and affliction, although the archaeological record suggests that the Hyksos were far more benign than the Theban propagandists would have it. In the Egyptian mindset of the Eighteenth Dynasty, the Hyksos were hated foreigners from Canaan, the land where Abraham and his seed were strangers, and the Hyksos era was one of Canaanite affliction.

Genesis depicts Abraham as wary of the pharaoh and fearing for his safety. He believed that when the pharaoh saw his wife, Sarai (later named Sarah), the monarch would want her for his own and would have him killed if he knew he was her husband. As a precaution, he directed Sarai to pretend to be his sister.

Abraham's fears were warranted. The king saw Sarai and wed her. Shortly thereafter the god of Abraham unleashed a series of household plagues to torment the Egyptian ruler, which led to a revelation of Sarai's relationship to Abraham. The pharaoh was taken aback. He returned Sarai to Abraham, bestowed many gifts upon them, and ordered them out of the country.

At this point Genesis contains a strange and puzzling passage. In the King James Version and many other translations, the text reads, "And Abraham went up out of Egypt, he and his wife, and all that he had, and Lot went with him, *into the south.*"[22] [Emphasis added.] If Abraham went "into the south" he did not go to Canaan, he went to Upper Egypt, where Thebes was located.

Obviously, this presents a problem in biblical interpretation. Did Abraham go south to Upper Egypt or north to Canaan? In the Revised Standard Version and other modern translations that same text is given a different twist. The phrase "into the south" has been replaced by the phrase "into the Negev." The Negev is the large desert area south of Canaan but *east* of Egypt.

The contradiction arises from the fact that in Hebrew *negev* means "south," and the Negev desert is obviously named for the fact that it is south of Israel.[23] Modern translators, recognizing that you can't get to Canaan by going "into the south," assumed that the Hebrew phrase referred to "the South"—the Negev desert. However, the

Bible does not use the Hebrew word *negev;* it uses *negevah,* which means "southerly," not "south." Abraham went in a *southerly* direction, not to "the South."

If Abraham went in a southerly direction to get out of the pharaoh's country, he had to be going to a portion of Egypt that remained outside Hyksos control, somewhere in Upper Egypt. In a chronological context, Abraham's movement from Lower Egypt in the north to Upper Egypt in the south serves as a backdrop to the conflict between Thebes and the Hyksos kings. Royal marriages served to cement treaties, and the story of the pharaoh and Sarai suggests a literary motif about political machinations in the Hyksos era. We'll have more to say about this story in later chapters.

The southerly journey represents an original remnant of the earliest version of the story, with Abraham as an Egyptian from the south rather than a Canaanite from the north. Sloppy editing may have caused the biblical redactors to overlook this clue to Israel's early roots.

Abraham's Birthplace

A question arises as to whether or not Abraham was ever outside of Egypt prior to his confrontation with the Hyksos king. Genesis implies that Abraham was born in Ur of the Chaldees, although it never specifically says that he was.[24] The text says that Abraham's father was born in Ur of the Chaldees and that he left there with Abraham and other family members to go to Haran, another Mesopotamian city.

After moving to Haran, Abraham, as noted above, received directions from God to leave Haran and go to Canaan, where the Israelites would become a great nation.[25] Almost immediately after his arrival they experienced a famine throughout the land and Abraham moved his family to Egypt. That is all we know about Abraham's residencies before his arrival in Egypt.

The entire claim, therefore, that Abraham was outside of Egypt prior to his seventy-fifth year is deduced from a few simple passages allegedly tracing his route from Ur of the Chaldees to Canaan. But Ur of the Chaldees is an anachronistic phrase that had to have been inserted into the text hundreds of years after the Exodus. It smacks of an effort by Hebrew scribes during the Babylonian Captivity (after

587 B.C.) to identify with the cultural roots of their Babylonian conquerors, the Chaldaeans.

The term "of the Chaldees" refers to either Chaldaea, a province
of Babylon, or Babylon itself. The Chaldaeans rose to prominence in
614 B.C., when they defeated the Assyrians and made Babylon the
capitol of their empire. Shortly thereafter they defeated the Hebrew
kingdom of Judah and moved its leadership to Babylon. Speiser observes that:

> [the] ancient and renowned city of Ur is never ascribed ex-
> pressly, in the many thousands of cuneiform records from that
> site, to the Chaldaean branch of the Aramaean group. The
> Chaldaeans, moreover, are late arrivals in Mesopotamia, and
> could not possibly be dated before the end of the second millen-
> nium. Nor could the Aramaeans be placed automatically in the
> Patriarchal period. Yet the pertinent tradition was apparently
> known not only to P (31) but also to J (28). And even if one were
> to follow LXX in reading "land" for "Ur," *the anachronism of the
> Chaldaeans would remain unsolved.*[26] [Emphasis added.]

This doesn't necessarily prove that Abraham didn't come from Ur,
but it does prove that the original Genesis author could not have
used the phrase "Ur of the Chaldees." The anachronism strongly
suggests that redactors inserted the entire pre-Egyptian portion of
Abraham's life in later times, more than seven hundred years after
the Exodus.

Another puzzling matter about Abraham's departure from Haran
concerns the command that he go to Canaan at the height of a
famine, when he would have to immediately leave Canaan and go to
Egypt. If Abraham's presence in Egypt fulfills a divine plan, why
doesn't he go there directly? Why should he need to first establish a
brief and insignificant presence in Canaan? Alternatively, if his presence in Egypt isn't necessary to the divine plan, why doesn't he delay
his departure until the famine is over? In truth, Egypt was the original locus of the early Abraham stories.

Amorites and Hyksos

The Genesis prophesy indicates that it will take four generations
before the iniquities of the Amorites come to an end. Biblical scholars suggest that God waited to deliver the Israelites out of Egypt

until the power of the Amorites in Canaan had come to an end. I suggest that the Amorites mentioned in the prophesy were the Hyksos rulers in Egypt.

The Amorites were an early Semitic-speaking people who inhabited the territory from Canaan to approximately Babylon. In the third millennium B.C. Babylonians called Syria and Palestine "the land of the Amorites."[27] By the time of the Eighteenth Dynasty the Amorites form just one of many tribes identified as inhabitants of Canaan. Speiser, commenting on the Amorite prophesy, says that the Bible uses the name Amorites both as a reference to a specific people and as a general reference to the pre-Israelite population of Canaan.[28] There is a third sense, however, in which such a name might have been used, and the one that I think was originally intended in Genesis. It would be a reference to a specific subset of a larger group. For example, during the American Revolution George Washington would have been fighting to end the iniquities of the Germans, where "Germans" would mean "the royal court of England's German king" rather than the German nation or the inhabitants of Germany.

In this third sense, the "iniquity of the Amorites" would refer neither to the Amorite people as a whole nor to the pre-Israelite population of Canaan as a whole, but to a small group of Amorites associated with evil. More specifically, given Abraham's chronological time frame and the dominance of the Hyksos over Lower Egypt and Canaan, the "iniquity of the Amorites" refers to the "iniquity" of the Hyksos conquerors of Egypt, where the Hyksos formed a subset of the Amorites.

Who the Hyksos were is something of a mystery. The name Hyksos originates with Manetho. Josephus says that in different manuscripts the word *Hyksos* has different meanings, "shepherd kings" in one, "captive kings" in another.[29] This latter interpretation led Josephus to identify the Hyksos with the children of Israel.

Gardiner notes that many Egyptologists still cling to this view.[30] "Although there are sound linguistic grounds for both etymologies," he writes, "neither is the true one."[31] He then translates *Hyksos* as "chieftains of a foreign hill-country," a usage that he says was applied from the Middle Kingdom on to designate Bedouin sheiks.[32] This alternative translation is now widely accepted among Egyptologists, and Gardiner notes its consistency with the Turin Canon reference to the "chieftains of a foreign country."[33]

In line with Gardiner's translation, "chieftains from a foreign hill-country," it's worth noting that at the time of the Exodus the Bible identifies the Amorites as living in the Canaanite hills.[34] In any event, whatever the origin of the name Hyksos, the contemporaneous Egyptians did not use it to describe the foreign conquerors. The Egyptian texts identify the Hyksos invaders by the name Aamu, which approximately means "Asiatics."[35]

While the meaning of the term *Amorite* in the Genesis prophesy is debatable, it is consistent with a description of the Hyksos kings. Both *Aamu* and *Amorite* refer to the people of Canaan and Mesopotamia, and the Hyksos kings certainly came from that region.

The Fourth Generation

The prophesy to Abraham says two things will happen in the fourth generation. First, there will be a return to some territory, and second, the "iniquities of the Amorites" will end. Consider, then, some coincidences.

Abraham left Egypt while the Hyksos ruled there. In the fourth generation (Abraham, Isaac, Jacob, and Joseph) Joseph returns to Egypt after the "iniquities" of the Hyksos have come to an end. Furthermore, Joseph's birth date coincides with the year in which the Hyksos suffered their last major defeat at the hands of the Thebans.

If we recognize Egypt as the place of return and the Hyksos as the Amorites, then that portion of the prophesy about the fourth generation makes logical sense. Unfortunately, the way the text reads, it implies that Canaan was the land of the return. But the prophesy also implies that Egypt is the strange land and, as we saw above, it is Canaan that is the strange land.

Apparently, the biblical redactors substituted Egypt for Canaan and Canaan for Egypt. Such an error is understandable. By the time of the redaction the tradition had already been established that the patriarchs were from Mesopotamia and Canaan. Therefore, any return home had to be to Canaan. Similarly, the strange land had to be somewhere other than the homeland—i.e., Egypt.

Placing the prophesy in the context of Egyptian history enables us to restore its true meaning: The return was to Egypt; the Amorites were the Hyksos; Joseph constituted the fourth generation, during which time the iniquities of the Amorites came to an end.

The Prophesy and the Exodus

Despite the longevity attributed to the early patriarchs, it is unlikely that the original Genesis chronographer intended to equate four hundred years with four generations, especially since most lived several centuries longer than a hundred years. What appears to have happened is that the redactor fused two separate but similar stories of affliction. One story talked of return, the other of departure. The redactor assumed both journeys were to the same location, Canaan.

As just explained, the one account, about a return home in the fourth generation when the "iniquity of the Amorites" ended, referred to the expulsion of the Hyksos in the generation of Joseph. In this story, the Hyksos of Lower Egypt, after some political maneuvering with rival kings in the territory, forced some northern nobles to flee into the south. Abraham and his family represented the departing Egyptians. In Abraham's fourth generation, his descendant Joseph returned to Lower Egypt, representing the reconsolidation of power under the southern kings of Thebes.

The second report referred to the actual Exodus. In this story the children of Israel, living in Egypt, were subjected to a period of affliction, and in the four-hundredth year of Abraham's seed they departed to a land where Abraham was a stranger—Canaan. The cause and nature of this affliction will be examined in the remaining chapters, but it is separate from the Hyksos affliction and could not have lasted four hundred years. The period of four hundred years originally encompassed not the time of affliction but rather the length of time between the birth of Abraham's son Isaac and the departure from Egypt.

The redactor's confusion originated in the belief that the children of Israel were Canaanites, not Egyptians. In his mind a return home meant a return to Canaan, and a strange land meant Egypt. Not familiar with the Hyksos conquest, the only affliction he knew of was that which led to the departure from Egypt. As a result, the two separate afflictions were thought of as a single continuous event, and in stitching together the narrative from diverse sources, he changed the places of origin and return so that they accorded with his own notions. Since Abraham's seed began with the birth of Isaac in 1715 B.C., this would date the Exodus to 1315 B.C.

The Exodus: 1310 or 1315?

We have previously shown that the 430-year sojourn in Egypt did not refer to a period of captivity in Egypt. Early on, the traditional notion developed that there was a 215-year period in Canaan and a 215-year period in Egypt. According to this theory, the sojourn began with Abraham's arrival, either in Canaan or Egypt, in his seventy-fifth year, 1740 B.C. This would indicate an Exodus date of 1310 B.C. But we also have an alternative Exodus date of 1315 based on the four-hundredth year of Abraham's seed.

The two dates are only five years apart, providing a very close correspondence and suggesting the two dating schemes draw upon similar chronological information and traditions. One might want to reconcile this five-year difference by arguing that the affliction ended in 1315, when Israel rose up in rebellion, and that it took five years of resistance before the Exodus occurred, but I suspect that the redactor simply made an arithmetic error in calculating the time between Jacob's arrival in Egypt and the Exodus, arriving at 215 years instead of 210.

In support of this view, I note that many of the Hellenistic sources used chronological data that differed from the biblical information. Demetrius, for example, a highly influential chronographer, wrote, "Now Joseph was at that time seventeen years old, and he was sold into Egypt, and had remained in prison thirteen years, so that he was then thirty years old; and Jacob was a hundred and ten years, one year before which time Isaac died, being a hundred and eighty years old."[36] While it is true that Joseph's thirtieth birthday occurred one year after Isaac died, Jacob was 121 years old on Joseph's thirtieth birthday, not 110. And, as we saw above, Demetrius also placed the birth of Kohath at least seventeen years later than Genesis had it.

In another example, Josephus, the highly influential Jewish historian raised in a priestly family, gives Isaac's age at death as 185 years, extending his life five years beyond the age given in Genesis (an interesting error given the five-year difference between the two Genesis dates).[37] And, of course, we have Josephus's massive inconsistency about a 215-year sojourn in Egypt and a 400-year period of slavery there.

Artapanus, another classical historian, in his *Concerning the Jews,* gives Moses's age at the time of the Exodus as eighty-nine years instead of eighty.[38]

Only in late Hellenistic writings and teachings do we find the doctrine of 215 years in Canaan and 215 years in Egypt. Demetrius provides us with the only specific chronology about how a 215-year period in Egypt was determined, but his data contradicts the Genesis evidence. The inconsistent numbers floating around among the Hellenistic writers of Jewish history, such as Demetrius, Josephus, and Artapanus, show that in this late time the Hellenistic Jews relied on a number of sources and traditions that differed from the Bible.

Given the high reliability of the Genesis chronology versus the untested and undocumented sources of Exodus, the Genesis-provided date of 1315 B.C. stands with greater authority than the Exodus-provided date of 1310. Additionally, other clues in the Bible also indicate that the Genesis dating scheme is to be preferred.

The Pharaoh of the Exodus

According to Exodus, Moses fled from Egypt after killing an Egyptian soldier. During his exile the sitting pharaoh died.[39] At this point God told Moses to go back to Egypt and liberate the Hebrew people.[40]

Although we are not told how much time elapsed between Moses's return and the Exodus, we are given to believe that it was a short period of time. Following the Israelites' departure, the pharaoh chased after them, arriving at a place where they were trapped in front of the sea. God caused the waters to part and "the Egyptians pursued, and went in after them to the midst of the sea, even all pharaoh's horses, his chariots, and his horsemen."[41]

Subsequently the waters closed over the Egyptian forces and "covered the chariots, and the horseman, and all the host of Pharaoh that came into the sea after them; there remained not so much as one of them."[42] The text doesn't explicitly say that the pharaoh drowned, but if all the chariots and horseman went into the sea, one should reasonably assume that the pharaoh rode in a chariot, joined in the chase, and drowned in the effort.

Scientifically, we cannot accept that this incident is literally true, but we can understand it as a figurative description of events. From such a perspective we may conclude that in the course of the Exodus the pharaoh died, indicating that he served only a very short term.

Chronologically, this gives us a pharaoh's death followed by a second pharaoh's death a short time thereafter.

The two possible Exodus dates, 1315 and 1310, place the event at the transition between the Eighteenth and Nineteenth dynasties. At this point the king sequence is: Horemheb, Ramesses I, and Sethos I. Horemheb is considered the last pharaoh of the Eighteenth Dynasty. Ramesses I served only about two years, part as coregent with Horemheb and part as coregent with Sethos I. He had perhaps only a few months as an independent ruler.

In the chronology adopted in our reconstruction of the Eighteenth Dynasty, Horemheb's reign ended at about 1315 B.C. and Sethos I's began at about 1314; Ramesses I overlapped the two. This coincides with the Genesis dating of the Exodus in 1315. The first pharaoh to die would have been Horemheb. This would leave Ramesses I as the monarch whom Moses confronted. He would also be the briefly ruling king who died during the Exodus. Sethos I would have been coregent at the time.

A particularly interesting coincidence that may have contributed to the image of a drowning pharaoh is that Ramesses I died at the start of a Sothic cycle, and the annual heliacal rising of Sothis signified the start of the flood season. The entire Sothic cycle signified the harmony between the flooding of the Nile and the movement of the sun. Coming only once every 1,460 years, the start of the cycle was an event of great religious import.

The death of Ramesses I at the start of a Sothic cycle in 1314 B.C. and the association of a Sothic cycle with the fruitful flooding of the Nile Valley may have suggested a literary metaphor for the drowning of the pharaoh and the flowering of Israel.

Moses and Akhenaten

Dating the Exodus to 1315 has significant implications for the origins of Israel. Moses was eighty years old at the time of the Exodus, which means he would have been born in 1395 B.C.

Akhenaten came to the throne between 1375 and 1372, at which time Moses would have been just over twenty years of age. We do not know Akhenaten's precise age at the time of his ascension, but the consensus holds that it occurred sometime between his late teens and early twenties. If Moses grew up in the royal household, as claimed in Exodus, then he and Akhenaten would have to have been raised together, receiving the same royal education.

The date of Moses's flight from Egypt provides another interesting piece of evidence connecting him to Akhenaten. Although the Bible doesn't say how old he was at the time, rabbinical tradition agrees that he spent forty years in the wilderness before the Exodus, making him forty years old when he left Egypt.[43] This would date his flight to 1355 B.C., a date which divided the reigns of Smenkhkare and Tutankhamen.

Smenkhkare was Akhenaten's successor, and served briefly as coregent with his predecessor. The end of Smenkhkare's reign marked the end of Akhenaten's revolution. When Tutankhamen took the throne, Atenism fell into disrepute.

That a counterrevolution took hold almost immediately upon Tutankhamen's ascension can be seen from the fact that he changed his name from Tutankh*aten*, to Tutankh*amen*.[44] The *aten* element in his original name refers to the Aten worshiped by Akhenaten, during whose reign Tutankhamen was born. The *amen* element signified the god Amen, the Theban god whose cult was the chief target of Akhenaten's religious revolution.

The Book of Exodus alleges that Moses fled Egypt because after he killed a soldier who was cruelly beating a Hebrew slave, he feared he would be put to death when his homicidal deed was discovered. Josephus, however, cites a different tradition. According to his account, political enemies feared that Moses would become pharaoh and plotted to kill him.[45] Warned of the murder plans ahead of time, Moses fled to safety.

Given the coincidence between the date of Moses's flight from Egypt and the death of Smenkhkare, Josephus appears to have preserved the true reason for Moses's flight: The death of Smenkhkare triggered a political struggle for the throne; Moses, as a key player in Akhenaten's revolution, may have been in line to succeed Smenkhkare, but the enemies of Akhenaten seized the upper hand and Moses had to flee to save his life.

9

Egypt Under Akhenaten

What angered Egyptians about Pharaoh Akhenaten was not his monotheism; it was his intolerance. Despite the polytheistic nature of Egyptian religion, it derived from an essentially monotheistic belief in a single Creator deity responsible for all that existed, including the other deities. Although different cults believed in different Creator deities, they all adhered to the same basic model of Creation.

In the beginning a great flood, known as the Nun or Nu, engulfed the universe. As in the Bible, the Creator's spirit caused the waters to stir, initiating the generative process. Out of the Nun arose the primeval hill and the self-created Creator. In Heliopolis the Creator was known as Atum, in Memphis he was Ptah, in Thebes he was Amen, and in Hermopolis he was Re.

Other deities, like angels in the Bible, were the creations of the one all-powerful deity, and each of the cult centers tried to argue that the Creator deities of the other cults were just lesser deities created by their own chief god. In Thebes, for example, the priests taught that Ptah, Atum, and Re were only aspects of Amen, the Theban Creator deity. Despite these disagreements, all cults flourished side by side, each free to teach what it wanted.

Egyptian literature has numerous references to a sole deity responsible for all of Creation, and not infrequently the texts often sound as if they were lifted from Hebrew prayer books. Sir Wallis Budge, a prominent Egyptologist in the early part of this century, collected several such expressions. Consider these examples:[1]

God is One and alone, and none other existeth with Him; God is the One, the One Who hath made all things.

God is from the beginning, and He hath been from the beginning; He hath existed from of old and was when nothing else had being. He existed when nothing else had existed, and what existeth He created after He had come into being. He is the father of beginnings.

God is the eternal One, He is eternal and infinite; and endureth for ever and aye; He hath endured for countless ages, and He shall endure to all eternity.

God is life, and through Him only man liveth. He giveth life to man, and he breatheth the breath of life into his nostrils.

God Himself is existence, He liveth in all things and liveth upon all things. He endureth without increase or diminution, He multiplieth Himself millions of times, and he possesseth multitudes of forms and multitudes of members.

God hath made the universe, and he hath created all that therein is: He is the Creator of what is in this world, of what was, of what is, and of what shall be. He is the Creator of the world and it was He who fashioned it with His hands before there was any beginning; and he established it with that which went forth from Him. He is the Creator of the heavens and the earth; the Creator of the heavens, and the earth, and the deep; the Creator of the heavens, and the earth, and the deep, and the waters, and the mountains. God had stretched out the heavens and founded the earth. What His heart conceived came to pass straightway, and when He had spoken His words came to pass, and it shall endure for ever.

And from the Egyptian Book of the Dead, we have:

I am the god Temu [Atum] in his rising. I am the only One. I came into being in Nu. I am Ra [Re] who rose in the beginning.[2]

The text goes on to identify other deities as aspects of Atum.

In a hymn to Re from the walls of the tomb of Sethos I we find a series of statements in which various gods are identified with the body of Re.[3] And a papyrus dating to about 1000 B.C. describes Amen as:

the being in whom every god existeth, the One of One, the Creator of the things which came into being when the earth took form in the beginning.[4]

Contrast these various passages with one of the most famous of all Hebrew prayers: "Hear O Israel, the Lord thy God, the Lord is one."

In retrospect, one can probably say that the monotheism of modern Judaism, Christianity, and Islam bears a closer resemblance to Egyptian polytheism than it does to Akhenaten's monotheism. All three religions, for example, recognize Satan as a powerful supernatural force aligned in opposition to the Creator deity. No amount of equivocation can deny the deistic nature of Satan. Though less powerful than the Creator, he enjoys the same status as lesser deities in Egyptian and other polytheistic religions.

These three monotheistic religions also acknowledge the existence of angels, deities who bear approximately the same relation to the Creator as the Egyptian lesser deities do to Egyptian Creator gods. And let's not forget the host of demons, genies, dybbuks, golems, and fairies that pop up with such frequency in religious literature. However, as Redford explains, Akhenaten would:

> brook no divine manifestations. The sun-disc was unique and supreme over all the universe, the only god there was. He did not change his shape or appear in other forms: he was always and only 'the living Sun-disc—there is none other than he.[5]

What we mistakenly describe as monotheistic about these other religions is their individual proclamations that there is only one all powerful god and it is only he whom one should obey and worship. In Judaism, Christianity, and Islam, other deities are to be ignored or feared, but not to be worshiped. Akhenaten, on the other hand, acknowledged no other deities at all, not even secondary ones.[6]

The Evolution of the Aten

The belief in a single Creator deity, coupled with the central role of the sun in Egyptian theology, led to a proliferation of deities identified with various solar aspects. In Heliopolis the sun was originally represented by Atum, and in Hermopolis by Re. Khepera was the

morning sun, Re the noon sun, and Atum the evening sun. Horus
was a sun god also, as was Osiris in some of his aspects. Evidence of
the solar influence on religious beliefs appears in several texts found
in the tombs of Eighteenth Dynasty pharaohs, documents such as
The Litany of the Sun from the reign of Thutmose III and The Book
of Gates found in the tomb of Horemheb, which describes Re as
"The Lord of the Aten."

As the number of solar gods increased, identities began to merge.
Heliopolitan Atum became Atum-Re, and by Akhenaten's time the
chief Heliopolitan deity was Re-Herakhte, a merger of Re and Horus. Even Amen, the chief god of Thebes, who was not originally a
solar god, had to be identified with the solar Re, becoming Amen-Re.
The proliferation of solar deities made it necessary to express the
word *sun* in a neutral form, devoid of anthropomorphic or religious
meaning, and the word *aten*, referring to the solar disk, came to fill
this need.[7]

During the Eighteenth Dynasty, the Aten slowly came to have
greater importance as a religious symbol, but its origins go back
much earlier, to at least the Twelfth Dynasty, when king Amenemhe
is referred to in the Story of Sinuhe as dying and flying to heaven to
unite with the Aten, the divine flesh mingling with him who had
begot him.[8] The same poetic expression announces the death of
Amenhotep I, the second pharaoh of the Eighteenth Dynasty.[9] Thutmose I, the next in line, chose as one of his titles "Horus-Re, mighty
bull with sharp horns, who comes from the Aten."[10]

Despite the Aten's original neutral tone, under Thutmose IV a
scarab inscription describes it as a "god of battles" who makes the
pharaoh mighty in his domains and brings all his subjects under the
sway of the sun disk,[11] a description not inconsistent with Jahweh
during the Canaanite conquest.

Under this same pharaoh evidence also appears for the growing
influence of the Heliopolitan solar cult. In a stele attributed to Thutmose IV, the king relates how as a child he had a dream in which he
was promised the kingship by the solar god Harmakhe (whom we
know as the great Sphinx) if he would free Harmakhe from the sand
in return.[12] The rest of the account is missing, but Gardiner believes
that the missing portion probably told of the king's efforts to uncover
the Sphinx from the sands in which it had been buried.[13]

With the reign of Amenhotep III, Akhenaten's father, Aten assumed an increased importance. For example, he named the state

barge Radiance of Aten, and at least one of his children (other than Akhenaten) had the name Aten as an element.[14]

Akhenaten as King

Finding evidence of Egypt's internal affairs under Akhenaten is difficult. His religious reforms, which sought to enjoin the worship of other deities, angered the Egyptian establishment, and subsequent to his death it attempted to obliterate all traces of his existence from the Egyptian mind and landscape. Most of the evidence would have been on monuments and walls, but wherever his works were found they were systematically destroyed or torn down, the stones recycled for other purposes.

Beginning in the last century, archaeologists discovered a significant amount of evidence relating to this pharaoh, including not only a number of inscribed stones removed from his capital at Akhetaten (now known as Amarna) and other sites, but also a substantial archive that shed light on many events from this period. These finds at Amarna and elsewhere have enabled us to piece together a rudimentary picture of what Akhenaten believed. It is ironic, as Aldred notes, that Egypt did all it could to forget this pharaoh and now he stands among our most celebrated of ancient kings.[15]

Akhenaten apparently came to the throne by accident. The evidence of the time suggests that Amenhotep III intended for one of his other sons to become king and that son went through the rigorous training in religious and administrative skills required of a monarch.[16] But the heir-apparent died prematurely, and Akhenaten, poorly trained in the necessary administrative skills, became the successor.

Aldred suggests that he was about sixteen when he became king,[17] making him about five years younger than Moses (according to our Genesis chronology). Others have suggested he was a few years older. We know little about his education or formal training.[18]

Redford notes only minimal evidence of contact between him and his father's court.[19] Nor, he adds, is there any evidence that he spent time studying in Heliopolis, the center of solar worship in Egypt.[20] Heliopolis, however, had been one of the leading centers of intellectual activity in Egypt and its wise men were long celebrated.[21] Aldred maintains that in light of what occurred during his reign the teachings of Heliopolis must have had a profound influence on Akhenaten's thinking.[22]

When he first took the throne, Akhenaten kept the family throne name, Amenhotep, the first part referring to the god Amen, chief deity of Thebes. On his ascension, however, he proclaimed his loyalty to "Re-Herakhte rejoicing on the horizon in his aspect of the light which is in the sun disk [the Aten],"[23] the chief deity of Heliopolis at the time. In the earlier stages of the king's religious progression Re-Herakhte was portrayed in his original form, a falcon-headed god bearing the uraeus-encircled disk of the sun on his vertex and his name in expanded form.[24]

Akhenaten's acceptance of a new patron god seems to have resulted from an ideological break with former ideas of deity. A fortunate discovery of two stones taken from Akhenaten's capital and reused in a fill by the pharaoh Horemheb gives us one of the few hints of the pharaoh's thoughts. The text, somewhat disjointed in its present form, is translated by Redford as follows:[25]

[. . .] Horus(?) [. . .]. [. . . Their temples(?)] fallen to ruin, [their bodies(?)] shall/do not [. . .]. [. . . Since the time of (?) the ancesto]rs; it is the wise men that [. . .]. [. . .] look, I am speaking that I might inform [you] [. . .]. [. . . The fo]rms(?) of the gods, I know [their(?)]temples [. . .]. [. . . The wri]tings of / and the inventory manual of their primeval bodies [. . .]. [. . .] they have ceased one after the other, whether of precious stones, [gold], [. . .]. [. . . Who himself gave birth] to himself, and no one knows the mystery of [. . .]. [. . .] he [go]es where he pleases, and they know not [his] g[oing . . .]. [. . .] to him(?) by(?) night, but I approach [. . .]. [. . . The . . .]s which he has made, how exalted they are! [. . .] their [. . .]s as stars. Hail to thee in [thy(?)] radiance! [. . .]. [. . .] What would he be like, another of thy kind? Thou are he who [. . .]. [. . .] [to them in that(?)] name of thine] [. . .].

According to Redford, this text reveals two significant thoughts. First, the king put on record his belief that somehow the gods have ceased or failed to be operative; second, he described his newly adopted god as absolutely unique and located in the heavens.[26]

Redford, who has been involved in the excavation of Amarna, believes that the text must have come from a particular location around which several surrounding vignettes have been preserved, and which make perfectly plain that the god in question is Re-Herakhte, "Re the horizon-Horus," the great sun god of Heliopolis.[27]

In the text just cited, Akhenaten makes reference to an important Egyptian practice, the use of manuals and formulas describing exactly how gods should be portrayed and carved. Egyptians believed strongly in magical practices by which precise formulations and recreations transformed image into reality. To produce a statue of a god in the proper form, they thought, would bring the god's presence into existence.

An attack on this form of idol worship played an important role in Akhenaten's religious reforms. He challenged the idea that gods have efficacy through statues and pictures.[28] In another inscription from his reign we learn that the Aten is "the one who built himself by himself, with his [own] hands—no craftsman knows him,"[29] implicitly challenging the idea that in designing statues, craftsmen can understand the true nature of a deity. Akhenaten's opposition to the use of statues to summon forth gods led him to ban the production of graven images of gods,[30] a ban that echoes in the Ten Commandments of Moses.

By the third year of his reign, Akhenaten replaced the falcon-headed god Horus with a solar disk from which emanate numerous straight sticklike arms ending in hands that either accept offerings or extend the symbols of life or health to the royal celebrants.[31] Eventually, this imagery was the only form in which this god could be displayed.

In the third year we also see another important change in the iconography associated with Re-Herakhte. In addition to the pictorial description of the solar disk with extended arms, the name and epithet of the god were enclosed within two upright cartouches, a pair on each side, a form that signified royalty.[32] To this he added a new epithet, "the great, living Disk which is in jubilee, lord of heaven and earth, who resides in [temple name]."[33]

The use of cartouches to enclose a god's name, signifying that the name belongs to a king, is most unusual. Even though Egyptians thought of other gods, such as Osiris and Amen, as kings and gave them kingly titles such as "Lord of the thrones of Upper and Lower Egypt," their names were never enclosed in cartouches the way that names of pharaohs were.[34]

This iconographic change reflected Akhenaten's belief that the

Aten ruled as king of the universe, just as the pharaoh served as king of the land. Akhenaten envisioned his god as a heavenly god, the "Good God," "Divine and Regal," and himself as virtually coregent with the Aten.[35]

Under Akhenaten, traditional representations of the gods no longer appear; their emblems, except for the Sed festivals, were ignored.[36] Even in the hieroglyphic script, figures of animals and humans are often avoided.[37] After the fifth year of his reign the plural form of *god* no longer appeared.[38]

Despite the eccentricity of these ideas, they would not have been difficult for Egyptians to tolerate if they were simply permitted to continue to follow their own beliefs. And, in the first five years, outside of Thebes, the gods seemed to have survived these reforms.[39] In the fifth year, however, matters took an aggressive turn.

The primary enemy of Akhenaten was the cult of Amen, and he set out on a campaign to erase the god's presence from Egypt. "The program of defacement that followed was so thorough," Redford observes, "that we must postulate either a small army of hatchet men dispatched throughout the realm, or parties of inspectors charged with seeing that local officials did the job. Everywhere, in temples, tombs, statuary, and casual inscriptions, the hieroglyphs for 'Amun' were chiseled out; objects sacred to him were likewise defaced. People who bore names compounded with 'Amun' were required to change them. . . . Osiris and his cycle of mortuary gods suffered a like anathematization."[40]

Also in the fifth year, Akhenaten sought to move his capital from Thebes to his newly constructed city of Akhetaten. Located in a deserted area never previously inhabited, he declared the land unclaimed by any other god. The young king asserted that Aten himself guided the monarch to this spot.[41]

Another unusual feature of Akhenaten's religious reforms concerned the change in the nature of the pharaoh's relation to the ruling god. Prior to Akhenaten every pharaoh constituted an embodiment of the god Horus. Akhenaten conceived of himself only as the First Prophet (i.e., high priest).[42] The Aten cult also appears to have had a second key official who ranked just below the pharaoh, a "Chief Seer of Re-Harakhte."[43] Redford believes that this title clearly derives from the Heliopolitan sun cult, and that this official was probably the managing head of the Aten cult.

Unfortunately, while we know much about the end product of

Akhenaten's revolution, we know little about the content of his teachings. The most important text we have on that subject is the "Hymn to the Aten," allegedly written by Akhenaten. Despite the contempt with which many Egyptologists hold Akhenaten, even his most serious detractors tend to agree that he was a talented poet. Many scholars have noted a resemblance between his hymn and the 104th Psalm, and arguments have been made that the two are related.[44] An excerpt from the hymn gives a sense of the nature of Akhenaten's god and his religious beliefs:

> How manifold are thy works! They are hidden from the sight of man, O Sole God, like unto whom there is no other! Thou didst fashion the earth according to thy desire when thou wast alone—all men, all cattle great and small, all that are upon the earth that run upon their feet or rise up on high flying with their wings. And the lands of Syria and Kush and Egypt—thou appointest every man to his place and satisfied his needs. Everyone receives his sustenance and his days are numbered. Their tongues are diverse in speech and their qualities likewise, and their color is differentiated, for thou hast distinguished the nations.[45]

Although we tend to refer to the deity that Akhenaten worshiped as the Aten (the solar disk), the Aten was only a generic representation of the god—the god's visible manifestation—not the god himself. Behind the Aten stood Re-Herakhte, the invisible source of the sun's creative power.[46]

Despite this dual aspect, there was only one god, a Creator god responsible for all other life and existence. Like the gods of the other cult centers, he was self-created; how, we do not know. But unlike the other Creator deities he brought no other gods into existence. The Aten was the only supernatural force that affects mankind.

Ethics and Akhenaten

Many scholars object to a connection between Akhenaten and Moses on the ground that the pharaoh appeared to lack any moral code. As Gardiner argues, "A defect in the Doctrine was its complete lack of ethical teaching. For this the elimination of Osiris was no doubt largely responsible. Not that his myth had ever been deeply spiritual, but it had recounted the triumph of good over evil and had told of wifely devotion and filial piety."[47] Redford, in the same vein, writes, "No text tells us he hears the cry of the poor man, or succors the sick, or forgives the sinner."[48] On the other hand, inscriptions of the time do portray him as "the Good Ruler who loves Mankind."[49]

The argument that Akhenaten's doctrines lacked an ethical base strike me as thoroughly unfounded. It implies that a different understanding of the nature of divinity requires a simultaneous adoption of a new moral code, no matter how just and ethical the prevailing moral code may be. In fact, the Eighteenth Dynasty had a very thorough and far-reaching ethical doctrine known as the Negative Confessions, a series of forty-two principles defining the kind of correct behavior which would permit you successful passage into the afterlife. It is not difficult, as we shall soon see, to find in the Negative Confessions the seeds of the Ten Commandments.

The Negative Confessions were part of a funerary ritual. The deceased, judged by Osiris and forty-two Assessor Judges (one for each confession), confesses to sins not committed.[50] Coupled with the ceremony of the weighing of the heart, Osiris would determine if the deceased could be permitted to enter the afterlife.[51]

Akhenaten would not have tolerated the connection to Osiris, but there is not the least reason to think that he would have had any problems promoting the ethical principles encompassed by the doctrine. Consider what the Negative Confessions say about proper behavior:

1. I have not done iniquity.
2. I have not robbed with violence.
3. I have not done violence to any man.
4. I have not committed theft.
5. I have slain neither man nor woman.
6. I have not made light the bushel.
7. I have not acted deceitfully.
8. I have not purloined the things which belong to God.
9. I have not uttered falsehood.
10. I have not carried off goods by force.
11. I have not uttered vile (or evil) words.
12. I have not carried off food by force.
13. I have not acted deceitfully.

14. I have not lost my temper and become angry.

15. I have invaded no man's land.

16. I have not slaughtered animals which are the possession of God.

17. I have not laid waste the lands which have been ploughed.

18. I have not pried into matters to make mischief.

19. I have not set my mouth in motion against any man.

20. I have not given way to wrath without due cause.

21. I have not committed fornication, and I have not committed sodomy.

22. I have not polluted myself.

23. I have not lain with the wife of a man.

24. I have not made any man to be afraid.

25. I have not made my speech to burn with anger.

26. I have not made myself deaf unto the words of right and truth.

27. I have not made another person to weep.

28. I have not uttered blasphemies.

29. I have not acted with violence.

30. I have not acted without due consideration.

31. I have not pierced [?] my skin [?] and I have not taken vengeance on the God.

32. I have not multiplied my speech beyond what should be said.

33. I have not committed fraud, and I have not looked upon evil.

34. I have never uttered curses against the king.

35. I have not fouled running water.

36. I have not exalted my speech.

37. I have not uttered curses against God.

38. I have not behaved with insolence.

39. I have not been guilty of favoritism.

40. I have not increased my wealth except by means of such things as are mine own possessions.

41. I have not uttered curses against that which belongeth to God and is with me.

42. I have not thought scorn of the god of the city.[52]

Compare these principles with the Ten Commandments, the fundamental ethical doctrine of Mosaic thought. Although there is some inconsistency in biblical descriptions of the Commandments, Exodus 20, considered a late reworking, summarizes them in the form with which we have become familiar.[53]

1. Thou shalt have no other gods before me.

2. Thou shalt not make unto thee any graven image, or any likeness of any thing that is in heaven above, or that is in the earth beneath, or that is in the water under the earth: Thou shalt not bow down thyself to them, nor serve them: for I the LORD thy God am a jealous God, visiting the iniquity of the fathers upon the children unto the third and fourth generation of them that hate me; And showing mercy unto thousands of them that love me, and keep my commandments.

3. Thou shalt not take the name of the LORD thy God in vain; for the LORD will not hold him guiltless that taketh his name in vain.

4. Remember the sabbath day, to keep it holy. Six days shalt thou labor, and do all thy work: But the seventh day is the sabbath of the LORD thy God: in it thou shalt not do any work, thou, nor thy son, nor thy daughter, thy manservant, nor thy maidservant, nor thy cattle, nor thy stranger that is within thy gates: For in six days the LORD made heaven and earth, the sea, and all that in them is, and rested the seventh day: wherefore the LORD blessed the sabbath day, and hallowed it.

5. Honour thy father and thy mother: that thy days may be long upon the land which the LORD thy God giveth thee.

6. Thou shalt not kill.

7. Thou shalt not commit adultery.

8. Thou shalt not steal.

9. Thou shalt not bear false witness against thy neighbor.

10. Thou shalt not covet thy neighbor's house, thou shalt not covet thy neighbor's wife, nor his manservant, nor his maidservant, nor his ox, nor his ass, nor anything that is thy neighbor's.

The first two commandments simply reflect pure Atenist principles introduced by Akhenaten. Akhenaten's attack on the images of various gods echoes in Exodus 34:13, where God commands Moses: "But ye shall destroy their altars, break their images, and cut down their groves."

The third commandment has its counterpart in the twenty-eighth, thirty-seventh, and forty-first Negative Confessions. The sixth through tenth commandments all have counterparts within the Negative Confessions. Among the Ten Commandments, the only ones unaccounted for are the fourth and fifth—honor the Sabbath and honor parents. But even the admonition about parents does have a parallel in Egyptian traditions. Diodorus Siculus, a Greek historian of the first century B.C., in his treatise on Egyptian customs, wrote:

> In the case of parents who have slain their children, though the laws did not prescribe death, yet the offenders had to hold the dead body in their arms for three successive days and nights, under the surveillance of a state guard; for it was not considered just to deprive of life those who had given life to their children, but by a warning which brought with it pain and repentance to turn them from such deeds. But for children who had killed their parents they reserved an extraordinary punishment; for it was required that those found guilty of this crime should have pieces of flesh about the size of a finger cut out of their bodies with sharp reeds and then be put upon a bed of thorns and burned alive; for they held that to take by violence the life of those who had given them life was the greatest crime possible to man.[54]

Diodorus Siculus implies that the law is ancient although he doesn't explicitly say so. It does suggest that Egyptians considered the relationship between parent and child special, due to the connection to the giving of life, and that a child owed special reverence to a parent.

However, even if we ignore this tradition, we find that the only difference between the Negative Confessions, amended by Akhenaten's religious principles, and the Ten Commandments, considered to be one of the great moral codes of all time, is the requirement that there be a Sabbath and that children honor their parents, a precariously fragile platform from which one could proclaim any grand moral distinction between the ideas of Moses and the thought of Akhenaten. In order to legitimately maintain such a claim, proponents need to prove that Akhenaten did not abide by the principles embodied in the Negative Confessions.

The Negative Confessions, as do the Sixth through Tenth commandments, reflect the general ethical principles of most societies, then and now. There is no reason to think that Akhenaten's embracing of monotheism in any way would require him to reject those values, any more than we would expect Moses to reject those principles when he adopted monotheism. The most that could be argued against any ethical link between the ideas of Moses and those of Akhenaten is that we have no written record of any moral principles advocated by Akhenaten. By the same token, we have no documents showing any disagreement with those principles. In fact, we have precious few documents at all that reflect Akhenaten's personal views, and what handful we do have barely elaborate fully on any aspect of his thoughts.

Against the image of the cold and distant reign of a heretic pharaoh, Aldred offers this observation: "The expressions his artists recorded—when he groped for Nefertiti's supporting arm in his daughter's death chamber, or registered grim distaste at the wringing of the neck of a sacrificial bird, or the affection between him and other members of his family, or the joy of his followers in his presence—all portray 'The Good Ruler who loves Mankind.' These and other touches strike a chord that is humane and sympathetic."[55]

Foreign Affairs Under Akhenaten

While we have little information about internal affairs in Egypt under Akhenaten, we have a good amount of information about foreign affairs in his time. This comes primarily from the discovery of his archives at Amarna, which held over 350 little pillow-shaped tablets of sun-dried clay containing correspondence from several Asian dignitaries to Akhenaten.[56]

Written mostly with cuneiform signs expressing either the Assyrian or Babylonian language, translation of the texts has been a difficult process. Scholars find that simple familiarity with the ancient Semitic languages fails to prepare one for the task.[57] Indeed, the job was difficult even in ancient times, with special training needed before the scribes could master the necessary skills.[58] Still, despite the difficulties, a general but incomplete picture has emerged concerning events in Asia at the time of Akhenaten.

The fundamental political unit in the Middle East in the second millennium B.C. appears to have been the fortified city ruled by a king. Frequently, minor kings formed alliances with other minor kings that gave them the collective force to dominate the surrounding territories. In addition, there were "Great Kings" from the larger cities, powerful enough to mobilize impressive armies capable of policing extensive domains and imposing vassal status on lesser kings.

All the Great Kings commanded the respect of the others and all considered themselves equals, frequently corresponding amongst themselves and addressing the others as brother. Treaties existed among all parties and territorial boundaries were generally respected. Marriages often helped cement these relationships.

Thutmose III, one of the Great Kings, had extended Egyptian influence as far as southern Syria and also to the east, establishing vassal relationships with the many kings in this region. He built fortress cities throughout the foreign territories from which Egyptian troops could rapidly strike into troubled areas, and, despite some occasional resistance, he successfully imposed a *pax Aegyptica* throughout the Egyptian sphere, a state of affairs that held for about eighty years after the king's death.

Just beyond the reach of the Egyptians were other kingdoms—Babylon, the Hittites of Anatolia in the north, Mittani to the east, and awaiting its moment in the background, Assyria.

During the latter part of the reign of Amenhotep III, the equilibrium was ruptured. Local rulers made claims against rival territories and allies constantly called upon their Egyptian overlords for protection. Early in the reign of Akhenaten, Suppuliliumas, the Hittite king, nurtured a more aggressive foreign policy, and when a falling out occurred between Akhenaten and Tushratta, king of Mittani, the Hittite ruler lost no time in exploiting this breach. In short order the Hittites conquered Mittani. Suppiluliumas next turned west, swept across the cities formerly allied with Mittani, and established a vast empire, significantly changing the geopolitical picture.

The redistribution of power had a radical influence throughout southern Syria, Lebanon, and Palestine. Although careful not to cross over into the Egyptian territory, thus denying Egypt an excuse for military response, the Hittite presence encouraged many of the lesser kings and Egyptian enemies to reassess their positions. Rebellions in the Egyptian provinces constantly erupted, and, remarkably, Akhenaten ignored repeated requests from his allies for military aid. The ability of Egypt to strike quickly had been the key to its dominance over the region, and its failure to act in the face of rebellion had severe consequences. Within a couple of years after Akhenaten took the throne the great Egyptian empire fell into disarray.

Labaya, King of Shechem

Among the many letters found in the Amarna archives, the scribes frequently mention groups of warriors known as the 'Apiru, the chief antagonists of the Egyptian allies. What little we know about them indicates that they were a people of mixed ethnic heritages, both Indo-European and Semitic, without any apparent territorial home. Primarily bands of mercenary soldiers, they hired out to whoever would have them, and their services were in high demand.

In the time of Akhenaten there was an 'Apiru leader named Labaya, the "Lion Man." Labaya ruled in the city of Shechem and held an especially hostile attitude towards Egypt. With the collapse of Egyptian support for the Canaanite kings, Labaya established a modest empire that dominated all of central Palestine. The boundaries of his kingdom loosely corresponded to the tribal territories of Manasseh and Ephraim, the two tribes descended from Joseph.

Shechem, a strategically important city along a major east-west trade route, played an important role in biblical history. It was the first place in Canaan visited by Abraham;[59] Jacob had purchased land there and formed an alliance with the king of Shechem;[60] Joseph's mummy was carried out of Egypt and buried in Shechem;[61] and it was here that Joshua established the confederation of Israeli tribes.[62] In later times, the city served briefly as the capital of Israel when it split from Judah.

One of the issues that intrigue biblical scholars about Shechem is that nowhere in the biblical account of the Canaanite conquest is there any reference to the capture of that city, yet it was obviously a safe haven in which the Hebrew troops and leaders could meet without any hostile reaction. What could account for such a situation? The presence of a Shechemite kingdom hostile to Egypt at a point in time close to the Exodus may provide some insight.

We first learn of Labaya in a letter to Akhenaten from Shuwardata of southern Judea:

> The 'Apiru chief has risen in arms against the lands which the god of the king, my lord, gave me, but (thy servant) has smitten

him. Also let the king, my lord, know that all my brethren have abandoned me, and that it is I and Abdi-Kheba who fight against the 'Apiru chief. And Zurata, chief of Accho, and Endaruta, chief of Achshaph pretended to come to my help in return for fifty chariots—I have been robbed(!)—and now they are fighting against me.[63]

While the text doesn't identify the 'Apiru chief by name, Albright notes that the territory ruled by the king as indicated by the letter corresponds to the region held or threatened by Labaya.[64] In a subsequent letter, Zurata is again called a traitor because of his friendship with Labaya.[65]

By one means or another Labaya extended his reach from the Mediterranean to the hills of Gilead and from the plain of Esdraelon to the frontiers of Jerusalem.[66] The rulers of Gezer, one of the chief cities in Palestine, and Gath were considered faithful allies of Labaya, and the princes of Megiddo and Jerusalem treated him with much apprehension.[67] One of his sons, Mut-Baal, established a foothold on the east side of the Jordan. After his death, during the reign of Akhenaten, his sons continued in his footsteps and were as fervently denounced to the king as their father was.[68]

Another letter, from Abdi-Kheba, reports:

And now Jerusalem—if this land does belong to the king, why like the city of Gaza does it [not] concern the king? See, the land of Ginti-kirmil belongs to Tagu and (yet) the men of Gintu (Gath in Sharon) are on garrison duty in Beth Shan.—Or shall we do like Labaya and [his sons who] have given the land of Shechem to the 'Apiru men?—Milkilu (of Gezer) has written to Tagu and the sons of Labaya, "As for you, go on and give all they want to the men of Keilah, and let us break away from the city of Jerusalem."[69]

The situation depicted in the Amarna archives in these and many other letters shows rapid disintegration of Egyptian authority in southern Syria and Palestine; Hittite influence expanding; kings in rebellion, often with the aid of 'Apiru warriors; and in central Palestine a powerful 'Apiru foothold established in Shechem, site of the formation of the confederation of Israel. Such was the state of affairs at the time of Akhenaten's death.

After Akhenaten

Smenkhkare, Akhenaten's coregent, continued to rule after Akhenaten, but for less than three years. Next came Tutankhamen, the boy king. The power behind the throne, however, was probably Ay, the politically ambitious general who succeeded Tutankhamen to the throne.

Under Tutankhamen, the pre-Atenist religions returned to the status quo ante.[70] As a sign of the change, the boy king immediately shed his birth name of Tutankh*aten* and adopted the throne name of Tutankh*amen,* a sure sign that the Theban opposition to Akhenaten had taken a firm hold. Still, despite the harsh suppression of the Amen cult by Akhenaten, for a short while after his death Thebes still permitted the Atenist temples to function.[71]

Redford notes that the speed with which the displaced establishment moved after Akhenaten's death to reclaim its privileged status can be seen from a proclamation inscribed on what Egyptologists refer to as the Restoration Stele.[72] Dating to the first year or so of Tutankhamen's reign, it describes a desperate state of affairs in the land, as the following excerpt shows:

> Now his majesty appeared as king at a time when the temples of gods and goddesses from Elephantine as far as the Delta marshes had fallen into ruin, and their shrines were dilapidated. They had turned into mounds overgrown with (weeds), and it seemed that their sanctuaries had never existed: their *enceintes* were (crisscrossed) with footpaths. This land had been struck by catastrophe: the gods had turned their backs on it. If (ever) the army was dispatched to the Levant (Djahy) to extend the borders of Egypt, they had no success. If (ever) one supplicated any goddess likewise, she would never come at all. Their hearts were weakened in their bodies, (for they) had destroyed what had been made.[73]

Egypt clearly suffered a crisis of confidence. Central to the pharaoh's complaint was the ruinous state of the temples all across the nation, an indication that Akhenaten, rightly or wrongly, was to be the scapegoat. (Note also the declaration of Egypt's military impotence in the Levant.)

Although issued under the name of the child king, the statement most likely reflects the views of his council of advisers, chief of whom was probably Ay. One can safely assume that the pressure for reform spread throughout the land. Ay, clearly worried about how his connection to Akhenaten would impede his political progress, no doubt saw the route of political accommodation as the best way to mollify his critics.

Towards the end of Akhenaten's reign, the Assyrian king sent a communication expressing hopes for an alliance and a joint military effort in Syria against the Hittites.[74] Akhenaten had rejected the plan, but it came to fruition under Tutankhamen's reign. At first it looked as if this bold move would succeed, but the Hittite chief, caught by surprise, soon regained the initiative and pushed both forces back.[75] Shortly afterward, Tutankhamen died.

Egyptian records don't contain any internal reactions to the Egyptian defeat or Tutankhamen's death.[76] Ay followed Tutankhamen to the throne, and, if we had only Egyptian records to go by, his ascension seemed to be without difficulty. Hittite documents, however, suggest an alternative scenario.

One text describes the Egyptians as being thrown into panic by the double tragedy of a military defeat and the loss of a king.[77] And in another document from the Hittite archives we find a most unusual proposal from Tutankhamen's widow to the king of the Hittites.

> My husband has died. A son have I not. But to thee, they say, the sons are many. If thou wouldst give me one son of thine, he would become my husband. Never shall I pick out a servant of mine and make him my husband . . . I am afraid.[78]

A subsequent note in the Hittite annals records the king as saying, "such a thing has never happened before in my life."[79] Scholars can only speculate about the Hittite king's reaction, but the widow's plea does suggest that Ay's ascension did not run as smoothly as would have appeared from the Egyptian record alone.

Warily, Suppiluliumas dispatched an ambassador to investigate the situation. The ambassador met with the queen and returned home with one of the queen's Egyptian representatives and a letter complaining about the Hittite's suspiciousness.[80]

Whether the Hittite ambassador knew about Ay's ascension to the throne we do not know, but Suppiluliumas rushed to seize the opportunity. He sent one of his sons off to marry Tutankhamen's widow, but Ay's intelligence network must have learned about the journey, and the prospective bridegroom was assassinated as soon as he set foot on Egyptian soil.[81]

The murder of Suppiluliumas's son led to a brief war between Egypt and the Hittites, but it appears not to have had a major impact on relations between the two countries.[82] Tutankhamen's widow was never heard from again.[83]

Ay had no male successor, so he turned his attention to Horemheb, Chief Overseer of the Army, a fellow military man who appeared, unlike Tutankhamen and Ay, to have been untainted by the Amarna heresy. One of Horemheb's chief goals was to eradicate all traces of Akhenaten's administration, a task he seems to have performed brick by brick. As Redford describes the process:

> Not one block was left upon another at Akhetaten. Walls were torn down to their foundations, mud-bricks pillaged, and steles and statuary hopelessly smashed. Thereafter the ruins provided a quarry for over a century, most of the known blocks gravitating across the river to Hermopolis where the Ramessides used them extensively; but some ended up as far away as Abydos, over one hundred miles to the south. The fate of the sun-temples at Memphis and Heliopolis can only be imagined; the one at Memphis was undoubtedly torn down. Today, *talatat* are found scattered throughout Cairo and the Delta.[84]

In the early years following Akhenaten's death, his sun temples were permitted to function alongside other temples; under Horemheb they were torn down, not simply as fill to be used in other constructions but to do away with the only surviving symbols of Akhenaten's regime.[85]

Attacks on Akhenaten in the years following his death were filled with allegations of corruption and maladministration. One of the most important documents of Horemheb's reign, partially preserved on a stele from Karnak, is the Edict of Reform. In it Horemheb announces two major goals: "to stamp out lawlessness on an official

level by the imposition of harsh penalties and to reform the judi-
ciary." According to Redford, there were three categories of crime:
extortion practiced by tax collectors, the connivance of royal inspectors, and lawless acts by the soldiery.[86] In this last category the
document mentions the extortion of goods and services from the
peasantry, outright robbery, and cattle rustling. Penalties included
not only restitution but mutilation and exile to Sinai.[87] As with most
bureaucratic institutions, many of the targeted officials would have
been hangers-on from an earlier administration, in this case from
the time of Akhenaten.

Whether corruption was real or just an excuse to remove and
punish administrators who had been associated with Akhenaten we
cannot say. But even giving Horemheb the benefit of the doubt,
under his administration we see the complete destruction of the
Atenist heresy and all those associated with its traditions. The destruction of the city of Akhetaten must have caused the displacement and possible enslavement of many thousands of people, priests,
civil servants, soldiers, and peasants, who served the heretic pharaoh
and administered the wealth of his temples. We can imagine the
wholesale seizure of wealth and property from his adherents and the
disillusionment of many noble families and priests. We can envision
extensive house cleaning, with hordes of administrators who traced
their patronage to the disgraced pharaoh being swept from office,
and large numbers of soldiers punished and exiled to—interestingly—Sinai, where Moses received the Law. It does not take great
imagination to envision under Horemheb large numbers of angry
and resentful citizens from all classes suffering humiliation, persecution, and banishment. They would easily provide a substantial reser-
voir of support for anyone who would challenge the source of their
discomfort.

Although students of this era confidently assert that Horemheb
must have regained Egyptian control over Palestine, no evidence
shows any significant Asian military campaigns during his reign.
That Egypt's hold on Palestine was precarious at best under
Horemheb is evident from the reports of Sethos I, who came to the
throne within months of Horemheb's death.

Sethos launched several foreign military expeditions into Palestine and Syria. One of the battle scenes in Karnak shows substantial
fighting between Sethos and hostile forces all along the 120-mile
military route from Egypt to Palestine.[88] Battles were also fought at

a number of Palestinian locations.[89] Many Palestinian city-states, hostile to Egypt, attacked towns loyal to the Egyptian leadership.[90] Upon Horemheb's death, Egypt obviously still had much to do to regain its influence in the Palestinian territory.

Approaching the Exodus

Historians generally agree that Akhenaten's reforms failed to gain mass acceptance among most of Egypt's population. Even if we accept this assumption, which we cannot accept or reject on the present state of the evidence, we have to acknowledge, at the very least, that many thousands of individuals had a personal stake in the maintenance of Akhenaten's temples and institutions. They included nobility, priests, civil servants, farmers, workers, soldiers, scribes, and their families, all of whom had an interest in maintaining some of the institutions established by Akhenaten.

The Bible indicates that after the Exodus, during the entry into Canaan, Shechem had a close relationship with the Hebrew people. In Palestine, during the reign of Akhenaten, King Labaya of Shechem rebelled against Egyptian authority and established a modest empire throughout central Palestine. Its boundaries coincided approximately with those of the Joseph tribes of Manasseh and Ephraim. After Labaya's death, in the reign of Akhenaten, his sons continued to rule and remained equally contentious toward Egypt. The difficulties faced by Sethos I in recapturing southern Palestine suggest that Horemheb failed to reestablish control over Egypt's foreign territories, and Shechem, no doubt, continued to remain a hotbed of anti-Egyptian rebellion.

Just before Moses returned to Egypt to confront the pharaoh, the Bible says, "And it came to pass in process of time, that the king of Egypt died; and the children of Israel sighed by reason of the bondage, and they cried, and their cry came up unto God by reason of the bondage."[91] In the previous chapter the king who died was identified as Horemheb, and this pharaoh was indeed persecuting the followers of a monotheistic religion. Egyptian records identify the victims as the followers of the Aten; the Bible identifies them as the Children of Israel.

As we approach the Exodus, we find a monotheistic religious cult persecuted by the pharaoh, its religious capital completely destroyed, the city's population dispersed, persecuted, and humiliated. Across the country the cult's temples are destroyed, its large network of loyalists ousted, and its wealth confiscated. Numerous Egyptian soldiers have been banished to the Sinai. In Palestine, the vast territories associated with the Joseph tribes are under the dominion of fierce military leaders openly hostile to Egypt.

Might not the 'Apiru of Shechem and the followers of the Aten have a mutual interest in joining together against the pharaoh?

10

Exodus:
The Egyptian Version

According to the Bible, the number of people joining the Exodus included "about six hundred thousand on foot that were men, beside children."[1] Joining them were a "mixed multitude," a large number of other peoples who didn't belong to the House of Israel.[2] Allowing for great exaggeration and reducing the number of refugees by ninety percent still leaves over sixty thousand male Hebrews, their families, and a "mixed multitude," a total that should have easily exceeded one hundred thousand people.

Of course, the lack of contemporaneous documentation makes it difficult to know whether the Exodus actually took place, let alone how many people participated. But the Merneptah Victory Stele, which contains the first known mention of Israel, implies that shortly after the time frame of the Exodus the Israelites constituted a strong military force without a specific homeland.

The text appears on a monument erected during the reign of pharaoh Merneptah, successor to Ramesses II. After describing the monarch's victory over a combined force of Libyans and Sea Peoples, it concludes with a few lines claiming victory over seven Middle Eastern powers—Israel, the Hittites, the Hurrians, Tehenu, Gezer, Ashkelon, and Yanoam. Although many scholars believe that the victories alleged were fictitious, merely a poetic form of praise to Merneptah's might, the inclusion of Israel among these seven major powers suggests that it had an important political and military presence during Merneptah's reign.

What particularly intrigues scholars about this passage is the grammatical parsing that defines Israel as a "people" but the other defeated groups as "territories." If these Israelites had no home territory, where did they come from?

167

This description encourages most biblical scholars to believe that here we have a picture of Israel in its post-Exodus, pre-Canaanite-conquest state. The majority of biblical scholars place the Exodus less than forty years earlier, in the latter part of the reign of Ramesses II. In chapter 8, we dated the Exodus to just after the death of Horemheb, about eighty years earlier than Merneptah. In either case, only a very short time frame would permit the Israelites to reach such an impressive political and military status. If Israel came out of Egypt at either of those times, they must have already been a powerful force to reckon with.

The Bible also indicates that prior to the Exodus Egypt suffered a series of great disasters at the hands of the Hebrew God. Again, allowing for significant amounts of exaggeration in the biblical account, we must still acknowledge that something unpleasant must have happened between the Israelites and the Egyptians. The departure of Israel could not have been without incident. Neither Sethos nor Ramesses II, both militaristic kings who battled continuously in Canaanite territory, would have allowed such a large opposition movement to peacefully depart so that it could later regroup and challenge Egyptian authority.

At the very least, there must have been some military confrontations between the Exodus group and the Egyptian government. It need not have escalated into a full-scale civil war, but it must have so threatened Egyptian stability that the two sides negotiated some sort of peace treaty granting the rebels safe passage out of the country. This is the historical context behind the story of the confrontation between Moses and the pharaoh, with endless negotiations, broken promises, and series of plagues leading up to the Israelites' departure.

Therefore, it stands to reason that if such an extraordinary event as the Exodus had occurred there should have been not only a Hebrew version but also an Egyptian account. Unfortunately, just as we have no evidence contemporaneous with the Exodus corroborating the biblical narrative, we have no contemporaneous evidence of an Egyptian viewpoint.

Still, between the fourth century B.C. and the first century A.D., Egyptian, Greek, Jewish, and Roman historians produced a body of literature presenting the Egyptian perspective on the Exodus. Despite the fragmentary nature of the material and occasional corruption in transmission, one can reasonably reconstruct the Egyptian version of the story and compare it to the biblical account.

Manetho wrote the most important of these histories, and it appears to have influenced most of what followed. But his account appears only in Josephus and is subject to possible corruption. According to Josephus's excerpt, Moses was an Egyptian priest named Osarseph who organized a rebellion among oppressed Egyptians suffering from leprosy and other diseases. After seizing power from the pharaoh, with the aid of Canaanite allies, he imposed a reign of terror over the country, destroying its temples, desecrating its sacred icons, and despoiling the land. Osarseph then ruled for thirteen years before the exiled pharaoh raised a new army and chased him and his followers into Canaan.

Egyptologists readily admit that Manetho's tale presents a disguised account of events under Akhenaten, but they reject the claim that Moses served as an Egyptian priest during his administration. Because the allegations equating Osarseph with Moses can be easily separated from the main story without doing any harm to the narrative thrust, commentators uniformly assert that the charge is false. Most go as far as to say that enemies of Judaea invented the allegation in order to discredit the Hebrew nation and that some scribe maliciously inserted the Osarseph-Moses passage into a Manetho text, which subsequently received wide circulation before it found its way into Josephus's hands. Others accept that Manetho probably relied on an earlier source text in a library, but even so, they still argue that the story about Moses is fictitious.

No solid evidence supports these critiques. The experts simply don't want these allegations to be true and consequently assert that they are false. In their zeal to deny the validity of Manetho's history they ignore or overlook a large amount of material indicating that the biblical and Egyptian versions not only tell essentially the same story, but utilize similar factual patterns and draw upon identical Egyptian literary themes.

The Manetho-Josephus Chronology

Before examining Manetho's Exodus story, we must briefly take note of the corrupted version of Manetho's chronology that found its way into Josephus. His Greek names for the Egyptian kings, as with earlier portions of his chronology, bear little resemblance to the known Egyptian names. He also listed more kings than actually served. But most important, in those cases where a correlation between the Manetho king list and the correct king list can be made, the Manetho kings appear in the wrong chronological sequence. For example, Amenhotep I, the second king of the Eighteenth Dynasty, appears in the third position.

For our purposes the most important problem concerns the placing of pharaoh Akhenaten. Manetho lists him after Ramesses I and before Sethos I.[3] He also makes Akhenaten the father of Sethos and refers to the latter as "Sethos also called Ramesses."

I should also note that neither Manetho nor Josephus seems to have any idea who Akhenaten was. They refer to him as Amenophis, using the Greek transliteration for Amenhotep, the original throne name of Akhenaten before he launched his religious revolution, and fail to distinguish him in any way from two other kings in the list with the same name. In fact, as we shall soon see, they didn't even realize that this Amenophis was the subject of the later Exodus account. These errors, I suspect, occur in large part due to earlier efforts to obliterate Akhenaten's reputation as a heretic, leading to confusion among the later scribes.

This identification of Akhenaten as the father and immediate predecessor of Sethos created chronological confusion in the recounting of the Egyptian Exodus story. The problem is that Moses departed Egypt twice, once after Akhenaten died and once at the beginning of the reign of Sethos, during the Exodus. Because the Egyptian scribes appear to have placed the end of Akhenaten's reign immediately before the start of Sethos's, they have dated the two departures of Moses to the same time, allowing for no intervening period. This caused Manetho to fuse the two events into a single occurrence and present a distorted chronological picture of what happened when.

The Story of Osarseph

According to Josephus, the Manetho Osarseph story takes place during the reign of a king named Amenophis. Josephus charges that this king was fictitious and that Manetho had attached certain legends to him in order to confuse the ancestors of the Jews with a crowd of Egyptians, "who for leprosy and other maladies had been condemned, he says, to banishment from Egypt."[4] As to Moses, Josephus adds that "the Egyptians regarded him as a wonderful, even a divine being, but wish to claim him as their own by an incredible calumny, alleging that he belonged to Heliopolis and was dismissed from his priesthood there owing to leprosy."[5] Despite this claim about how Egyptians felt about Moses, Josephus offers no explanation as to why, if the Egyptians held Moses to be a "wonderful, even divine being," he appears as such a monstrous figure in the Manetho story.

Chronologically, Josephus places the story after the reign of Ramesses II. Of course, this has the effect of isolating the Amenophis in the story from the Amenophis corresponding to Akhenaten in the king list. Nevertheless, Egyptologists generally agree that, except for the Moses-Akhenaten connection, the Osarseph story refers to events in the reign of Pharaoh Akhenaten.

That Josephus placed the story after the reign of Ramesses II shows that he had no familiarity with the events of Akhenaten's reign or with Akhenaten himself. When he says that the king Amenophis in the story is fictitious because "[Manetho] did not venture to define the length of his reign, although in the case of the other kings he adds their years precisely,"[6] he overlooks the fact that his own king list has three rulers named Amenophis and each has a precisely defined reign.

The Josephus copy of Manetho's chronology shows no dynastic break between the start of the Eighteenth Dynasty and the end of the reign of Ramesses II. No doubt Manetho inserted the story of Osarseph after the reign of Ramesses II because he saw that as a natural breaking point in his history of the kings and chose that place in his manuscript to tell about some of the events in the lives of the kings just mentioned. Obviously, Josephus didn't make the connection.

As we relate the story of Osarseph[7], keep in mind that Josephus believed that the Hyksos and the Children of Israel were one and the same and that the expulsion of the Hyksos constituted the Exodus. Also keep in mind that the Josephus king list places Amenophis (Akhenaten) just before a king named "Sethos also called Ramesses."

The Osarseph Story

The first writer upon whom I shall dwell is one whom I used a little earlier as a witness to our antiquity. I refer to Manetho. This writer, who had undertaken to translate the history of Egypt from the sacred books, began by stating that our ancestors came against Egypt with many tens of thousands and gained the mastery over the inhabitants; and then he himself admitted that at a later date again they were driven out of the country, occupied what is now Judaea, founded Jerusalem, and built the temple. [Josephus, here, is identifying the Hyksos with the House of Israel, and the expulsion of the Hyksos with the Exodus of Israel.] Up to this point he followed the chronicles: thereafter, by offering to record the legends and current talk about the Jews, he took the liberty of interpolating improbable tales in his desire to confuse us with a crowd of Egyptians, who for leprosy and other maladies had been condemned, he says, to banishment from Egypt. After citing a king Amenophis, a fictitious person—for which reason he did not venture to define the length of his reign, although in the case of the other kings he adds their years precisely—Manetho attaches to him certain legends, having doubtless forgotten that according to his own chronicle the exodus of the Shepherds [i.e., Hyksos] to Jerusalem took place 518 years earlier.[8] [Again, Josephus is identifying the expulsion of the Hyksos with the Exodus.] For Tethmosis was king when they set out; and, according to Manetho, the intervening reigns thereafter occupied 393 years down to the two brothers Sethos and Hermaeus [later in the text the spelling changes from Hermaeus to Harmais], the former of whom, he says, took the new name Aegyptus, the latter that of Danaus.[9] Sethos drove out Hermaeus and reigned for fifty-nine years; then Rampses, the elder of his sons, for sixty-six years. [Rampses would correspond to Ramesses II, who ruled for sixty-six years and ten months.] Thus, after admitting that so many years had elapsed since our forefathers left Egypt, Manetho now interpolates this intruding Amenophis. This king, he states, conceived a desire to behold the gods, as Or, one of his predecessors on the throne, had done; and he communicated this desire to his namesake Amenophis, Paapis's son, who, in virtue of his wisdom and knowledge of the future, was reputed to be a partaker in the divine nature.[10] This namesake, then, replied that he would be able to see the gods if he cleansed the whole land of lepers and other polluted persons. The king was delighted and assembled all those in Egypt whose bodies were wasted by disease: they numbered 80,000 persons.[11] These he cast into the stone-quarries to the east of the Nile, there to work segregated from the rest of the Egyptians. Among them, Manetho adds, there were some of the learned priests, who had been attacked by leprosy. Then this wise seer Amenophis was filled with dread of divine wrath against himself and the king if the outrage done to these persons should be discovered; and he added a prediction that certain allies would join the polluted people and would take possession of Egypt for thirteen years. Not venturing to make this prophecy himself to the king, he left a full account of it in writing, and then took his own life. The king was filled with despondency. Then Manetho continues as follows (I quote his account *verbatim*):

"When the men in the stone-quarries had suffered hardships for a considerable time, they begged the king to assign to them as a dwelling-place and a refuge the deserted city of the Shepherds, Auaris [i.e., Avaris], and he consented. According to religious tradition this city was from earliest times dedicated to Typhon [Set]. Occupying this city and using the region as a base for revolt, *they appointed as their leader one of the priests of Heliopolis called Osarseph* [emphasis added], and took an oath of obedience to him in everything. First of all, he made it a law that they should neither worship the gods nor refrain from any of the animals prescribed as especially sacred in Egypt, but should sacrifice and consume all alike, and that they should have intercourse with none save those of their own confederacy. After framing a great number of laws like these, completely opposed to Egyptian custom, he ordered them with their multitude of hands, to repair the walls of the city and make ready for war against King Amenophis. Then, acting in concert with certain other priests and polluted persons like himself, he sent an embassy to the Shepherds who had been expelled by Tethmosis, in the city called Jerusalem; and, setting forth the circumstances of himself and his companions in distress, he begged them to unite wholeheartedly in an attack upon Egypt. He offered to conduct them first to their ancestral home at Auaris [Avaris], to provide their hosts with lavish supplies, to fight on their behalf whenever need arose, and to bring Egypt without difficulty under their sway. Overjoyed at the proposal, all the Shepherds, to the number of 200,000, eagerly set out, and before long arrived at Auaris. When Amenophis, king of Egypt, learned of their invasion, he was sorely troubled, for he recalled the prediction of Amenophis, son of Paapis. First, he gathered a multitude of Egyptians; and having taken counsel with the leading men among them, he summoned to his presence the sacred animals which were held in greatest reverence in the temples, and gave instructions to each group of priests to conceal the images of the gods as securely as possible. *As for his five-year-old son Sethos, also called Ramesses, after his grandfather Rapses* [emphasis added], he sent him safely away to his friend. He then crossed the Nile with as many as 300,000 of the bravest warriors of Egypt, and met the enemy. But, instead of joining battle, he decided that he must not fight against the gods, and made a hasty retreat to Memphis. There he took into his charge Apis and the other sacred animals which he had summoned to that place; and forthwith he set off for Ethiopia with his whole army and the host of Egyptians. The Ethiopian king, who, in gratitude for a service, had become his subject, welcomed him, maintained the whole multitude with such products of the country as were fit for human consumption, assigned to them cities and villages sufficient for the destined period of thirteen years' banishment from his realm, and especially stationed an Ethiopian army on the frontiers of Egypt to guard King Amenophis and his followers. Such was the situation in Ethiopia. Meanwhile, the Solymites [or dwellers in Jerusalem] made a descent along with the polluted Egyptians, and treated the people so impiously and savagely that the domination of the Shepherds seemed like a golden age to those who witnessed the present enormities. For not only did they set towns and villages on fire, pillaging the temples and mutilating images of the gods without restraint, but they also made a practice of using the sanctuaries as kitchens to roast the sacred animals which the people worshipped: and they would compel the priests and prophets to sacrifice and butcher the beasts, afterwards casting the men forth naked. *It is said that the priest who framed their constitution and their laws was a native of Heliopolis, named Osarseph after the god Osiris, worshipped at Heliopolis; but when he joined this people, he changed his name and was called Moses.* " [Emphasis added.]

Such, then, are the Egyptian stories about the Jews, together with many other tales which I pass by for brevity's sake. *Manetho adds, however, that, at a later date, Amenophis advanced from Ethiopia with a large army, his son Rampses*—[earlier in the story his son is identified as "Sethos Also Called Ramesses, after his grandfather, Rapses"]—*also leading a force, and that the two together joined battle with the Shepherds and their polluted allies, and defeated them, killing many and pursuing the others to the frontiers of Syria.* [Emphasis added.] This then, with other tales of a like nature, is Manetho's account.

Osarseph and Akhenaten

Several elements make clear that the Osarseph story is derived from an account of Akhenaten's reign. The pharaoh involved is named Amenophis, Akhenaten's original throne name as well as the name of his father; Osarseph banned the worship of Egyptian gods and destroyed the images of the gods, one of the most important aspects of Akhenaten's reforms; and the period of exile lasted thirteen years, the number of years Akhenaten ruled after launching his revolution in the fifth year of his reign.

In regard to this last point, Redford observes "the thirteen years of woe wrought by lepers and shepherds [i.e., Hyksos] can only be the term of Akhenaten's stay in his new city."[12] Note also that Manetho describes the child "Sethos also called Ramesses" as five years old in what corresponds to the fifth year of Akhenaten's reign.

While the story clearly talks about Akhenaten's administration, the heretic pharaoh seems to have been removed from responsibility. Manetho shifts the blame to Osarseph, who no doubt functioned as the chief priest of Akhenaten's cult.

Another indication that the Amenophis in the story corresponds to Akhenaten comes from the claim that he wanted to see god, as did Or, one of his predecessors. In the Josephus king list, one of the kings has the name Orus, and Egyptologists generally accept that this king corresponds to Amenhotep III, Akhenaten's father.[13] In Greek, Or, Orus, and Horus are essentially the same name, all transliterations of the Egyptian god-name Heru.

The only king Amenophis (Amenhotep) to rule after Orus (Amenhotep III) was Amenhotep IV, the original throne name for Akhenaten. If the Amenophis in the Osarseph story followed after Or, he had to be Akhenaten.

"Sethos Also Called Ramesses"

In the Osarseph story, Amenophis is the father of "Sethos also called Ramesses." In the Josephus chronology, Amenophis again appears as the father of "Sethos also called Ramesses." While this coincidence seems to have escaped Josephus's attention (he thinks the Osarseph story happened 125 years after the reign of Sethos), clearly the two sets of father and son are both the same—Akhenaten and Sethos.

But we have a problem. The Manetho chronology wrongly places Sethos on the throne immediately after Akhenaten. The same thing occurs in the Osarseph story. As noted above, this led to the confusing conclusion that the Exodus occurred both at the end of Akhenaten's reign and in the beginning of Sethos's. Only one of those propositions can be true, but it must be more than a random coincidence that both the Genesis chronology and Manetho date the Exodus to the beginning of the reign of king Sethos.

Biblical Parallels

The Osarseph story shares a number of parallels with the biblical Exodus story: A pharaoh fears trouble from a group of Egyptian inhabitants; he makes them slaves; he keeps the slaves relatively isolated from the rest of the population;[14] the slave leader is raised as an Egyptian; the slaves ask permission to go to another destination; plague afflicts large numbers of Egyptians; when the slave alliance confronts the pharaoh, the pharaoh has a change of heart, first taking a strong stance against them and then withdrawing his opposition; the slave leader brings great devastation upon the land of Egypt and its people; and the Egyptian pharaoh chases the slaves and their allies out of Egypt.

In addition, the slaves worked at the city of Avaris. Many Egyptologists identify Avaris as the site of Pi-Ramses, one of the two cities in the Bible that employed Hebrews as slaves. Although some Egyptologists dispute the shared identity of Pi-Ramses and Avaris, they usually place the two sites only a couple of miles apart.

As for the proposition that Pi-Ramses and Avaris were one and the same, consider the following: Ramesses II, who gave Pi-Ramses its name, had a family identification with the city of Avaris. Sethos I, his father, not only celebrated the four hundredth anniversary of the city's founding, but was named for the god Set, worshiped at Avaris. Its not unlikely that Avaris held a special place in the heart of Sethos and his father Ramesses II.

While many parallels exist, there are also some differences. In

Manetho, Moses and his followers are native Egyptians, not Asians (although the slaves are aided by Asian allies). Additionally, Moses doesn't seek to leave Egypt; initially he seeks only to move to Avaris, and later attempts to become king. Also, as the story is presented, it is the pharaoh who flees Egypt and later returns to liberate his people, whereas in the Bible it is Moses who flees Egypt and later returns to liberate his people.

Chaeremon's Version of the Exodus

After giving Manetho's account of the Exodus, Josephus tells of another Egyptian writer named Chaeremon, who, he says, also prepared a history of Egypt and included a story similar to Manetho's account of Osarseph. Josephus writes:

> The next witness I shall cross-examine is Chaeremon. This writer likewise professes to write the history of Egypt, and agrees with Manetho in giving the names Amenophis and Ramesses to the king and his son. He then proceeds to state that Isis appeared to Amenophis in his sleep, and reproached him for the destruction of her temple in war-time. The sacred scribe Phritobautes told him that, if he purged Egypt of its contaminated population, he might cease to be alarmed. The king thereupon collected 250,000 afflicted persons and banished them from the country. Their leaders were scribes, Moses and another sacred scribe—Joseph. Their Egyptian names were Tisithen (for Moses) and Peteseph (Joseph). The exiles on reaching Pelusium fell in with a body of 380,000 persons, left there by Amenophis, who had refused them permission to cross the Egyptian frontier. With these the exiles concluded an alliance and marched upon Egypt. Amenophis, without waiting for their attack, fled to Ethiopia, leaving his wife pregnant. Concealing herself in a cavern she gave birth to a son named Ramesses, who, on reaching manhood, drove the Jews, to the number of about 200,000 into Syria, and brought home his father Amenophis from Ethiopia.[15]

Josephus acknowledges that Chaeremon's story is a variation of the Osarseph story, but quickly points out many differences between the two, believing that to be sufficient to undermine the credibility of both. We need not itemize every inconsistency, but some are worth mentioning.

Manetho talks about the pharaoh's desire to "see god," whereas Chaeremon says that the pharaoh had a vision of the goddess Isis. Both situations involve a vision of a deity, and in both stories the vision is connected to an expulsion of the diseased population. In Manetho, the pharaoh failed to follow the advice; in Chaeremon, the advice was followed. In Manetho the lepers made common cause with the Hyksos; in Chaeremon they allied with an expelled army belonging to Amenophis (i.e., Akhenaten.) In Manetho, the pharaoh's son was five years old when Moses comes to power and eighteen when Moses was chased from Egypt; in Chaeremon, the pharaoh's son was an infant when Moses came to power and an adult of unspecified age when Moses was expelled.

The names in the two stories also differ slightly. In Chaeremon's story Amenophis's son is called Ramesses; in Manetho he is "Sethos also called Ramesses." In Chaeremon's account the leaders of the rebellion are scribes named Peteseph and Tisithen; in Manetho the leader is a priest named Osarseph. While the similarity between Osarseph and Peteseph is obvious, Chaeremon identifies the latter with Joseph instead of Moses. But this inconsistency may be due to Chaeremon's observation of the similarity between the names Joseph and Peteseph. However, Chaeremon's version does include Moses as a coleader.

Redford suggests that the differences between Chaeremon and Manetho indicate that Chaeremon's version is a "contaminated descent, not a free and equal variant."[16] That the two are different, though, proves nothing about which, if either one, is the more contaminated.

Redford appears to give Manetho preference because Manetho is earlier than Chaeremon and therefore closer to the original source. But the version of Manetho that we have comes from Josephus, contemporaneous with Chaeremon and already in a very corrupt form. Josephus also worked from two inconsistent versions of Manetho, had a badly mixed-up king sequence, was poorly informed about the chronological sequences pertaining to Akhenaten and Sethos, and had no idea that the Osarseph story belonged with the pharaohs of the Eighteenth Dynasty.

Chaeremon worked at the library at Alexandria and had access to its resources. He likely quoted from a direct source, and since he and

Josephus were contemporaries, Josephus's Chaeremon quote is unlikely to have been corrupted. However, Chaeremon's story, though based on a similar set of episodes as that in the Manetho story, appears to stem from a different source document than Manetho's. Who is to say which was more faithful to the original source, or which source was more faithful to the original events? The two versions together, Manetho and Chaeremon, suggest that the libraries had more than one text about what happened at the time of the Exodus, but how old those sources were we cannot know.

Biblical Parallels

While the Osarseph story has numerous structural parallels to the biblical account, Chaeremon's version adds more consistency. The biblical account requires that Moses depart Egypt and then return. That occurs in the Chaeremon account—the lepers are expelled but then return with an army of Akhenaten's former soldiers—but the return is placed at the beginning of Akhenaten's reign rather than at the beginning of Sethos's. This may be due to the confusion about when Akhenaten's reign ended.

Another interesting coincidence concerns the number of soldiers involved in the rebel army. Chaeremon says that there were 250,000 diseased Egyptians allied with 380,000 soldiers once belonging to Amenophis, a total that corresponds to the biblical figure of 600,000 males plus a mixed multitude.

In both stories Akhenaten flees Egypt during the reign of the usurpers. This reflects the chronological distortion due to the misplacing of Akhenaten's reign. It would have been Akhenaten's forces under Osarseph (Moses) who fled to Ethiopia, and the flight would have occurred at the end of Akhenaten's reign. (This may be when Moses acquired the Ethiopian wife that caused so much trouble between him and his sister Miriam.[17]) These forces would be the Egyptian soldiers in Chaeremon's account that allied with Moses. They would have been reinforced by the Asian army described as Shepherds in the Josephus story.

However, because the Egyptian scribes mistakenly placed Akhenaten's reign just before Sethos's, there was no room to have a flight from Egypt by Moses after Akhenaten's reign, a return to Egypt by Moses sometime later, and a second flight from Egypt by

Moses during the reign of Sethos. So the first departure was placed at the beginning of Akhenaten's reign instead of at the end.

Shepherds and Shechemites

The reference by Josephus to "shepherds" results from his mistranslation of the name Hyksos. It should mean "chieftain of a foreign hill-country," but Josephus had two different Manetho manuscripts, each with a different definition of Hyksos. One translated it as "Shepherd-Kings," the other as "captive shepherds."[18] It does not necessarily refer only to the followers of the Hyksos kings expelled by Ahmose. When Manetho says Osarseph (Moses) made an alliance with the Hyksos, it only tells us that Moses formed an alliance with some group of unspecified Canaanite or Syrian chieftains.

Historically, however, we can make a pretty good guess as to who these chieftains were. Josephus says the allies came from Jerusalem. As we noted in the previous chapter, beginning with the reign of Amenhotep III, Labaya, the king of Shechem, established a large kingdom that dominated central Palestine. Albright notes that the kingdom extended to the frontiers of Jerusalem, and that the rulers of Jerusalem were troubled by his presence.[19] Labaya and his sons who succeeded him maintained a hostile attitude towards the Egyptians.

If Osarseph formed an alliance with any strong military presence in the region of Jerusalem, it would have been the Shechemites. This would go a long way to explaining why Shechem had such a close relationship to the Israelites during the conquest of Canaan.

Horus and Set / Moses and Pharaoh

We already have noted some interesting parallels between the biblical and Egyptian accounts of the Exodus. But there is a very strange inconsistency between them. According to the Egyptian view, a powerful enemy usurps the Egyptian throne from the rightful ruler and persecutes the Egyptian people; the Egyptian king flees from Egypt; the king has a son, Ramesses (or "Ramesses also called Sethos"), born in secrecy and hidden away by his mother; this child comes back in his adult years, confronts the evil king, defeats him in battle, and liberates his people from oppression.

This presents a near perfect mirror image of the biblical account in which an evil king takes the throne; Moses is born in secrecy and hidden away for a short time, eventually to become the adopted son of the pharaoh and presumptive heir to the throne; he flees from Egypt to avoid being killed but later returns, confronts an evil pharaoh, subjects him to a great military defeat, and liberates his people.

The two plot lines share identical themes, but the identities of the hero and villain are switched. In the Egyptian story the pharaoh, as a child, is hidden away from the cruel and oppressive Moses but returns in adulthood to liberate the Egyptians. In the bible, Moses, as a child, is hidden away from the cruel and oppressive pharaoh but returns in adulthood to liberate the Hebrews. In other respects the two stories share the same viewpoint: Moses inflicts damage upon the Egyptian people and subsequently the pharaoh chases him and his followers from Egypt. Why should the two sides portray the same cycle of events with the same characters but reverse the roles in such an irreconcilable way?

The answer is that both stories drew upon the same antecedent literary themes, the most obvious one being the mythical conflict between Horus and Set following the death of Osiris. In that legend Osiris had been the king of the gods, but his brother Set, seeking the throne, arranged to have Osiris killed. He did so by tricking him into entering a chest, killing him, sealing the chest, and floating it out to sea. In this manner Set usurped the throne. Isis, wife of Osiris and mother of Horus, recognizing Set's ambitious plans, feared for the safety of the infant Horus and hid him away on the floating island of Chemmis. Horus, as Osiris's son, was the lawful heir to the throne and was raised with the prospect of avenging his father's death. Subsequently he challenged Set for the kingship, and after a series of battles defeated him.

The similarity between the Horus-Set theme and the Moses/Osarseph stories should be obvious. Iconographically, Osiris is the displaced king, Set is the usurping king, Isis is the mother who hides the child away, and Horus is the returning son who defeats the usurping king. In the conflicting Egyptian and biblical versions, the pharaoh and Moses correspond to either Horus or Set, depending upon which side tells the story.

The role reversal between the two antagonists arose from competing claims to the throne after Horemheb's death, with Moses seeking to return the Atenists to power and Ramesses I seeking the support of the Theban establishment.

Horemheb died without a blood heir to the Egyptian throne. His appointment of Ramesses I as coregent, a northern military officer, must have been a shock to the southern Theban establishment. Not only did Ramesses I come from outside traditional political circles, he and his family had a strong devotion to the god Set, as signified by the name of his son, Sethos I. Sethos I even celebrated the four hundredth year of the god Set, an event that Egyptologists routinely identify as referring to the foundation of Avaris, the Hyksos stronghold. The elevation of a northern-based, Set-worshiping pharaoh who identified with the Hyksos stronghold of Avaris could not have been pleasing to the southern-based, Amen-worshiping, Hyksos-hating Theban establishment. Such a situation must have generated considerable resentment at the beginning of this pharaoh's reign.

Among the many ambitious factions plotting a way to capture the throne from this northern family would have been the remnants of the Atenist faction, who, as victims of Horemheb's anti-Atenist reign of terror, had good reason to hate Horemheb and his appointed coregent.

Since Egypt identified the king with Horus, competitors for the throne had to convince Egyptians that the claimant represented Horus and the rival represented Set the Usurper. As politicians and priests jockeyed for position after Horemheb's death, rival claimants needed to wrap themselves in the royal iconography, a task complicated for Ramesses I by the fact the he had to identify with Horus at the same time that his public image identified him with Set the Usurper.

The Atenists also had a complicated task. Not only had their power base shrunk considerably, they rejected the traditional Osiris-Horus mythology. Nevertheless, they did worship Re-Herakhte (Re, the Horizon Horus) as their chief deity. Therefore, they could identify themselves with Horus. Since there was no blood heir to turn to, the Atenist leader, Osarseph (Moses), depicted himself (truthfully, perhaps) as the adopted son of a pharaoh, entitling him to royal succession.

Because Atenism diminished the role of the gods, the Mosaic version of the conflict passed into Hebrew literature without most of the traditional Osiris-Horus-Set iconography, but the act of hiding the infant and floating him down the Nile in an ark serves as a powerful reminder of the original literary theme.

While Moses portrayed himself as the adopted son of a pharaoh, giving him claim to a Horus title, the Egyptians portrayed him as based in Avaris, the Hyksos capital dedicated to Set. This identified him with Set the Usurper. In fact, Moses and his followers may have had a connection to Avaris. If, as many Egyptologists believe, Avaris and Pi-Ramses were the same city, it would explain why both the biblical and Egyptian stories portray the followers of Moses as working there.

Sethos and Harmais

The story of Osarseph (and the companion story about Peteseph) already indicates that fighting broke out between the Atenists and Sethos at the transition between the end of Akhenaten's and Sethos's reigns. But the placing of the two events together eliminates about forty years in between and leads to some confusion as to where in that forty-year period the Exodus occurred. Therefore, let's look at another story by Manetho, one describing a civil war and flight during the reign of Sethos.

Immediately after bringing his chronology up to "Sethos also called Ramesses," Josephus tells a story (attributed to Manetho) about a power struggle between that pharaoh and a brother named Harmais. On the surface it appears to have nothing to do with the Egyptian version of the Exodus. But later, when placed in context, it will be seen as a crucial part of our reconstruction. Here is what Josephus says about the incident:

> [Sethos] appointed his brother Harmais viceroy of Egypt, and invested him with all the royal prerogatives, except that he charged him not to wear a diadem, nor to wrong the queen, the mother of his children, and to refrain likewise from the royal concubines. He then set out on an expedition to Cyprus and Phoenicia and later against the Assyrians and the Medes; and he subjugated them all, some by the sword, others with a blow and merely by the menace of his mighty host. In the pride of his conquests, he continued his advance with still greater boldness, and subdued the cities and lands of the east. When a consider-

able time had elapsed, Harmais who had been left behind in Egypt, contravened all his brother's injunctions. He outraged the queen and proceeded to make free with the concubines; then, following the advice of his friends, he began to wear a diadem and rose in revolt against his brother. The warden of the priests of Egypt then wrote a letter which he sent to Sethos, revealing all the details, including the revolt of his bother Harmais. Sethosis[20] forthwith returned to Pelusium and took possession of his kingdom; and the land was named Aegyptus after him. It is said that Sethos was called Aegyptus and his brother Harmais, Danaus.[21]

No known evidence corroborates Manetho's account of this civil war, and Egyptologists routinely dismiss it as a piece of folklore. Herodotus, as Redford notes, attributed a similar conflict to the reign of the Twelfth Dynasty pharaoh Sesostris, as does Diodorus Siculus, who renders the pharaoh's name as Sesoosis. Note here that during the story Josephus changed the name of Sethos to Sethosis. Substituting his *th* (the Greek letter theta) for the *so* in Diodorus's Sesoosis produces the same name, casting some doubt on the source of this Manetho story. (In an oral transmission this could easily occur because of a lisp.)

In the Herodotus tale, Sesostris returned from his foreign conquests and attended a banquet given by his brother, who ruled in the king's absence. Hoping to trap Sesostris, the brother set fire to the dining hall, but the king's sons formed a human bridge that enabled their father to escape. Later, Sesostris returned and punished his brother and his brother's allies.[22]

Diodorus tells a similar story, but omits the part about the human bridge.[23] Neither historian, however, refers to a connection between Sesostris and either Danaus or Aegyptus, about whom we shall speak in a moment.

Because Harmais in Manetho's story serves as an appointee, Redford identifies him with Horemheb, who was not of royal birth.[24] Subsequently, he argues, the story became badly confused for two reasons.[25] First, Sethos became confused with Ramesses II due to the use of the name "Sethos also called Ramesses." Second, he says, scribes mistook a series of sea battle scenes in the reliefs of Medinet Habu with those at Karnak.[26] The Medinet Habu inscriptions, he notes, may have also been partly responsible for influencing the legends of great military conquests by Sesostris.[27]

Although Redford's thesis cannot be verified, it does show a great tolerance for the idea that in ancient times different events at different times and places can easily be confused with each other. But, in addition to the problem of where the main story comes from, we have a second problem, the identification of Sethos and Harmais with Aegyptus and Danaus. This is a separate myth cycle from that involving Sesostris in the Twelfth Dynasty.

Danaus and Aegyptus

The story of Danaus and Aegyptus belongs to a Greek cycle that traces the roots of Perseus, the great Greek mythic hero, to ancient Egypt.

As the story has been handed down to us, Danaus and Aegyptus were the sons of Belus and Nile.[28] Belus was king of Egypt who appointed Danaus king of Libya and Aegyptus king of Arabia. Aegyptus then brought Egypt under his control and named the land for himself. After some quarrels between the two brothers, Danaus fled for his life to Argos, where he became king upon the surrender of the reigning monarch. Aegyptus's sons followed Danaus to Argos and, claiming that they wanted to end their hostilities, asked to marry Danaus's daughters. Danaus agreed to the merger but didn't trust Aegyptus. So the frightened brother instructed each of his daughters to kill her husband on their wedding night. All but one daughter carried out the plan. That daughter and her husband, a son of Aegyptus, founded the Danoi branch of the Greeks from which Perseus was descended.

The story of Danaus and Aegyptus does not originate in an account of a civil war in the reign of Sethos. The evidence suggests that it belongs to a much earlier age. Danaus is the eponymous ancestor of the Danoi, a name that Homer appears to have equated with the pre–Trojan War Greeks.[29] Among his descendants are Perseus and Heracles, both of whom belong to the Mycenaean age. By all traditions, Perseus is the founder of Mycenae.[30]

Scholars generally accept that Danaus belongs to the earliest phase of the Greek heroic age, and the consensus is that he belongs in the sphere of the sixteenth century B.C.[31] Because scholars associate the myth with the sixteenth century, and because it talks about Danaus departing from Egypt under hostile circumstances, a number of scholars believe that Danaus symbolically represents the expulsion of the Hyksos.

In essence, the Danaus story tells of a family's flight from Egypt; the pursuit of them by the Egyptians (i.e., the sons of Aegyptus); the near total destruction of the Egyptian forces (the wedding night deaths of Aegyptus's sons at the hands of Danaus's daughters); the conquest of a foreign territory by the fleeing brother; and the foundation of a new nation. These are also the basic elements of the Exodus story. What led Manetho to think that there were some parallels between the story of Danaus and Aegyptus and that of Sethos and his brother?

Moses and Danaus

If the Exodus occurred in the reign of Sethos, then it is easy to see how Manetho's redactors could confuse the story of Moses with the story of Danaus, just as Redford suggests that the Egyptian scribes confused the story of Sesostris with that of Sethos. That the myth of Danaus may have been confused with the story of Moses introduces us to another historical account, one attributed to Hecataeus, a Greek writer of the fourth century B.C., who thus precedes Manetho by about a century. His original manuscript is lost, but Diodorus Siculus preserved the relevant piece.[32]

According to Hecataeus, Egypt had suffered greatly from plague, and the authorities blamed it on the presence of alien people and alien religious rites. These alien practices had caused the Egyptian gods to be displaced. In order to restore the Egyptian gods to their rightful place the aliens were driven out. The expulsion, says Hecataeus, resulted in Danaus and Cadmus going to Greece, and Moses to Jerusalem.

This story, which is the earliest of the nonbiblical Exodus stories, introduces us to the theme of widespread plague caused by the presence of alien religious rites, a theme that is central to the Osarseph story. That the Egyptian gods were displaced and needed to be restored hints strongly at the events of Akhenaten's reign.

Of immediate importance to our discussion is the claim that Danaus and Moses left Egypt at the same time. From the Sethos-Harmais story above, we saw that something in the reign of Sethos caused the Egyptians to believe that some sort of Exodus had occurred, and Manetho identified it with Danaus. Hecataeus, writing perhaps a century before Manetho, says Moses and Danaus were part of the same cycle, a strong clue that the Exodus belongs in the reign of Sethos.

Redford accepts that Hecataeus derived his information from Egyptian sources, but believes it resulted from an oral tradition.[33] He also adds that the absence of names and places indicates a lack of interest in the details of Egyptian traditions. It should be remembered, however, that the absence of detail may be due to Diodorus writing about two hundred years later. We don't know how good a Hecataeus source Diodorus had, or whether Diodorus quoted him exactly or prepared a summary.

Although Hecataeus hints at events associated with the reign of Akhenaten, he identifies the offenders not as allies of Akhenaten but as aliens to Egypt. This may be due to Hecataeus's efforts at reconciling Egyptian and Hebrew history. He knew both Egyptian and Hebrew sources. According to Josephus, Hecataeus had written a book about Jewish history.[34]

By itself, this story could easily be consistent with the biblical account and need not be taken as any connection to Akhenaten. That the Egyptian gods fell into disfavor may only reflect the defeat suffered at the hands of the Hebrew god. But the perspective of the story, referring to problems of plague created by the presence of alien people and alien religious rites, seems to reflect an Egyptian point of view rather than a biblical one. It attributes the failure of the gods to the presence of alien rites rather than to a confrontation with the aliens. This seems more consistent with the role of Akhenaten than the role of a confrontational Moses.

In any event, Hecataeus shows that well before Manetho, Egyptian tradition identified the Exodus of Danaus with the Exodus of Moses, and Manetho tied that event to a civil war in the reign of Sethos. Is there any other evidence connecting Moses to Harmais?

Moses and Harmais

The name Moses, as many scholars now recognize, is not of Hebrew, but of Egyptian derivation.[35] According to Exodus, Moses received his name from the pharaoh's daughter, who gave him that name because "I drew him out of the water."[36] This gloss on the origin of the name derives from a similarity between the name Moses (Mosheh in Hebrew) and the Hebrew word *mashah,* which means "to draw out."[37] Scholars generally reject this explanation.

The name Moses actually originates from the Egyptian word *ms,* meaning "is born," as in Thutmose and Ramose.[38] "Moses" is an anglicized version of a Hellenized transliteration (i.e., *mosis*) of the original Egyptian. In addition, there seems to be no reason for the Egyptian princess who adopted and named Moses to give him a Hebrew name when the pharaoh had ordered all male Hebrew children to be killed at birth.

If the name Moses does derive from the Egyptian *ms,* then it would probably have been preceded by the name of a god, as in the names Ptahmose or Ramose.[39] Under Akhenaten, however, the Amen and Osiris cults were two of the chief targets of his regime. Individuals who had such god-names as elements in their own names had to change them.[40] Therefore, if an Osarseph served under Akhenaten, he would have been required to change his Osiris-derived name to something more acceptable.

In the Manetho account, Osarseph does just that, allegedly choosing the name Moses or, more properly, *ms.* The taking of *ms* as an element of his name suggests that he also prefaced it with the name of a god acceptable to Akhenaten. That would have been either Re or Horus, since Re-Herakhte, "Re the Horizon Horus," was the god whom Akhenaten worshiped. There was, for example, an important official in Akhenaten's regime known as Ramose.[41] Moses, therefore, may have been actually known as either Ramose or Hormose (or Harmose, to use an alternative transliteration). In Egyptian, those names would have been rendered as either *Rms* or *Hrms,* without vowels.

Artapanus, a historian of the second century B.C., wrote that while Moses was still with the Egyptian court he was highly honored by the priests, and in recognition of his skills in hieroglyphics he was named Hermes.[42] Hermes was the Greek god identified with the Egyptian Thoth, the god of writing. But Egyptians at the time of Moses wouldn't have used the name Hermes; they would have used Thoth. Also, as a member of Akhenaten's court, Moses would not have used such an impermissible god-name. While the Artapanus story may simply be an unsubstantiated folk tale, it may be that there was a remembered tradition in which Moses was originally know as either *Rms* or *Hrms,* and Artapanus mistakenly thought the name was Hermes. It is not difficult to see how an Egyptian *Rms* or *Hrms* could be rendered as the Greek Hermes.

This brings us to the connection between Moses and Harmais, the brother who challenged Sethos for the throne. Although the names Hormose (or Harmose) and Harmais are not literally identical they are close enough in pronunciation and spelling to be confused with the original Egyptian spelling. Furthermore, it is not clear that the name Harmais is an accurate transmission. Josephus actually has two different spellings, again, no doubt, from his two different editions of Manetho, one being Harmais and the other Hermaeus.[43] (Here the English spelling is a transliteration of the Greek.) Dropping the vowels in either case leaves us with Hrms.

Was Moses also Hermais? If Moses, or Ms, was short for Hrms, then the two names share enough similarity to be confused. Unfortunately, we don't know Moses's true name. The fact that only the Ms survived in the Bible suggests that the scribes dropped the prefix because it consisted of a god-name offensive to the Hebrew tradition. If that is true, then the god name would have to have been either Re or Horus, leading to the Egyptian names of either Rms or Hrms.

The Sethos-Harmais story describes the two rivals as brothers. Earlier we saw that the Exodus story line is derived from literary themes associated with the conflict for the throne between Horus and Set. Horus and Set were brothers and the Sethos-Harmais story may have drawn on those mythic images.

Josephus, in the course of introducing the story of Osarseph, mentions the struggle between Sethos and Harmais and suggests it occurred at the beginning of Sethos's reign, at which time we have dated the Exodus. This battle occurs almost simultaneously with the expulsion of Osarseph (Moses) by Sethos and his father. So in quick succession, the scribes imply a confrontation between "Ms" and Sethos and another conflict between "Hrms" and Sethos. The two battles were originally one and the same, but the stories came from alternative source documents and the connection between them was lost.

Northern Invasion and Plague Themes

While many commentators think that the Osarseph story is a fraud—a pseudo-Manetho created by an enemy of the Jews—Redford suggests that Manetho probably relied on a source in the library but the source was fictitious.[44] He believes that it was nothing more than a composite account derived from two late first-millennium literary themes: invasion from the north and expulsion of the "polluted ones."[45] In support of his argument, he rounded up fourteen examples of such stories, including Manetho's Osarseph story, Chaeremon's variation on the Osarseph story, and the Hecataeus excerpt.

These themes, he argues, arose in response to the increasingly frequent and successful invasions of Egypt by foreign forces—Assyrians, Ethiopians, Persians, and Greeks—in the latter part of the first millennium B.C. According to his view, the foreign victories over Egyptian forces undermined Egyptian self-confidence, leading the nation's writers to draw upon the more successful past for inspirational guidance. For such purposes the most significant model was the expulsion of the Set-worshiping Hyksos.

Plague Stories

With regard to the plague-expulsion theme, Redford cites Poseidonus of Apamea, Polemo, and Strabo.

Poseidonus wrote that the Jews were expelled from Egypt because of leprosy, and they migrated to Jerusalem.[46]

The Polemo material is quite vague. It refers to a time when Phoroneus, the son of Apis, served as king, and indicates that a part of the Egyptian army was expelled and established itself in Palestine.[47] Although plague isn't specifically mentioned, Redford believes the expulsion of the army to be derived from the plague-expulsion theme.[48] However, the story reminds us of Chaeremon's claim that Moses joined up with an army of expelled Egyptians. Additionally, Phoroneus and Apis are ancestors of Danaus and Aegyptus, bringing us back to themes found in Manetho and Hecataeus.

Strabo simply indicates that Moses was an Egyptian priest who held part of Lower Egypt, preached monotheism, was unhappy with Egyptian religion, and persuaded thoughtful men to follow him to Jerusalem.[49] Redford believes that this, too, was derived from the plague-expulsion theme but that it was favorably reworked in the light of the biblical tradition.[50] But the piece is not in accord with the biblical tradition. It makes Moses an Egyptian priest and gives him rule over part of Lower Egypt, supporting the general outline of the Osarseph story.

Of the three plague stories cited here, only one actually refers to plague, and it follows the Osarseph story in claiming that the Jews suffered from leprosy at the time of the Exodus. Another describes Moses as an Egyptian priest who ruled over part of Egypt and persuaded people to follow him to Jerusalem. This, too, derives from the Osarseph story. As derivatives of the story in question, they cannot be used to argue that the parent story is part of a larger literary theme. One can only use independent stories to support such a claim.

The third story doesn't directly mention the Jews, Moses, or plague, but in line with Chaeremon's allegations, it does refer to an Egyptian army expelled into Palestine, and hints at the Danaus-Exodus theme.

An Oracle

Continuing his survey, Redford cites another story known as the Oracle of the Potter.[51] Here, too, the king is Amenophis. On the king's visit to Hermopolis a potter predicts that alien worshipers of Typhon will conquer Egypt and defile the temples, causing the king and his court to flee to Nubia for seven years. Then, says the oracle, a legitimate king will arise and purge the foreigners.[52]

Typhon is the Greek name used for Set. The Typhon worshipers would be the Hyksos kings. But since the king is Amenophis and the court flees to Nubia (Ethiopia), the Hyksos referred to would be the ones who aided Osarseph. Here, too, we then have a corrupted descendant of the Osarseph story.

King Bocchoris

Next, Redford brings together a group of four stories that take place in the reign of a pharaoh named Bocchoris. They come from Lysimachus, Tacitus, and Apion, and one tale is known as the Oracle of the Lamb. The first three talk about the Exodus and place the event in Bocchoris's reign. The fourth has nothing to do with the Jews.

The placing of the Exodus in the reign of Bocchoris introduces some confusion among these later sources concerning the Exodus date. History knows of a King Bocchoris who ruled during Egypt's Twenty-fourth Dynasty in the eighth century B.C. But Josephus seems to think that the Bocchoris in these stories ruled about 1,700 years before his own time.[53] On the other hand, Apion, Josephus's contemporary and the target of Josephus's *Against Apion,* dates the Exodus to the seventh Olympiad, which is close in time to the reign of Bocchoris.[54]

While Apion's Exodus date is clearly wrong, the error may have to do with whether the Bocchoris in the stories actually refers to the eighth-century ruler or to some earlier pharaoh whose name became corrupted in transmission.[55] Josephus says that the existence of Bocchoris was "discovered" by Lysimachus and that Lysimachus had invented a "fresh name" for him.[56]

According to Lysimachus, as preserved by Josephus,[57] the Jews under King Bocchoris were suffering from leprosy and other diseases, causing a crop failure throughout Egypt. The oracle of Ammon directed the king to purge the temples of these peoples because the "sun was indignant that such persons should live." Bocchoris had the diseased rounded up; the lepers were drowned and the others were left exposed in the desert. Among them was Moses, who raised their spirits and led them on a march to inhabited territory. He also instructed them to destroy the temples and altars of the gods wherever they were found. In the territory where they arrived (presumably in Egypt, but not specifically identified) they maltreated the people, plundered their wealth, and burned the temples. Eventually they arrived in Judea.

When you consider Lysimachus's account, there is not much that differs from the biblical account other than the claim of Jewish diseases. The Jews were rounded up, the ten plagues caused much destruction and burning in Egypt, and Moses did lead the people out of the desert. Still, as Josephus realizes, the story is essentially a derivative of the Osarseph story, in which the writer "differs from the previous writers [Manetho and Chaeremon] . . . neglecting the dream and the Egyptian prophet, [and] has gone [instead] to Ammon for an oracle concerning the victims of scurvy and leprosy."[58] The Jews are still diseased native Egyptians. An oracle directs the king to round them up and expel them. Moses becomes their leader, plunders property, and destroys the temples of the gods.

A second Bocchoris story comes from Tacitus, the Roman historian who, like Apion, bitterly opposed the Jews. He writes: "Most authorities, however, agree on the following account. The whole of Egypt was once plagued by a wasting disease which caused bodily disfigurement. So pharaoh Bocchoris went to the Oracle of Hammon [Amen] to ask for a cure, and was told to purify his kingdom by expelling the victims to other lands, as they lay under a divine curse."[59] The leader of the exiles, says Tacitus, was Moses, who led them into Canaan and conquered the territory.

The Tacitus comment about most agreeing with this story appears in the context of his discussing several theories about Jewish origins. His remarks suggest that outside Jewish circles the theory he sets forth had much support. It appears to be a variation of the Lysimachus account, and both must have drawn on similar sources. Each, of course, ultimately derives from the Osarseph story, with Bocchoris substituted for Amenophis.

The third Bocchoris-Exodus story was written by Apion, and, as so often is the case, Josephus is our source. Josephus doesn't actually say that Apion made Bocchoris the pharaoh of the Exodus but he does say that Apion agrees with Lysimachus in claiming that the fugitives numbered 110,000, indicating that he followed Lysimachus or used a similar or common source.[60] He also adds that Apion placed the Exodus at the time of the Seventh Olympiad, a point in time close to when the true Bocchoris ruled.[61]

According to Apion: "Moses, as I have heard from old people in Egypt, was a native of Heliopolis, who, being pledged to the customs of his country [Egypt], erected prayer-houses open to the air, in the various precincts of the city, all facing eastward; such being the orientation also of Heliopolis. In place of obelisks he set up pillars, beneath which was a model of a boat; and the shadow cast on this basin by the statue described a circle corresponding to the course of the sun in the heaven."[62]

Josephus doesn't give Apion's full account of the Exodus; he just makes allusions to it in a vitriolic and insulting manner. In essence, he says that Apion follows the others in claiming that the Jews were of the Egyptian race and were expelled from Egypt because of plague.

The last of the Bocchoris stories is known as the Oracle of the Lamb. It has nothing to do with the Jews or the Exodus. Redford summarizes the story as being about a lamb that predicted that after nine hundred years Egypt would be desecrated by foreign invaders and the shrines of the gods would be taken to Ninevah and Amor.[63]

Subsequently, someone (Bocchoris?) would bring the shrines back to Egypt.[64]

Absent from this story is the plague motif, and the invading forces are identified with Assyrian territories. Assyria was one of the dominant political forces at the time of Bocchoris, and it is not unreasonable to believe that this story may be unrelated to the other Bocchoris accounts.

Conclusions

Of Redford's fourteen stories, we have now touched on eleven—Manetho, Chaeremon, Hecataeus, Poseidonus of Apamea, Polemo, Strabo, Oracle of the Potter, Lysimachus, Apion, Tacitus, and the Oracle of the Lamb. The remaining three are all variations of the mythic struggle between Horus and Set.[65] None have any connection to specific historical events (unless, Redford observes, one can discern a connection to the expulsion of the Hyksos). They appear in Redford's collection because they deal with the theme of invasion from the north (Set being identified with the northern invaders) and date to the fourth century B.C. or later.

If we exclude these three myths from the survey, as well as the Oracle of the Lamb, all of which deal with some sort of northern invasion, we are left with ten stories. Eight of them specifically refer to the Exodus—Manetho, Chaeremon, Hecataeus, Poseidonus, Strabo, Lysimachus, Apion, and Tacitus. A ninth, the Oracle of the Potter, is clearly derived from the Osarseph story, although it makes no specific mention of Moses or the Jews. The tenth, by Polemo, makes reference to Danaus's ancestors and corroborates Chaeremon's claim that an Egyptian army had been expelled.

What Redford offers as literary evidence of a plague-expulsion motif is actually a collection of stories all based on an Egyptian version of the Exodus, the broad outlines of which correspond to the Osarseph story. The plague-and-expulsion theme is not a random collection of unrelated stories developed in the late first millennium; it is specifically derived from the confrontation between Moses and the pharaoh. The overall thrust holds that Moses served as a Heliopolitan priest and helped bring about the religious reforms associated with Pharaoh Akhenaten; that plague was widespread among the followers of Moses; that Moses brought great destruction upon the land; and the deposed pharaoh chased Moses and his followers from Egypt.

While all the accounts appear very late in the historical record—the fourth century B.C. or later—they are based on earlier sources of indeterminate age. The differences between Manetho and Chaeremon indicate that Egyptian libraries had more than one version of how the Exodus occurred. The only reason we have any record of these stories at all is because of the influence of the Hellenistic age. Greek and Roman writers, interested in history, started to write down what they learned. Manetho and Chaeremon, both Egyptians, wrote in Greek for Greek audiences, while Josephus, a Jew, wrote in Greek. That these later writers, under Hellenistic influence, finally preserved the evidence tells us nothing at all about how much older the original sources were.

Leprosy Among the Hebrews

I suspect that the chief reason for rejecting the credibility of the Osarseph thesis, aside from its connection to Akhenaten, is the association of the Hebrews with leprosy and wasting diseases. Commentators consider the identification of the Jews as a source of plague, disease, and leprosy as little more than an anti-Semitic slur without any historical foundation. (Never mind that the heart of the Exodus story specifically relates how the god of Moses subjected Egypt to a number of dangerous and deadly plagues.)

Josephus particularly condemned the claim that the first Jews were Egyptians plagued by leprosy and other wasting diseases. He writes, that Moses "suffered from no such affliction is clear from his own words."[66] He then goes on to cite a number of ordinances issued by Moses in relation to leprosy, including the isolation of lepers from the general community and a ban of lepers from the priesthood.[67] However, an examination of the biblical and historical evidence shows that Moses probably did suffer from leprosy and that leprosy and plague were widespread among the Hebrews at the time of the Exodus, lending strong support to Manetho's identification of Osarseph with Moses.

In the fourteenth century B.C. plague was endemic throughout the Middle East and Egypt.[68] References to its effect appear in many documents of the time, such as in the Amarna letters and Hittite archives.[69] Under Amenhotep III, over seven hundred statues were erected of the goddess Sekhmet, the Egyptian goddess of pestilence, possibly providing evidence of the presence of plague in his time.[70]

During Akhenaten's reign plague was ravaging the Phoenician coast, and twenty years later it was widespread among the Hittites.[71] In Amarna, numerous sudden deaths occurred after the eleventh year of Akhenaten's reign, and the plagues ravaging the land have been thought responsible.[72] If plague was so widespread among the Egyptians and other regional peoples of that time, why would we expect those associated with the Israelites to be any less susceptible?

The Hand of Moses

The first relevant biblical reference to leprosy occurs when Moses asks God for some sign by which he can demonstrate to the Hebrews that he is the Lord's messenger come to deliver them. God instructs Moses to place his hand inside his robe and then remove it. He does so, and his hand appears "leprous as snow."[73] He is then directed to place his hand back in his robe. The next time he brings it out the flesh is cured.[74] This passage certainly suggests the possibility that Moses suffered from leprosy and that in later times priests reinterpreted the nature of his affliction so as to remove any taint.

The Veil of Moses

We also have the curious incident of Moses's veil. While Moses dwelled in the wilderness he asked of God: "I beseech thee, shew me thy glory [i.e., his face]."[75] But God said, "Thou canst not see my face: for there shall no man see me, and live."[76] God then arranged for Moses to stand nearby, telling him, "And it shall come to pass, while my glory passeth by, that I will put thee in a clift of the rock, and will cover thee with my hand while I pass by; And I will take away my hand, and thou shall see my back parts; but my face shall not be seen."[77]

As a result of this incident something happened to Moses's face that frightened the people. "And when Aaron and all the children of Israel saw Moses, behold, the skin of his face shone; and they were afraid to come nigh him."[78] From that time on, Moses wore a veil over his face whenever he appeared before the people.[79]

There has always been disagreement among scholars about the

correct translation for the description of Moses's face. At one time it was thought that the words meant that he had horns emanating from his head, as depicted in Michelangelo's Moses.[80] Biblical translations now tend to say that his face "shone" but do not indicate what it is about a shining face that should so frighten the people. Some scholars presently believe that the passage should be understood to mean that his face was disfigured, and this seems to be the most sensible solution given the context.[81]

Was this disfigurement a form of leprosy? Given the fear that existed at the appearance of Moses's face, coupled with the earlier reference to his hand becoming "leprous as snow," there is good reason to think that Moses must have been suffering from some form of unpleasant skin disease.

The story of Moses's veil is doubly interesting for our purposes. First, the Osarseph story says that Moses had leprosy. Second, we have an unexplained connection between the desire of the pharaoh "to see god" and the rounding up of lepers. In the biblical story, not only is it suggested that Moses has leprosy or some form of severe skin disease, but his affliction has a connection to his desire "to see god." We should also note that when Moses's hand turned leprous, it did so while in the presence of God, who at the time took the form of a burning bush:[82] God's voice came out of the bush, but his face couldn't be seen.

Snow White Miriam

The Book of Numbers tells us that Miriam and Aaron, sister and brother to Moses, fomented a revolt against their brother's leadership. "Miriam and Aaron spake against Moses because of the Ethiopian woman; for he had married an Ethiopian woman. And they said, Hath the Lord indeed spoken only by Moses? Hath he not spoken also by us?"[83] What caused this anger is not clear.

Their challenge to Moses angered God. As a punishment "Miriam became leprous, white as snow."[84] Only through Moses's special pleading did God spare her.[85] Interestingly, though, Aaron is equally guilty: "And Aaron said unto Moses, Alas my lord, I beseech thee, lay not the sin upon *us*, wherein *we* have done foolishly, and wherein *we* have sinned."[86] [Emphasis added.] But only Miriam receives the punishment of leprosy. Why isn't Aaron made to suffer the same affliction?

Aaron is the father of the line of Israel's chief priests, but under biblical law priests had to be free of leprosy and other skin diseases. In the original story Aaron may also have had leprosy, but later scribes loyal to the Aaronites may have expunged the reference.

Special Ordinances

One of Josephus's arguments against Manetho's charge of leprosy among the Hebrews was his citation of numerous ordinances about leprosy. Indeed, several chapters of Leviticus (the Third Book of Moses) are devoted to the disease. The Bible devotes more space to this issue than to the entire life of Moses, from his birth to his flight from Egypt. It also takes up more space in Leviticus than the discussion of any other problem.

Leviticus tells us that when leprosy was suspected, the victim was brought before Aaron or one of his sons for inspection.[87] Numerous instructions are given and alternative treatments, based on different stages of the infections, are mentioned. That so much space is devoted to this issue, with detailed instructions requiring the direct participation of Aaron and his sons as observers, suggests that leprosy was a significant problem among the Egyptian exiles, just as Manetho indicated.

Among these ordinances is one that says a leper "shall put a covering upon his upper lip," which reminds one of Moses's veil.[88] Another regulation indicates that when "the seed of Aaron is a leper . . . he shall not eat of the holy things, until he be clean."[89] Here, the ordinance specifically excludes Aaron from the directive, another indication that he himself may have suffered from the disease.

Seeing God

The incident of Moses's veil reminds us of Manetho's claim that Amenophis desired "to see god." Since this Amenophis is actually Akhenaten, the inability to see god raises some interesting questions.

Since all pharaohs prior to Akhenaten identified with Horus, the desire of this particular pharaoh to see god suggests that there was some sort of breech in this pharaoh's identification with Horus. And under Akhenaten, the pharaoh acted not as a god but as the chief prophet of the god. So if the pharaoh was no longer a god, he could no longer see god.

That Akhenaten wanted to see god provides another parallel with Moses, whom the Egyptian stories identify as the ruling priest in Akhenaten's reign. In the Manetho story the desire to see god is closely linked to the wide-scale presence of plague and leprosy. In the biblical account we saw that the desire of Moses to see god caused him to experience some sort of diseased condition and that leprosy was probably widespread among the Hebrew exiles. Therefore, we should note that Akhenaten himself suffered from debilitating diseases.

Redford observes that Akhenaten is conspicuously absent from artistic scenes in his father's reign, and speculates that he suffered from "a congenital ailment that made him hideous to behold."[90] Summarizing the later depictions of Akhenaten, Redford adds, "The repertoire of Amarna art has made us familiar with the effeminate appearance of the young man; elongated skull, fleshy lips, slanting eyes, lengthened ear lobes, prominent jaw, narrow shoulders, potbelly, enormous hips and thighs, and spindly legs. Of late experts have tended to identify his problem with some sort of endocrine disorder in which the secondary characteristics failed to develop, and eunuchoidism resulted."[91]

Aldred, referring to these same artistic depictions, writes, "It is not simply that Akhenaten had himself represented as effeminate or androgynous, he specified certain distortions that belong to neither normal man or normal woman. In an exaggerated form these are the abnormalities that have enabled a number of pathologists independently to diagnose that the subject depicted in this way may have suffered from a disorder of the endocrine system, more specifically from a malfunctioning of the pituitary gland."[92]

Aldred also observes that "the pathological condition in which Akhenaten chose to have himself represented is shared to a lesser extent by all his family and his entourage."[93] The extension of this depiction to others, however, appears not to be the result of sharing the disease, but of an attempt to portray Akhenaten as the ideal figure. As evidence of this proposition, Aldred cites a change in the portrayal of Ramose, an important official in Akhenaten's court. In the earlier scenes Ramose has a normal appearance, then the images suddenly record distortions similar to those used in depicting Akhenaten.[94]

Given the diseased state of Akhenaten's body, I can't help but wonder if Manetho hasn't given us a vital clue as to what happened in the early years of the pharaoh's reign. The pharaoh's desire to see god took place prior to the religious revolution. Prior to declaring himself for Re-Herakhte, I suspect that he sought to cure his diseased body through prayer to Amen, the chief god after whom Akhenaten was originally named. The desire to see god was a prayer for a cure, for relief from disease and plague. But no cure came. Perhaps the combination of his own disease and widespread plague was responsible for his declaration that the gods were no longer effective. Seeing himself abandoned by the traditional gods, he was ripe for a new religious turn, easily influenced by Osarseph or another priest.

Manetho says that Amenophis was told that he could see god (i.e., become cured) if he would expel the lepers and "polluted ones," a suggestion that on its face seems reasonable; one way to fight disease is to isolate the diseased. Instead, we find the advice ignored and the lepers brought together, eventually to a city of their own. Did Akhenaten's own diseased state lead him to sympathize with others who experienced wasting diseases? Did he bring them to his new city of Akhetaten, or perhaps to Avaris? Did such kindness and generosity build a large fanatical following among those people who suffered indignity and disapprobation elsewhere?

On the other hand, Redford finds nothing unusual about the pharaoh's desire to see god. "Seeing the gods," he says, "and the desire to do so are themes well known in Egyptian literature, sometimes signifying the desire to attend upon a god, as when the famous sage Amenophis, son of Hapu,[95] calls the Thebans 'Ye who desire to see Amen.' "[96] He also tells us that "seeing the sun god" was a popular theme during the reign of Amenhotep III, on the eve of the Amarna period.[97]

Still, Redford offers no explanation for the direct link between Amenophis's desire to see god and the horrendous calamities that befell Egypt as a result. Why was the ability to see god related to an expulsion of the lepers?

In any event, with regard to seeing god, the Manetho and biblical accounts agree. Akhenaten and Moses each desired this, and in both accounts the desire to see god is associated with bodily disfigurement. Also, leprosy was widespread, and the exiles included a large contingent of diseased individuals. And, we should add, both

Akhenaten and Moses suffered bodily deformities. This is not to say that Akhenaten and Moses were one and the same. Moses is only the scapegoat. The correlations, however, do show that Manetho and the Bible both present the same story, but from slightly different perspectives.

Civil War and the Ten Plagues

On the basis of biblical chronology we have been able to date Moses to the court of Akhenaten and the Exodus to the coregency of Sethos and Ramesses I. Furthermore, the sequence of a king dying just before the Exodus and another king dying during the Exodus (at the Red Sea) corresponds closely to the fact that Horemheb and Ramesses I died within a year of each other. The Egyptian view of the Exodus, despite the chronological confusion caused by the misordering of the reigns of Akhenaten and Sethos, agrees with the biblical chronology in that it also places Moses in the court of Akhenaten and the Exodus in the reign of Sethos.

We have also seen that with the exception of the role reversal caused by the Horus-Set theme, both the Egyptian and biblical versions of the Exodus tell the same basic story: Moses was a spokesman for the enslaved people; he exhibited signs of leprosy; he challenged the power of the Egyptian gods; he confronted the pharaoh; he inflicted great damage upon the Egyptian people; and he led his followers out of the country.

One apparent difference between the two accounts, though, is that the Egyptians tell of a civil war fought between Sethos and Moses, whereas the Bible talks only of Moses single-handedly taking on the Egyptian establishment and subjecting the country to ten horrible plagues, including the death of the first-born son of every Egyptian family.

Just as the image of Moses as a threatened child growing up to confront the enemy draws upon the Horus-Set theme, the idea of Moses as a lone hero successfully challenging the might of a powerful army also draws upon Egyptian literary precedents. One of the more famous such instances occurs in an account by Ramesses II of his battle with the Hittites at Kadesh. Historians generally agree that in that battle Ramesses II suffered a major setback, but you wouldn't know it from what he wrote:

Then His Majesty started forth at a gallop, and entered into the host of the fallen ones of Khatti [the Hittites], *being alone by himself, none other with him.* [Emphasis added.] And His Majesty went to look about him, and found surrounding him on his outer side 2500 pairs of horses with all the champions of the fallen ones of Khatti and of the many countries that were with them . . . they were three men to a pair of horses as a unit, whereas there was no captain with me, no charioteer, no soldier of the army, no shield-bearer; my infantry and chariotry melted away before them, *not one of them stood firm to fight with them.*[98] [Emphasis added.]

Ramesses, the story continues, then called upon Amen for assistance. Gardiner summarizes the rest of the text as an account of how the king single-handedly routed the foe and hurled them into the river Orontes.[99]

A Hittite document describing the same battle narrates Ramesses's defeat and retreat.[100] Shortly after the battle of Kadesh, the Egyptians and Hittites signed a peace treaty.[101]

Ramesses, with the aid of Amen, and Moses, with the aid of Jahweh, each single-handedly wreaked devastation upon a powerful army, eventually driving the enemy to defeat through drowning. But as Gardiner observes, what saved Ramesses at Kadesh was not so much his valor as the arrival of reinforcements in the nick of time.[102] And however brave Moses may have been, like Ramesses he had a large powerful army of his own waiting in the wings. The story of Moses's single-handed victory over the Egyptians is the same sort of fictitious braggadocio as Ramesses describing his victory over the Hittites.

The story of the ten plagues also draws upon Egyptian literary traditions. Evidence of this can be seen from an ancient document known as the "Admonitions of an Egyptian Sage," also referred to as the Ipuwer Papyrus.[103] Although the manuscript itself may date to the Nineteenth Dynasty, the writing style embraces Middle Egyptian, a clear indication that the text was copied from a much older document.[104]

The papyrus tells of an era of great anarchy, perhaps the First Intermediate Period.[105] Some of the events described bear a remarkable similarity to the effects of the plagues unleashed by Moses.

Consider the following comparisons between the papyrus and the biblical account of the ten plagues:[106]

Papyrus: Indeed the river is blood, yet men drink of it. Men [shrink] from human beings and thirst after water.
Exodus: And all the waters that were in the river were turned into blood. . . . The Egyptians could not drink of the water of the river; and there was blood throughout all the land of Egypt.[107]

Papyrus: Indeed, gates, columns, and [walls] are burnt up. . . . Behold, the fire has gone up on high, and its burning goes forth against the enemies of the land.
Exodus: [A]nd the fire ran along upon the ground.[108]

Papyrus: Indeed, trees are felled and branches are stripped off.
Exodus: And the hail smote every herb of the field and brake every tree of the field.[109]

Papyrus: Neither fruit nor herbage can be found . . . everywhere barley has perished.
Exodus: And there remained not any green thing in the trees, or in the herbs of the fields, through all the land of Egypt.[110]

Papyrus: [The land] is not bright because of it.
Exodus: And there was a thick darkness in all the land of Egypt.[111]

Papyrus: Indeed, all animals, their hearts weep; cattle moan because of the state of the land.
Exodus: And all the cattle of Egypt died.[112]

Papyrus: Indeed men are few, and he who places his brother in the ground is everywhere. . . . Indeed [hearts] are violent, pestilence is throughout the land, blood is everywhere, death is not lacking, and the mummy-cloth speaks even before one comes near it.
Exodus: And all the firstborn in the land of Egypt shall die. . . .[113]

Reading the two sets of passages side-by-side, one might easily conclude that in the First Intermediate Period Egypt was not very much different from Egypt during the Ten Plagues of Moses. But what the Bible describes as the effects of Ten Plagues is simply an embellished account of the war between Moses and Sethos, and from a literary standpoint it is not much of a jump to describe the effects of that war as the heavenly infliction of plague. In this sense the story of the Ten Plagues rings true. The devastation and destruction did occur, and the army of Moses may have been the instrument of infliction, but it was the hand of God, according to the priests, which guided the events.

The Exodus

The biblical and Egyptian accounts of the Exodus each combine a mixture of fact and fiction, but one can now be easily separated from the other. Reading the two versions side-by-side and placing them in chronological and historical context, we can recover the nature and origins of the Exodus.

During the reign of Amenophis III (Akhenaten's father and the pharaoh who "knew not Joseph") plague and leprosy were widespread. As a preventive measure, many of the diseased people were rounded up and placed into forced labor camps. When Akhenaten became pharaoh he appointed Moses, his childhood friend, to a high position in the administration, most likely chief priest and administrative head of the Aten cult.

Moses, suffering from some form of skin disease (perhaps leprosy) championed the cause of the lepers and the "polluted ones," pleading their case before the pharaoh. Akhenaten, himself a victim of debilitating diseases, sympathized, and in the fifth year of his reign had the lepers and "polluted ones" brought together to live a more protected lifestyle.

During Akhenaten's reign new religious reforms were introduced. He desecrated the temples of the opposing cults, discouraged the worship of gods other than the Aten, and disrupted the power of the Theban priesthood. Moses, as chief priest, took responsibility for administering these reforms and became the most visible target of Theban wrath.

When Akhenaten died, a vengeful Amen priesthood marked Moses for death. Fortunately, he (but not Amenophis, the patron with whom he was confused) escaped to Ethiopia, where he had good relations with the king. (You may recall from the story of "snow white Miriam" that Moses had somehow acquired an Ethiopian wife.)

During the priest's exile, Horemheb came to the throne and launched a campaign of retribution against the Atenists. He destroyed their buildings and temples, harassed their priests, removed leaders from office, dismissed civil servants, confiscated wealth, and banished Atenist soldiers to Sinai. This was no small group of people.

The institutions established by Akhenaten would have involved tens of thousands of people. Priests alone would have numbered several thousand. In addition, soldiers, civil servants, wealthy nobles, merchants, farmers, religious converts, and the "polluted ones" all owed allegiance and thanks to Akhenaten for their good fortunes. To this must be added the many members of their families.

Horemheb appointed as his coregent Ramesses I, a northern, Set-worshiping general with no royal blood and no other claim to the throne. In turn, Ramesses appointed his son Sethos as coregent, which would no doubt have disappointed the southern-based, Set-hating Theban establishment.

With the death of Horemheb and a nonroyal heir designate in the wings, political ambition led various political factions to jockey for position (as reflected in the story of Harmais). Into this milieu came Moses, seeking to restore the Atenists to the throne and, as the adopted son of Amenhotep III, claiming a right of title.

Moses found ready support among the bitter remnant of Akhenaten's regime, many of them anxious to return to power. Additionally, Moses made common cause with the king of Shechem, one of the stronger powers in Canaan at the time and someone who had no desire to see Sethos reclaim hegemony over his empire. He may also have had temporary alliances with "a mixed multitude" of other southern Egyptians who thought a combined military campaign could dislodge the northern-based coregency of Ramesses and Sethos.

The Atenist and Shechemite forces staged a two-front assault. Moses rallied his forces from the south, perhaps at the old capitol of Akhetaten, and the Shechemites attacked from the north. Sethos halted the Asian advance at Pelusium and then turned his attentions to the south. Realizing that eventually Sethos would get the upper hand, Moses negotiated a cease-fire and safe passage for his southern troops. They marched due east towards the northern edge of the Red Sea, where it narrowed into the Gulf of Suez. There they crossed into Sinai and marched across the Exodus route. Sethos, like Horemheb, wanted no public record to acknowledge the existence of the Aten cult, and no monuments, inscriptions, or paintings recounted the battle between Moses and Sethos. Privately, however, stories circulated.

In time, Sethos reasserted military authority over Canaan, the Shechemites were brought to heel, and, in keeping with the treaty between Moses and the pharaoh, the Atenists were left alone, later to evolve into the House of Israel.

11

Who Were the Genesis Patriarchs?

The Book of Genesis presents the history of ancient Israel prior to the Exodus. It focuses mostly on the stories of the Hebrew patriarchs, Abraham, Isaac, and Jacob, all of whom died before Akhenaten was born. Abraham was the father of Isaac and Isaac was the father of Jacob. According to the Bible, these Hebrew patriarchs and their families lived in the Canaanite-Syrian territories.

Jacob had twelve sons. In his middle years he changed his name to Israel. His sons and their families came to be known as the Children of Israel, or the Twelve Tribes. The heir to Jacob's blessing was Joseph, who had become the prime minister of Egypt. Toward the end of his life, Jacob joined Joseph in Egypt and moved his family to the Nile Delta, where they remained until the Exodus.

That the Hebrew patriarchs lived in Canaan and Syria does not necessarily conflict with the thesis proposed herein, that the House of Israel arose in the aftermath of Akhenaten's monotheistic revolution. Centuries before Akhenaten became king, Egypt's prosperous and bountiful northern delta served as a magnet for large numbers of Canaanite immigrants. Many Egyptologists believe that this alien influx provided the Hyksos kings with the political base that enabled them to take control of Egypt.

With the Hyksos model before us, one can easily see how a small group of monotheistic Semitic-speaking tribes might have immigrated to the Nile Delta and evolved into a large political, religious, and social unit with a strong presence on the Egyptian scene. Such an entity would have no trouble supporting a pharaoh whose monotheistic views coincided with their own, and in the oppression following Akhenaten's death one can understand how it could become a victim of the counter-revolution against the Atenist heresy.

Nevertheless, no archaeological evidence or contemporaneous documentation prior to the Exodus corroborates the existence of Abraham, Isaac, Jacob, or the Twelve Tribes. Only Genesis provides any evidence that they ever lived or came from outside of Egypt. While few biblical scholars take the biblical account as literally true, many, if not most, accept that the stories most likely reflect tales and legends handed down about real characters, or that the struggles among the various family members for position and power symbolize tribal wars or mergers. The stories, they argue, have too much narrative detail, too many well-developed plots, too much fully developed characterization of the personalities to be fictional accounts.

In this and the next two chapters we will take a closer look at the patriarchal history. I plan to show that it is pure myth, derived from Egypt stories about the god Osiris and his family, and that ancient Israel had no genealogical history prior to the Exodus.

When Moses led his followers out of Egypt they would have naturally brought with them many of the tales and legends about Egyptian gods who were thought to be the ancestors of the Egyptian people. Atenists, however, didn't believe in these other Egyptian deities. They had to transform these well-known stories about ancestral gods with magical powers into tales about human forefathers who interacted with the one and only supernatural being.

After several centuries of living in their new homeland, the Israelites took on more and more of the cultural trappings of their Canaanite neighbors. The Egyptian characters accumulated more and more Canaanite features as Canaanite-trained scribes reworked the stories. Over time, the locales changed from Egypt to Canaan.

Confusion in the Biblical Record

The Book of Genesis exhibits frequent confusion about who did what or when and where events occurred. Consider, for example, the differences between the E and P sources regarding the origin of the name Israel.

In the E source, Jacob changed his name to Israel after he wrestled with an angel (or God) at Peniel; in the P source the name became Israel at Bethel.[1] Richard Elliott Friedman, in his very informative *Who Wrote the Bible*, observes that politically, the E source closely identified with Moses and with king Jeroboam, the first king of Israel

after the split from Judah.[2] The P source, he adds, supported the
Aaronite wing of priests and tended to downplay the role of Moses.[3]
P also opposed the anthropomorphic imagery of God.[4] (In this latter
sense the P source corresponds closely to the Atenist view of deity.)

Friedman points out that the difference in viewpoint between E
and P affected the choice as to which city to associate with the
change of Jacob's name to Israel. Bethel was one of the two chief cult
centers of the northern kingdom; Peniel was a city fortified by Jeroboam in defense against Judah.

To P, therefore, the Bethel cult center was more important than
the Peniel government center. P also needed to challenge E's anthropomorphic image of Jacob wrestling with an angel. E, on the other
hand, considered the political fortress of Peniel more important than
the cult center of Bethel. Consequently, rival political factions disagreed over where and why Jacob's name became Israel.

The P source wrote later than E and put forward an alternative
history that transferred locales and omitted mythic incidents. Here
the redactor kept both stories, but who knows how many such mythic
incidents were dropped or transformed to accommodate the conflicting sources.

In this one example we can see how religious and political disputes
can cause the site of a patriarchal story to shift from one locale to
another. Later we will see that the wrestling story is derived from an
Egyptian myth.

The Wife / Sister Stories

The redactors not only confused locations, they lost track of time,
place, and actor, as demonstrated by the "wife/sister" stories. Genesis has three stories about how a patriarch visiting a foreign king had
his wife pretend to be his sister. Two of the incidents involved Abraham and one involved Isaac.

The first of these incidents occurred shortly after Abraham arrived in Canaan during a famine. Because of the shortages, Abraham
had to go to Egypt. Fearing that the Pharaoh would have designs on
Sarah and want to kill her husband, Abraham had his wife pretend to
be his sister. The ruse worked, and when Pharaoh took Sarah for a
wife he spared Abraham. Despite the king's lack of knowledge about
the deception, Abraham's god punished the Egyptian monarch and

sent a plague to persecute the royal household. When Pharaoh learned the truth he let Abraham and Sarah leave Egypt.

After returning to Canaan, Abraham had a similar encounter with Abimelech, king of Gerar, a city outside of but near Egypt. In this incident, Genesis identifies the king as a Philistine,[5] and the captain of the Philistine army as a man named Phicol.[6] This time, before the king could sleep with Sarah, God appeared to him in a dream and warned of impending death if he consummated the relationship. Abimelech returned Sarah to Abraham and the two men made peace. Subsequently, hostilities broke out when Abimelech's troops seized a well belonging to Abraham. Once again, however, the two sides made peace.

The third incident involved Isaac and his wife Rebekah. Once again, Canaan experienced a famine. This time, though, God specifically directed Isaac not to go to Egypt, sending him instead to Gerar, the scene of the second Abraham story.[7] Again, the Philistine king was named Abimelech[8] and the captain of the Philistine guard was named Phicol.[9]

For the same reason as in the other stories, Isaac pretended that his wife was his sister. This Abimelech, however, discovered the truth when he saw Isaac and Rebekah acting in a romantic manner. As with Abraham and Abimelech in the earlier incident, both parties made peace. Afterwards Abimelech also tried to seize a well belonging to Isaac. Subsequently, they reached a new peace accord.

The Isaac story takes place after Abraham's death, at least forty-five to sixty-five years after Abraham's encounter with a King Abimelech in Gerar.[10] While a substantial time differential appears between the two Abimelech stories, it is not impossible that the same king and army captain were involved with both Abraham and Isaac, and that on both occasions a peaceful resolution was followed by a dispute over a well. However, Genesis never identifies this Abimelech as the earlier one, nor does it connect the second Phicol with the first.

Scholars generally agree that these three stories have a common source. The Isaac story, for example, combines the famine episode from the first Abraham encounter with the Abimelech story from the second. Unfortunately, we have no way to distinguish which story is the original and which is imitation.

The existence of three stories describing essentially the same incident demonstrates some of the problems facing the biblical redactor.

His source materials disagreed as to whether the locale of the incident was Egypt or Canaan, whether the patriarch was Abraham or Isaac, and whether the incident occurred during Abraham's lifetime or after his death. One of the stories takes place in Egypt, and if that is the original version it supports the idea that the patriarchal stories originated in Egypt and were subsequently transferred to a Canaanite locality.

In support of Egypt as the original site, we note that the other two stories have Abraham and Isaac confronting a Philistine king with a Philistine army occupying a Philistine city in Canaan, but the Philistines didn't arrive in Canaan for more than four hundred years after the Isaac incident,[11] which suggests a very late editing of the sources by someone who was out of touch with the original version.

Another consideration in favor of the wife/sister story having an Egyptian locale is the unusual direction given to Isaac during the famine. God specifically instructed him to go to Gerar, not Egypt. Why should he go to Gerar? Egypt is the major food center. It is where both Abraham and Jacob went in times of famine. Furthermore, Gerar resides close to the Palestinian-Egyptian border.[12] It reads as if the author of Isaac's adventure deliberately tried to break any link between the wife/sister story and Egypt. In later times a confused redactor included all three stories, no longer cognizant that all three derive from a single source.

Osiris and His Family

Egyptian records present a confusing picture of Osiris and his family relationships, a confusion that we shall see duplicated in the Genesis patriarchal history. The problem stems in major part from the merger into a single deity of at least three different gods named Horus: Horus the Elder, Horus the Child, and Horus the Son of Isis. The relationship of this merged Horus god to Osiris and Set presents a major problem in our analysis.

Egyptians also seemed to be confused about the identity of Set, with Egyptian myths giving him conflicting roles. In some sources Set corresponds to Apophis, the serpent that attacks Re (the sun) at the end of each day. For this reason, Greeks identified Set with Typhon, a monster serpent from Greek mythology. Other sources portray Set as a mighty warrior who defends Re against Apophis.

For purposes of our examination, we need not look at the complicated mythological and philosophical issues underlying the many
contradictions in Egyptian myth. Our concern is only with the broad
outline of two basic mythological cycles—the rivalry between Osiris
and Set and that between Horus and Set.

According to Heliopolitan Creation myths, Atum was the first deity and responsible for Creation. Without the benefit of a mate he
brought forth two deities, the male Shu (air) and the female Tefnut
(moisture). These two deities gave birth to the male Geb (earth) and
the female Nut (heaven). Geb and Nut had children, and at this
point Egyptian stories disagree about who the children were and who
the parents were.

In the most widespread version of the myth, Geb and Nut gave
birth to four gods at one time—Osiris, Isis, Set, and Nephthys. Osiris
married Isis and Set married Nephthys. In the Egyptian theology,
these first nine gods formed a unit known as the Great Ennead,
which Egyptians thought of as some sort of ruling council of gods.
Subsequently, Osiris and Isis had a child named Horus, known as
Horus the Son of Isis. As the tenth god born, he did not belong to the
Great Ennead.

An alternative version makes Geb and Nut the parents of five
children born in the following order: Osiris, Horus the Elder (a different god from Horus the Son of Isis), Set, Isis, and Nephthys. Egyptians memorialized this birth sequence in their solar calendar,
naming the last five days of the solar year after these five gods in the
order of their births.

The two versions disagree on the identity of Horus and the place-
ment of his birth. In an attempt to integrate the two genealogies, the
Egyptians came up with the idea that Osiris and Isis conceived Horus while they still lived in Nut's womb with Set and Nephthys, but
that doesn't resolve all the inconsistencies. The second genealogy
places the birth of Horus before the birth of Isis and contradicts the
idea of a Great Ennead that excludes Horus as one of the first nine
gods.

In one account, preserved in the first century A.D. by the Greco-
Roman writer Plutarch, this second genealogy, involving Horus the
Elder, went through a further refinement. While Nut still gave birth
to all five children, there were different fathers. Re fathered Osiris
and Horus the Elder, Thoth fathered Isis, and Geb fathered Set and

Nephthys. Also, at a later time Osiris and Isis had a child named Horus the Child.(different from Horus the Son of Isis).

While Plutarch makes Horus the Elder the son of Re and Nut, earlier myths make Horus the son of Re and Hathor. The name Hathor means "House of Horus," and the goddess Hathor, like Nut, represented the heavens. The substitution of the heaven goddess Nut for the heaven goddess Hathor may have been an evolutionary step in the Horus myth that attempted to integrate various contradictions.

In summary, Egyptians had two basic Horus genealogies. In one, Horus is the son of Re and a heaven goddess, either Hathor or Nut. In the other Horus is the son of Osiris and Isis. Also, in one line of descent, Set is Horus's younger brother. In the other, Set is Horus's older uncle. Note also that Isis functions as both wife and sister to Osiris. Both genealogies, as we shall see, were incorporated into the Genesis patriarchal history.

Early References to the Osiris Cycle

The Osiris cycle consists of two separate mythological accounts that were subsequently fused into one story. One described the attempts of Set to replace his brother Osiris as king of Egypt. The other concerned the attempts of Set to replace his brother Horus as king of Egypt.

The Egyptians left no full account of the Osiris story. Consequently, we only have bits and pieces in various inscriptions and illustrations, but we do have a lengthy account of the myth from Plutarch. His version is problematic and will be considered further below.

Several pieces of the Osiris myth appear in the Pyramid Texts of the Fifth Dynasty. According to Rudolf Anthes, one of the experts on Egyptian mythology, as the Osiris myth appears in the Pyramid Texts it can be summarized as follows:

The king, Osiris, was killed by his brother Set in Nedyt (or Gehasty). Isis and Nephthys, the sisters of Osiris, sought for the body, found it in Nedyt, and lamented over it. Isis restored Osiris to life temporarily so that he might get her with child. She then gave birth to Horus, suckled him, and brought him up

in Khemmis, a place in the Delta. As a child, Horus overpow-
ered a snake. He reached manhood through a ceremony which
centered on the fastening of a belt, which Isis performed, and
went out to "see" his father (*Pyr*. 1214–15). Apparently he
found him. Then a court over which Geb presided was held at
Heliopolis. Set denied the murder of Osiris; presumably, too,
the question arose whether or not Horus was the true heir to
Osiris; in any event, Isis testified on behalf of her son by taking
him to her breasts. Horus was made king by the acclaim of the
court.[13]

Anthes also refers to two other elements of the Osiris story that
appear in the Pyramid Texts but which he says were not yet fused
into the main story.[14] One concerns his drowning, a throwback to his
early role as an agricultural deity. The other describes the dismemberment of the deceased king, who symbolized Osiris. He says that
in later Greek transmissions of the myth the dismemberment of
Osiris by Set plays an important role.

The Pyramid Texts also introduce some of the confusion over the
identity of Horus. As Anthes observes, "in early sections of the Pyramid Texts, Horus and Seth appear as brothers and equal rulers of
the two parts of Egypt, Lower and Upper."[15] He also adds that in the
Second Dynasty kings were identified not just as Horus but as Horus
and Seth.[16]

The Plutarch Account

The fullest account of the Osiris cycle comes from the Greco-Roman
writer Plutarch. Although ancient Egyptian inscriptions and texts
indicate that Plutarch followed traditional Egyptian beliefs, his text
presents many problems. For one, he often substitutes the names of
Greek gods for the Egyptian gods, and we have to rely on generally
accepted identifications. On other occasions he may have added in
elements from Greek myths with similar themes. He also records a
version of the myth current in the first century A.D. that may have
significantly evolved over thousands of years from earlier versions.

Plutarch begins his story with the birth of the Osirian gods.[17]
Apparently Re had forbidden Nut to have sexual relations with Geb
but she ignored the prohibition. Re punished her by declaring that

she could not give birth during any month or year. Thoth, in a game of draughts, managed to win a portion of the moon's light, enough to form five extra days. Since these didn't fall within any month of the calendar year, Nut could give birth on those days, and she did. She bore five children: Osiris, Horus the Elder, Set, Isis, and Nephthys, one on each day, and in that order. Set, according to Plutarch, was born out of turn because he forced his way out through a wound that he made in his mother's side.[18] Plutarch observed that these are the five gods associated with the five extra days added to the Egyptian calendar.[19]

Although Nut was the mother of all five gods, Plutarch records that the children had several fathers. Re fathered Osiris and Horus the Elder; Thoth fathered Isis; and Geb fathered Set and Nephthys.[20] After making Re the father of Horus the Elder, Plutarch introduces into his story the general Egyptian confusion about the identity of Horus. For instance, after stating that Re was the father of Horus the Elder, he says that Horus was the offspring of Osiris and Isis while they were still in the womb.[21] This Horus would be Horus the Son of Isis. Then, later in the story, he makes Osiris and Isis the parents of another Horus, Horus the Child who was born lame in the leg.[22]

The main elements of Plutarch's story can be summarized as follows: Osiris had a civilizing influence on what was then a barbarous Egyptian culture. He taught agricultural skills, passed laws to regulate conduct, and instructed Egyptians in the proper manner to worship the gods. After ruling for a while, he decided to travel abroad to spread his teachings. During his absence Isis safeguarded the throne against Set's covetous actions.

When Osiris returned, Set tricked him into entering a chest, which Set immediately sealed with the help of seventy-two accomplices and an Ethiopian queen named Aso. Set floated the chest out to sea and it eventually drifted to Byblos, where it had become enmeshed within a tree. These events occurred either in Osiris's twenty-eighth year of reign or twenty-eighth year of life.

Isis sought after Osiris's body and arrived in Byblos, where she became a nurse for the king and queen, Melkart and Astarte. One incident of note concerns her efforts at giving immortality to one of the king's children. Each day she passed him through a fire to burn away the mortal parts. The procedure failed when Isis's actions were accidentally discovered by the queen.

Isis recovered Osiris's body and brought it back to Egypt, where she hid it in a remote area. Then she went to visit her son Horus, whom she had also hidden away to protect him from Set. While she was away, Set discovered Osiris's body and hacked it into fourteen pieces. These he distributed around the country, except for the penis, which had been devoured by a fish. Isis searched for the parts of Osiris's body but found only the thirteen buried pieces. These she buried in the vicinity where they were found.

The balance of Plutarch's account briefly summarizes a series of conflicts between Horus and Set, with Horus emerging victorious. His account concludes with the story of how Isis accompanied Osiris after his death and became impregnated with Horus the Child, who was born "before his time and lame in the lower limbs."

The Contendings of Horus and Set

So far we have been concerned mostly with that branch of the Osiris Cycle dealing with the conflict between Osiris and Set. Now we turn to the conflicts between Set and Horus. The fullest account appears to be a New Kingdom story known as "The Contendings of Horus and Set."[23]

The story recounts the deliberations of the Ennead as they wrestle with the problem of who should succeed Osiris, Horus the Child or Set. According to the text, the deliberations had been going on for over eighty years.[24] Despite the passage of time, Horus still appears in the story as a child, but also as a mighty warrior.[25] The Horus in this story is Harpokrates (Horus the Child). In the Plutarch account, Harpokrates was born after Osiris's death and is separate from the Horus who fought with Set.

Horus, as son of Osiris, argued that the son of the king was rightfully entitled to succeed him. Set, the brother of Osiris, argued that he was the mightiest of warriors, more powerful than Horus, and as such was entitled to succeed Osiris.

Strangely, given Set's well-documented role in killing Osiris, in the course of the deliberations no one raises the issue. At one point Osiris himself is consulted on who should succeed him, and, while endorsing his son's claim, no mention is made of Set's earlier foul play.[26]

With the exception of Re-Herakhte, the chief deity who has to make the decision, all the gods on the council want Horus to become king. But Re-Herakhte wants to appoint Set, the mighty warrior who protects him against the serpent Apophis. (Obviously, Set here is the "good" Set who defends Re rather than the "evil" Apophis.) Horus's chief defender is his mother Isis, and together she and Horus use trickery and deceit to beat Set.

The Contendings consists of about a half-dozen stories interspersed with various arguments and assertions by different Egyptian deities. With one exception each of the incidents features a conflict between Horus and Set. Horus manages to overcome Set time and again, but Set refuses to concede until the very end, when Atum orders that Set be brought before the council in manacles.

The Patriarchal Family

The central theme of patriarchal history concerns the passage of God's covenant from generation to generation. The first patriarch receiving God's blessing was Abram, who was married to Sarai. On the birth of their son Isaac, God changed their names to Abraham and Sarah.

While Isaac was Sarai's first son, Abraham had another son, Ishmael, born thirteen years earlier. The mother of Ishmael was Hagar, an Egyptian maidservant of Sarai. Abram greatly favored Ishmael, but God decreed that Isaac, not Ishmael, should be Abraham's heir. Sarai forced Hagar out of Abram's household and Hagar went into the wilderness, where she expected to die with her son. But God had promised Abram that he would protect Hagar and make Ishmael the father of a mighty nation.

Isaac married Rebekah, and together they had twin sons, Jacob and Esau. These were rivals and fought, even in the womb. Esau emerged first and became Isaac's favorite son and prospective heir. Later, however, Jacob, with the help of his mother Rebekah, tricked Isaac and Esau into giving him his father's blessing, enabling Jacob to receive the covenant with God.

Jacob's deception infuriated Esau, and the younger brother fled north to Syria, where he sought to marry Rachel, the daughter of his uncle Laban (and Rebekah's brother). His uncle agreed to the marriage on condition that Jacob work for him for seven years. Jacob accepted, but after the seven years were up Laban reneged, insisting

that Jacob first marry his older daughter Leah and then work another seven years for Rachel. This, too, Jacob agreed to, and after
seven more years he finally married his beloved Rachel.

Leah bore Jacob six sons and a daughter. Jacob also had four other
sons by two concubines, Bilhah and Zilpah. These children were all
born before Rachel could give Jacob a child of her own. But eventually she and Jacob had a son, Joseph, who immediately became Jacob's favorite.

After the birth of his eleven sons, Jacob and his wives chose to
leave Laban's household and return to Canaan. On the return journey Jacob visited Esau, at which time the two brothers made peace.
At about this time God changed Jacob's name to Israel. While in
Canaan, Rachel gave birth to Benjamin, Jacob's twelfth son, but she
died in childbirth.

During Jacob's sojourn in Syria, Esau moved to the Jordanian side
of Canaan where, according to the Bible, he became the founder of
the nation of Edom, in the vicinity of Mount Seir.

Jacob loved Joseph more than any of his other sons and made
Joseph his heir. While in Egypt, Joseph married the daughter of the
priest of Heliopolis and they had two children, Manasseh and
Ephraim. Jacob had thought that the blessing would go to Manasseh,
the older of the two children, but Joseph passed it on to the younger
son, Ephraim. Genesis ends with the death of Joseph.

In the next two chapters we will take a closer look at the stories of
Abraham, Isaac, and Jacob, examining the plot lines and looking at
the character descriptions and iconographic representations. These
elements will then be cross-referenced to the Egyptian Osiris and
Horus stories. It will then become clear that the core elements of
patriarchal history derive from Egyptian myths about the family of
Osiris.

While the genealogical contradictions in the Egyptian myths prevent us from making an exact one-to-one correspondence between
the Egyptian deities and the Genesis patriarchs, a broad set of parallels can be established.

In the Jacob cycle, which draws primarily on the struggle between
Horus and Set, the Jacob-Israel story represents Horus in all three of
his aspects, while Esau corresponds to Set. Jacob's mother Rebekah
plays the role of Isis.

In the Isaac cycle, which draws primarily on the relationship between Osiris and his family members, Isaac has a dual role. In his

adult years, as husband of Rebekah and father of Jacob, he plays the role of Osiris, but in his early years he plays the role of Horus. His brother Ishmael corresponds to Set. Isaac's parents, Abram (Abraham) and Sarai (Sarah) represent the various gods and goddesses that fathered the Osirian family.

While these relationships are not immediately obvious, they will become clear when we compare the Genesis material with the Egyptian sources.

12

The Horus Cycle: Jacob and Esau

In this chapter we examine the major episodes in Genesis about Jacob and Esau, the twin brothers born to Isaac and Rebekah. The evidence will show that most of the main material for the Jacob cycle is derived from the Egyptian accounts of the struggles between Horus and Set. In this regard Jacob represents Horus, Esau represents Set, and Rebekah represents Isis.

In a true one-to-one correspondence, the Set character (Esau) should be the brother, not the son of Isis. But in order to accommodate genealogical contradictions in the Egyptian myths, the role of Set had to be divided into two separate Genesis characters, Ishmael and Esau. In this way the author of the original Genesis stories attempted to preserve the appropriate relationships among the Osirian gods.

The division of responsibility between Ishmael and Esau stems from Set's relationship to Horus. The Horus in Egyptian myth fuses together three different Horus deities: Horus the Elder, Horus the Child, and Horus the Son of Isis. Horus the Elder is brother to both Set and Isis as well as *older* brother to Set; the other two Horuses are the sons of Isis and *younger* nephew of Set. Since one Horus is older than Set and one is younger, it is not possible to have only one character represent Horus and only one represent Set and still provide a perfect genealogical correlation between the Osirian gods and the Genesis characters. Therefore, the role of Set had to be divided between two different people in Genesis, Ishmael and Esau. To accommodate the two Set characters in Genesis, the roles of the three Horus deities have also been distributed between two Genesis characters, Jacob and Isaac. We will deal with the Isaac-Ishmael relationship in the next chapter.

220

The Births of Jacob and Esau

Jacob and Esau were the twin sons of Isaac and Rebekah. They did not get along and struggled even in the womb. Esau forced his way out first and Jacob unsuccessfully tried to stop him by grabbing at his brother's heel.[1]

At birth, Esau "came out red, all over like a hairy garment."[2] As he grew up he became a "cunning hunter"[3] and had become Isaac's favorite son because of his ability to provide his father with tasty meat.[4] By virtue of his status as first born, Esau should have been heir to the covenant with God and leader of the Hebrew people. Instead, Jacob, with the help of Rebekah, tricked Isaac into giving him the birthright.

When Esau learned about what happened he threatened to kill Jacob. "The days of mourning for my father are at hand; then will I slay my brother Jacob."[5] Fearing for Jacob's safety, Rebekah advised her son to flee to Syria and stay with his uncle Laban (Rebekah's brother). Jacob remained there for twenty years and married Leah and Rachel, Laban's daughters. By these two wives and their two maidservants, Jacob fathered twelve sons and a daughter.

While Jacob lived in Syria, Esau moved east of the Jordan to the country of Edom, where he defeated a mysterious people known as the Horites. Genesis identifies Esau as the ancestor of the Edomites, a people with whom the Hebrews in the first millennium had numerous battles. When Jacob decided to return home he made a courtesy visit to Esau, hoping to make peace. To his surprise, Esau greeted him in a friendly manner, said he was no longer angry, and invited Jacob and his family to come stay with him for a while. Afraid that Esau still nursed a desire for vengeance, Jacob offered to follow after Esau but instead headed to the Canaanite city of Shechem.

On his trip from Syria to Canaan, Jacob had two unrelated experiences in which his name changed from Jacob to Israel. One incident, occurring just before his visit with Esau, involved an all-night wrestling match with a stranger. In the course of the struggle Jacob suffered an injury that left him lame in the lower leg. The other incident happened at a later time, when Jacob returned to Bethel, a place where he had previously dreamed about angels climbing a ladder to heaven.

Looking at the stories of Jacob and Esau at only surface level, it is hard to see the elements of the Egyptian Horus cycle. But when we burrow below the surface the Egyptian precedents become clear. Consider some of the biblical plot lines: The older brother wants to succeed to the leadership; the head of the family supports the older brother's claim; the younger brother, aided by his mother's trickery, obtains the right to rule; the mother, fearing for the younger brother's safety, hides him away from the older brother; and eventually the older brother makes peace with the younger brother and acknowledges his role as leader. This story line, as we shall soon see, closely parallels the account in *The Contendings of Horus and Set*.

The birth of Esau also suggests a connection close to Egyptian sources. According to Genesis, Esau forced his way out of the womb and came out with red hair so thick it was like a garment. According to Plutarch, Set, too, forced his way to an early birth, coming "into the world, being born neither at the proper time, nor by the proper place, but forcing his way through a wound which he had made in his mother's side."[6] And the Egyptians also identified Set as a red-haired beast, which was often associated with the donkey. Some ancient texts describe him as having a red mane, and Plutarch tells us that the Coptites threw an ass over a precipice because in its redness it resembled Set.[7] Therefore, Esau's early birth and thick red hair suggest a close correspondence to the red-haired image of Set.

The birth of Jacob fails to evoke a parallel Egyptian image, as Esau's does, but his subsequent laming in the course of changing his name from Jacob to Israel suggests another Egyptian Horus birth. In Plutarch, Horus the Child was born lame, and in *The Contendings* Set's rival is Horus the Child. An examination of other stories in Genesis will reinforce the connection between Jacob and Esau, and Horus and Set.

The Birthright

How Jacob obtained the birthright from Esau is the central incident in Jacob's life. Genesis has two stories about how that happened. In one, Esau returned home famished after a day in the fields. Upon his arrival he found Jacob with a bowl of lentils. Taking advantage of his brother's hunger, Jacob offered to exchange the lentils for Esau's birthright: "And Esau said, Behold, I am at the point to die: and what profit shall this birthright do to me?"[8]

In the second story, Rebekah conspired with Jacob to deceive Isaac, who was then old and nearly blind. One day Isaac told Esau to go out and get him some venison and that after eating he would give Esau the blessing. Rebekah overheard Isaac's promise and went to Jacob. She told him to go to the flock and kill two young goats so she could prepare a stew for Isaac and have Jacob deliver it, pretending to be Esau. At first Jacob balked at Rebekah's plan: "And Jacob said to Rebekah his mother, Behold, Esau my brother is a hairy man, and I am a smooth man: My father peradventure will feel me, and I shall seem to him as a deceiver; and I shall bring a curse upon me, and not a blessing."[9] But Rebekah responded, "Upon me be thy curse, my son: only obey my voice, and go fetch me them."[10]

Rebekah then prepared the meal, placed Esau's clothing on Jacob, and, to simulate Esau's hairy body, placed the goat skins on Jacob's hands and neck. Jacob's disguise easily fooled Isaac, and he mistakenly gave the blessing to Jacob.

The first of these stories involves the sale of Esau's birthright for a bowl of food; the second involves a deception by which Jacob obtained Esau's blessing, again involving a bowl of food. The entire incident seems to share a common source with a very similar story in *The Contendings of Horus and Set*.

The Island in the Middle

In *The Contendings*, Horus's chief defender is his mother Isis, and, with the exception of Re, who favors Set, she successfully unites all the gods against Set. Angered at Isis's role, Set declares, "I shall not go to law in the tribunal while Isis is (still) in it."[11]

In response, Re directs all the gods to assemble at the Island in the Middle, with orders to the ferryman not to allow Isis or anyone looking like her to come across. But Isis disguises herself as an elderly woman and tells the ferryman that she has a bowl of porridge for the young man who has been tending cattle and is hungry. The ferryman is hesitant, saying that he has been forbidden to ferry women across, but Isis reminds him that the proscription was only against women looking like Isis. She then offers him a bribe and he takes her across.

When she arrives on the island she sees Set and transforms herself into the most beautiful woman in the country. Set immediately lusts after her and approaches. She then tells him a tale of woe:

> I was a wife (living) with a cattleman to whom I bore a son. My husband died, and the lad started tending his father's cattle. But then a stranger came and settled in my stable. He said thus in speaking to my son, "I shall beat you and confiscate your father's cattle and evict you." Now it is my desire to have you afford him protection.[12]

Set, sympathizing with her plight, replies, "Is it while the son of the male is still living that the cattle are to be given to the stranger."[13]

No sooner are the words out of his mouth than Isis transforms herself into a bird and calls out to the god that his own words did him in.[14] When Re learns of this he writes to the Ennead that the crown should be given to Horus. Of course, Re's decision doesn't end the dispute. Set continues to challenge Horus's claim, and the gods continue to argue over who should be enthroned.

Parallel Themes

Consider the basic elements in the Egyptian story. The chief of the clan (Re) favors the older brother for the crown. Isis wants to obtain the crown for her son Horus, the younger brother. She puts on a disguise and approaches with a bowl of food. She says that the food is for the hungry man who was tending cattle all day. Set is tricked into giving his blessing to Horus. Re has to sadly declare that Horus has won the title. Set refuses to concede and challenges Horus further.

With only very slight changes, Genesis and *The Contendings* tell the same tale, but the Egyptian story combines both Genesis birthright stories into a single incident. A person wearing a disguise approaches someone with a bowl of food. She says it is for someone who worked hard all day in the field (the first birthright story). She then tricks that person into uttering the words that bestow the crown on the opposing party (the second birthright story).

The only minor differences between the Egyptian and biblical accounts concern which persons perform which deeds. In the Egyptian story, the mother does the deed on behalf of her son; in Genesis, the mother plots out the plan, takes responsibility for it, and has the son wear the disguise. In the Egyptian story, the older brother is the one tricked into uttering the damning words; in Genesis, the person tricked is the father who favors the older son.

The Flight

In the traditional Horus-Set story, after Set kills Osiris, Isis realizes that he also planned to kill Horus, so she hides her son away in order to protect him. In Genesis we have a similar situation. When Isaac blesses Jacob instead of Esau, Esau threatens to kill his younger brother. Rebekah, then, arranges for him to be hidden away with her uncle. While the correlations aren't perfect, they are quite close.

One difference is that at the time of the hiding, Horus is a child while Jacob is an adult. Another is that Set kills Horus's father, whereas Esau does not kill Isaac. Both events in the Egyptian story are related to the death of Osiris. Osiris's death, however, presented a special problem to the Atenist-Genesis scribes, and the nature of that problem will be examined in the next chapter. In Genesis, the death of Osiris as the defining moment is replaced by Isaac giving the blessing to Jacob. However, we should note that according to Genesis, Isaac chooses to give the blessing because he thinks he is close to death.[15]

The Wife / Sister Issue

In the story of Isis in disguise, I believe we have a clue to the origins of the wife/sister stories in Genesis. As you may recall, there are three instances in which a patriarch's wife pretends to be his sister instead of his wife. In each of the stories the patriarch and his wife enter into a foreign territory where they believe the king wants to have a sexual relationship with the wife.

In the Egyptian myths, Isis is both wife and sister to Osiris and the mother of Horus. Set is the enemy of both her husband and her son and plans to kill both. He successfully murders Osiris but, due to Isis's protection, he fails in his efforts to kill Horus. Ultimately, Horus triumphs, and according to a number of Egyptian texts, he banishes Set to the desert areas outside of Egypt.

The desert territory ruled by Set corresponds to the Bible's Wilderness of Shur, on the northeast corner of the Egyptian border. It is also the site of Gerar, the city where two of the three wife/sister stories take place. (The third incident occurs in Egypt.)

I submit that originally Set is the foreign king in the Wilderness of Shur and that he had already killed Osiris, the husband/brother of Isis, and continued to threaten Horus. As in *The Contendings*, Isis adopts a disguise to arouse Set's lust and tricks him into saying the words that would destroy his claim to the title. The two stories in Gerar even feature a dispute over territorial claims, with the foreign king, after hostilities, eventually recognizing the patriarch's title to the property.

The broad outlines of these stories were incorporated into Genesis as a wife/sister story, but confusion developed between Set's two separate confrontations with Isis's family. As the Egyptian deities were transformed into human characters the stories underwent further transformation, with some of the magical elements being edited out or replaced. Centuries later, the redactors read the intermediary sources and saw two separate instances with a wife/sister confronting a king in the Wilderness of Shur. In both stories the king has the same name and lusts after the wife/sister, who appears in disguise.

In considering this solution, we should note that the king's name in the biblical account, Abimelech, constitutes nothing more than a generic title meaning "father-king." More important, Genesis anachronistically identifies the king as a Philistine, but four hundred years will pass before Philistines come to Canaan. Clearly, some form of alteration of the original story occurred.

Esau Against the Horites

After Jacob fled from Canaan to Syria to avoid his brother's wrath, Esau moved to the east side of the Jordan, where Genesis says he became the eponymous ancestor of the Edomites.[16] But before establishing his claim to the territory he first had to defeat a mysterious people known as the Horites.[17]

Unfortunately, archaeologists have yet to identify an Edomite people known as Horites. Some biblical scholars theorize that "Horite" refers to the Hurrians, but, as Speiser points out, no evidence places the Hurrians in Edom.[18] He also notes that the Hurrians were non-Semitic, whereas Genesis gives the Horites Semitic names.[19]

The biblical text also gives evidence of some confusion about the identity of the Horites. On one occasion Genesis mentions a Horite branch headed by a man named Zibeon who has a son named Anah and a granddaughter named Aholibamah.[20] Elsewhere, Genesis says that Esau married Aholibamah, daughter of Anah, the daughter of Zibeon the Hivite.[21] Are Hivites the same as the Horites, or a subgroup?

Genesis has three references to the Hivites. In the Family of Nations, Hivites are the descendants of Canaan.[22] Later Genesis locates them in the Canaanite city of Shechem.[23] The third reference is simply to "Zibeon the Hivite," leaving his origin up in the air. So we are left with a list of Horites that may include Hivites, who belong in Canaan, not Edom.

The situation becomes even more complicated when we look at the passages naming the wives of Esau. Initially, we are told that Esau had three wives: Judith, the daughter of Beeri the Hittite; Bashemath, the daughter of Elon the Hittite; and Mahalath, Ishmael's daughter, the sister of Nebajoth.[24] Here his wives are two Hittites and Ishmael's daughter—no Hivites or Horites.

Later, however, Genesis says that his three wives were: Adah, daughter of Elon the Hittite; Aholibamah, daughter of Anah, daughter of Zibeon the Hivite; and Bashemath, daughter of Ishmael and sister of Nebajoth.[25] This list differs from the first in a number of respects. To begin with, both lists have only one name in common, Bashemath, and the first list makes her a Hittite daughter while the second makes her Ishmael's daughter (from the Wilderness of Shur). Also, the first list has two Hittites, the second list only one. Also, since neither Ishmael, nor the Hittites, nor the Hivites live in Edom, neither list has any Edomites. And lastly, the name of Ishmael's daughter differs in the two lists.

The placing of Esau in Edom appears to be the result of a linguistic misunderstanding. According to Genesis, Esau is identified with Edom because Esau accepted a bowl of *red* pottage in exchange for his birthright.[26] In Hebrew, the name Edom closely corresponds to the Hebrew word for the color red. The color red also reminds us that Esau was covered with a thick coat of red hair. Also, some scholars have noted that Seir, the name of the chief mountain in Edom, can be construed as "hairy."[27] Biblical redactors must have assumed that Esau's association with the color red and his hairy red body was responsible for the naming of the country of Edom.

That Esau's association with Edom must have been a late gloss seems to be corroborated by Isaac's blessing to Esau. After Jacob tricked Isaac into giving him the birthright, Isaac gave this blessing to his older son:

> And Isaac his father answered and said unto him, Behold, thy dwelling shall be the fatness of the earth, and of the dew of heaven from above; And by thy sword shalt thou live, and shalt serve thy brother; and it shall come to pass when thou shalt have the dominion, that thou shalt break his yoke from off they neck.[28]

The latter part of the blessing indicates that Edom will be subjugated to Israel but that there will be a time when Edom breaks free of Israel's domination. This suggests that the author of the blessing wrote in the mid–first millennium, when Edom had become independent of Israel. This would be the time when biblical redactors assumed that Esau belonged in Edom.

This brings us back to the question, who were the Horites? When we acknowledge that Esau represents the Egyptian god Set, the answer becomes obvious. The Horites were originally the allies of the god Horus in his struggles with Set. In later times, based on Set's red hairy body, the redactors simply identified him with the nation of Edom and moved him and his Horite enemies into that territory.

Jacob and Israel

Genesis gives us two accounts of how Jacob changed his name to Israel. One incident occurred upon the occasion of Jacob's wrestling through the night with a stranger. The other happened in connection with Jacob's dream about a ladder to heaven. We will now look at both incidents and see that they derived from Egyptian stories about Horus and Set, and that the two changes of Jacob's name corresponded to the merger of the three Horus deities into a single personality.

Jacob Wrestles With a Stranger

Jacob remained with Laban for twenty years. While there he married two of Laban's daughters, Rachel and Leah, and by them and their two handmaids had eleven sons and a daughter. His twelfth son was born after returning to Canaan.

On the way home, Jacob decided to make a peace offering to Esau and sent messengers to his brother bearing the news and an offer of gifts. The messengers returned to Jacob and told them that Esau would come to meet him and that he was bringing four hundred men with him. Jacob became nervous at this news, fearing that Esau meant to do him harm, and took various precautions to protect his family against attack.

During the night, while awaiting Esau's arrival at the Jabbok ford by the Jordan River, Jacob had a strange experience:

And Jacob was left alone; and there wrestled a man with him until the breaking of the day. And when he saw that he prevailed not against him, he touched the hollow of his thigh; and the hollow of Jacob's thigh was out of joint, as he wrestled with him. And he said, *Let me go, for the day breaketh.* And he said, I will not let thee go, except thou bless me. And he said unto him, What is thy name? And he said, Jacob. And he said, Thy name shall be called no more Jacob, but Israel: for as a prince hast thou power with God and with men, and hast prevailed. And Jacob asked him, and said, Tell me, I pray thee, thy name. And he said, Wherefore is it that thou dost ask after my name? And he blessed him there. And Jacob called the name of the place Peniel: for I have seen God face to face, and my life is preserved. And as he passed over Penuel[29] *the sun rose upon him, and he halted upon his thigh.* Therefore the children of Israel eat not of the sinew which shrank, which is upon the hollow of the thigh, unto this day: because he touched the hollow of Jacob's thigh in the sinew that shrank. *And Jacob lifted up his eyes, and looked, and, behold, Esau came,* and with him four hundred men.[30] [Emphasis added.]

Jacob was initially frightened by Esau's arrival and separated his family into separate groups, but when Esau approached:

Esau ran to meet him, and embraced him, and fell on his neck, and kissed him: and they wept. And he lifted up his eyes, and saw the women and the children; and said, Who are those with thee? And he said, The children which God hath graciously given they servant. Then the handmaidens came near, they and their children, and they bowed themselves. And Leah also with

her children came near, and bowed themselves: and after came
Joseph near and Rachel, and they bowed themselves. And he
said, What meanest thou by all this drove which I met? And he
said, These are to find grace in the sight of my lord. And Esau
said, I have enough, my brother; keep that thou hast unto thyself. And Jacob said, Nay, I pray thee, if now I have found grace
in thy sight, then receive my present at my hand: for therefore *I
have seen thy face, as though I had seen the face of God,* and thou wast
pleased with me.[31] [Emphasis added.]

The two brothers made peace, and Esau invited Jacob to come visit
him. But Jacob still feared Esau and made excuses for not following
immediately after. Esau offered to leave some of his men with Jacob,
but Jacob said it wasn't necessary. Finally, Jacob said:

Let my lord, I pray thee, pass over before his servant: and I will
lead on softly, according as the cattle that goeth before me and
the children be able to endure, until I come unto my lord unto
Seir."[32]

Esau then returned to Seir, but Jacob did not follow after. He
moved on to Shechem.

Jacob's Opponent

The most immediate question is: With whom did Jacob wrestle? At
first Genesis says that he wrestled with a man through the night.
This man remains unidentified, but Jacob assumed that he had been
wrestling with God and named the place Peniel because "I have seen
God face to face, and my life is preserved." (Peniel means "face of
God.")

Jacob's claim that he had looked on the face of God must be erroneous, though, because we know from the story of Moses that no
mortal can look on the face of God and live; mere presence in its
vicinity would cause great physical harm. Also, it would not be possible for Jacob to have wrestled God to a standstill. For these reasons,
it is usually maintained that Jacob wrestled with an angel.

However, the identity of the stranger is suggested by the circumstances of the fight—a battle through the night in which the
stranger cannot overcome his opponent. As Egyptologists have generally noted, in the Old Kingdom Pyramid Texts the battles between

Set and Horus the Elder symbolized the battle between dark and light, night and day. Therefore, it is significant that Jacob's battle not only continued through the night and ended at daybreak, but at the conclusion Jacob lifts up his eyes and suddenly Esau appears.

The sudden appearance of Esau suggests that he was the stranger. In support of this view, recall how shortly thereafter Jacob says to Esau, "I have seen thy face, as though I had seen the face of God."

Jacob's wrestling match is nothing more than a corrupted account of the original daily struggles between Set and Horus the Elder. But why did this lead to the name change from Jacob to Israel?

A change of name suggests a form of rebirth. In connection with the name change Jacob suffered an injury to his leg that left him with a permanent limp. In Plutarch's story of Osiris, we note that after Set and Horus made peace, Osiris temporarily returned from the dead to father a child with Isis. This was Horus the Child, and he was born lame in the leg.

The laming of Jacob also occurs in the context of peace between Horus and Set. Initially, Jacob represents Horus the Son of Isis. When he wrestles with the stranger he represents Horus the Elder. When peace arrives he receives a new name, a rebirth, and in his lame condition becomes Horus the Child.

In describing the wrestling incident as a throwback to the earlier daily battles between Horus and Set, another point to consider is that Jacob and Esau each have twelve sons. The ancient Egyptians divided the day into twenty-four parts, twelve day portions and twelve night portions, giving us what eventually became the twenty-four-hour day. Therefore, the twelve sons in each family may represent the twelve parts of day and the twelve parts of night.

The Ladder to Heaven

After Jacob leaves Esau, the family moves to Shechem, and we have a strange story about Jacob's daughter Dinah, but we will consider that a little later. After the incident involving Jacob's daughter, the family moves to Bethel, where the second name change of Jacob to Israel occurs.

So Jacob came to Luz, which is in the land of Canaan, that is, Bethel, he and all the people that were with him. And he built there an altar, and called the place Elbethel: because there God appeared unto him, when he fled from the face of his brother. But Deborah Rebekah's nurse died, and she was buried beneath Bethel under an oak: and the name of it was called Allonbachuth. And God appeared unto Jacob again, when he came out of Padanaram, and blessed him. And God said unto him, Thy name is Jacob: thy name shall not be called any more Jacob, but Israel shall be thy name: and he called his name Israel.[33]

Although we saw that as a result of the wrestling incident Jacob's name was changed to Israel, we have here a second version of the name change. No explanation appears for this second transformation, but the passage tells us that when he fled from his brother Esau, Jacob had an unusual experience in this city. On that earlier occasion:

he lighted upon a certain place, and tarried there all night, because the sun was set; and he took of the stones of that place, and put them for his pillows, and lay down in that place to sleep. And he dreamed, and behold a ladder set up on the earth, and the top of it reached to heaven: and behold the angels of God ascending and descending on it. And, behold, the LORD stood above it, and said, I am the LORD God of Abraham thy father, and the God of Isaac: the land whereon thou liest, to thee will I give it, and to thy seed.[34]

After he awoke,

he was afraid, and said, How dreadful is this place! this is none other but the house of God, and this is the gate of heaven. And Jacob rose up early in the morning, and took the stone that he had put for his pillows, and set it up for a pillar, and poured oil upon the top of it. And he called the name of that place Bethel: but the name of that city was called Luz at the first.[35]

This image of a ladder to heaven has puzzled biblical scholars looking for Semitic antecedents for the concept. Some have tried to identify the ladder to heaven with the Babylonian ziggurats. Speiser, for example, finds it hard to imagine a steady stream of angels going up and down an ordinary ladder, and considers "stairway" a better translation than "ladder." Since the ziggurats had a stairway leading to the top, Speiser concludes, "only such a stairway can account for Jacob's later description of it as a 'gateway to heaven.' "[36]

But this was no ordinary ladder. To find its origin we need look no further than the Egyptian Pyramid Texts. Consider this example from the tomb of the Fifth Dynasty pharaoh Unas:

Ra setteth upright the ladder for Osiris, and Horus *raiseth up the ladder for his father Osiris, when Osiris goeth to [find] his soul;* one standeth on the one side, and the other standeth on the other, and Unas is betwixt them. Unas standeth up and is Horus, he sitteth down and he is Set.[37] [Emphasis added.]

Or this from the Pyramid of Pepi I (Sixth Dynasty):

Hail to thee, O Ladder of God, Hail to thee, O Ladder of Set. Stand up O Ladder of God, stand up O Ladder of Set, stand up O Ladder of Horus, *whereon Osiris went forth into heaven.*[38] [Emphasis added.]

Jacob's ladder dream comes straight out of Egyptian imagery. The Egyptian passages quoted come from funerary rituals. As the Unas passage says, Osiris has to climb the ladder to find his soul. Osiris represents the deceased king, and it is the deceased king who will climb the ladder. The ladder itself consists of the bodies of the gods Horus and Set.

Jacob's dream depicts the same ladder. He even recognizes that he stands at the gate to heaven. In place of the deities, however, Genesis has angels.

As the gateway to heaven, Jacob renamed the city Bethel, "House of God." Coincidentally, the Egyptians identified heaven with the goddess Hathor, whose name means "House of Horus" (i.e., where the sun lives). Thus, Bethel, as the gateway to heaven and the place where God lives, would be the Hebrew equivalent of the House of Horus, which coincides with Jacob's presence there as a Horus figure.

If Jacob's ladder originated as a funeral image, then one should expect the dream to be associated with a death, but no death appears in the story. However, when Jacob returned to Bethel and changed his name, a death occurred. Immediately before the name change, Genesis says that Deborah, nurse to Rebekah, died. Also, Jacob's name change symbolically represents both birth and death. The old king, Jacob, died and was replaced by the new king, Israel. In

Egyptian terms, Jacob died and became Osiris, who climbed the ladder, while the naming of Israel signified the substitution of a new Horus for the deceased Jacob.

Genesis, together with Plutarch's Osiris story, provides some evidence for this interpretation. Just before the name change, Deborah, nurse to Rebekah, dies. Genesis has no previous mention of her. All we know about her comes from her obituary notice—that she was Rebekah's nurse and died at the tree named Allonbacuth, which in Hebrew means "Tree of Weeping."

The tree reminds us of the incident in the Plutarch story in which Isis finds the body of her dead husband Osiris in a tree trunk in the house of the king and queen of Byblos. To be with her husband, Isis takes a job as nurse to the royal couple's child. In the story, Isis tries to confer immortality on the child through ritual magic involving the passing of the child's body through fire. During the process Isis transforms herself into a swallow and flits around the tree bemoaning her fate. The child never receives immortality because the queen accidentally discovers what Isis was doing and the transformation ends. At about that point Isis lets out a shriek that frightens one of the king's children to death.

In Plutarch's story we have a nurse flying sadly about a tree that contains the dead body of Osiris. In Genesis the nurse appears at the Tree of Weeping, but instead of Rebekah/Isis as the nurse, the role has been transferred to someone identified as Rebekah's nurse, and her appearance coincides with the transformation of Jacob into Israel.

The Deborah story has all the appearance of a truncated insert. There must have been more to it, and the Plutarch account hints at what this was. In all probability Deborah would have tried to confer immortality on Jacob, aiding his transformation into Israel. And perhaps, as in Plutarch, the nurse's actions would have been interrupted. But the polytheistic symbolism, as well as the Osirian connections, may have been too much for the Atenists to swallow, so they might have heavily edited the original.

The Banquet of Peace

As *The Contendings of Horus and Set* unfolds, the gods begin to weary of the continuous arguing between Horus and Set. Re directs the two brothers to share a peaceful meal in the hope of resolving the dispute. Set, with ulterior motives, invites Horus over to his house and Horus accepts. During the night, while Horus is asleep, Set manages to sodomize his rival, which, if proven, would cause the gods to favor Set over Horus. When Horus realizes what has happened he goes to Isis, who first purges her son of Set's semen and then secretly places Horus's semen in Set's food. When the two disputants appear before the council the next day Set brags of his deed, but Horus denies the deed was done. To resolve the issue, the god Thoth called forth semen to see where it resided. As a result, the semen of Horus came out from Set: This caused the gods to believe it is Horus who has sodomized Set. Once again they declare Horus king, but Set continues to assert new claims and propose new challenges.

A similar version of this story appears to have been introduced into Genesis but in a disjointed and highly disguised form.

Esau's Invitation

As previously noted, immediately after Jacob's night of wrestling with a stranger he lifted his eyes and saw Esau. Although Esau offered to let bygones be bygones, Jacob (now Israel) remained afraid. When Esau invited Jacob back to his house for a celebration, Jacob agreed to follow, but instead he headed toward the city of Shechem. Genesis doesn't record Esau's reaction to this snub.

If Genesis were following the story line in *The Contendings* we would expect that Jacob should have followed Esau back and suffered some sort of humiliating sexual incident, after which the tables would have been turned on the offending brother. Instead, Jacob departs. However, right after Jacob leaves for Shechem, Genesis tells us about a startling incident in that city, one that suggests that it had been substituted for the expected banquet incident. It concerns the rape of Dinah, Jacob's daughter.

The Rape of Dinah

It seems that Prince Shechem, the son of King Hamor, ruler of Shechem, took a fancy to Jacob's daughter Dinah and raped her. Then he begged his father to arrange a marriage between himself and Dinah.

King Hamor approached Jacob with an offer of a mass marriage between his daughters and Jacob's sons. Simeon and Levi, two of Jacob's sons, urged Jacob to agree but insisted that a condition be imposed. The men of Shechem must agree to be circumcised.

The Shechemites accepted these terms and during the night, while the men of Shechem were in pain from the operation, Simeon and Levi slipped into the Shechemite camp and slew all the men. Jacob reacted in horror to what his sons did and berated them, but the sons replied, "Should he deal with our sister as with an harlot?"[39] Fearful of what Hamor's allies might do to his family, Jacob again fled, this time to Bethel, and immediately thereafter God changed the patriarch's name to Israel.

Parallel Themes

In *The Contendings of Horus and Set* we have a pretense of peace by Set, who invites Horus to his home for a banquet to celebrate their arrangement. At the banquet, Set rapes his guest, but through Isis's magic it appears to be Set who was violated.

In Genesis we also begin with the Set character declaring peace and inviting his opponent back to the house for a celebration. Through Jacob's actions, however, we are given to believe that Esau's invitation is as phony as Set's. But then the story takes a twist.

By following the Egyptian account, we would expect Jacob to follow Esau home and then suffer some sort of sexual humiliation, followed by Jacob's revenge. Instead, Jacob departs, leaving Esau to wonder where his brother went.

However, at the very point where the twist takes place, we have another story in which the child of Jacob is raped and punishment is meted out to the violators, providing a close parallel to the Egyptian plot line.

Furthermore, there is something interesting about the name of the Shechemite king, Hamor. Strong's Dictionary, a standard reference work on the meaning of biblical words, defines the name Hamor as meaning "a male ass (*from its dun red*):—(he) ass." [Emphasis added.][40] Hamor's name, then, coincides with a defining characteristic of Set—a red donkey. Hamor is Set and substitutes for Esau.

The rape of Jacob's daughter by the son of a Set character has obviously replaced what should have been the story of Esau's sexual violation of Jacob and Jacob's revenge. The near perfect thematic parallel between the Egyptian and Genesis story lines suggests that the original Egyptian account may have been too strong for the Genesis author: The Hebrew priests could not allow Jacob to be humiliated by Esau in such a horrible fashion. An alternative story with a similar plot had to be substituted, and the story of Dinah filled the requirement.

In the later period of Israel's monarchy, the partisans of Judah used this story to disqualify Simeon and Levi from royal succession. Simeon and Levi were Judah's older brothers, and by legal tradition had a better claim to the Hebrew throne. Therefore, the Judaean scribes added a passage to Genesis in which Jacob disqualifies Dinah's avengers:

> Simeon and Levi are brethren; instruments of cruelty are in their habitations. O my soul, come not thou into their secret; unto their assembly, mine honour, be not thou united: for in their anger they slew a man, and in their selfwill they digged down a wall. Cursed be their anger, for it was fierce; and their wrath, for it was cruel: I will divide them in Jacob, and scatter them in Israel. Judah, thou art he whom thy brethren shall praise: thy hand shall be in the neck of thine enemies; thy father's children shall bow down before thee. Judah is a lion's whelp: from the prey, my son, thou art gone up: he stooped down, he couched as a lion, and as an old lion; who shall rouse him up? The sceptre shall not depart from Judah, nor a lawgiver from between his feet, until Shiloh come; and unto him shall the gathering of the people be.[41]

Summary

With the exception of Jacob's stay in Syria, where he married and had children, and Jacob's final days in Egypt, we have now examined the major incidents in Jacob's life and seen that they were derived from Egyptian sources. In several incidents we saw that the relationship between Jacob and Esau was drawn from various stories in Egyptian mythology that defined Horus and Set. Similarly, the relationship of Rebekah to Jacob corresponds to that between Isis and Horus.

In the story of the birth of Jacob and Esau we find similarities in Egyptian myth. Esau forced his way to a premature birth and came out with thick red hair all over his body. In Plutarch's account Set, too, forces his way to an early birth and in Egyptian depictions of Set he often has the appearance of a red donkey. Later, Esau threatened to kill Jacob and Jacob's mother had to hide him away in Syria. In Egyptian myth Isis had to hide Horus away to prevent Set from killing him.

The most important event in Jacob's life concerns how he obtained the birthright. A comparison between that story and the Egyptian account of Isis and Set on the Island in the Middle provides a near perfect parallel. In both stories, a mother (Isis or Rebekah) and her son (Horus or Jacob) compete with an older brother (Set or Esau) for the blessing of the clan leader (Re or Isaac). The clan leader favors the older brother and the mother arranges for a disguised person to carry a bowl of food to an opponent and trick him into saying the words that give title to the younger child.

The story of Isis on the Island in the Middle also suggests a number of correspondences to the wife/sister stories in Genesis, in which a patriarch's wife pretended to be a sister because a foreign king evinced sexual interest in her. In the Egyptian story, Isis, who is both wife and sister to Osiris, dons a disguise in order to deceive a violent foreign king who has a sexual interest in her.

The story of Jacob's dream about a ladder to heaven has almost identical parallels in the Pyramid Texts, in which Horus and Set form the ladder to heaven, and the deceased king, in the role of Osiris, rises to heaven. In the Genesis story angels replace Osiris.

In the incident where Jacob wrestled through the night with a stranger we find a close parallel to the image of Horus and Set fighting all night long in a daily struggle between the forces of darkness and the forces of light. In the conflict between Set and the Horites we find another echo of the ongoing battles between the two deities. In the laming of Jacob prior to his taking the name of Israel we see a comparison to the birth of Horus the Child, who was born lame. And lastly, in *The Contendings of Horus and Set* we find precedents for Esau's invitation to Horus and the subsequent story of the rape of Dinah. Both stories follow the plot line of *The Contendings,* in which Set feigns peace, invites Horus to dinner, and then sodomizes him in his sleep. Afterwards, Isis makes Set appear to be the victim of the sexual attack.

In Genesis, Esau feigns peace, despite his arrival with a large military force, and invites Jacob to his house for a celebration. Jacob refuses, but immediately thereafter the son of Hamor rapes Jacob's daughter. Hamor's name means "red ass," which suggests that he corresponds to Set. He, too, gets his comeuppance when his sons submit to circumcision and are killed while recuperating.

The chief story line omitted above has to do with Jacob's stay in Syria, where he married and had the children (except for Benjamin, born later) who became the Twelve Tribes of Israel. We will deal with questions relating to the origin of the Twelve Tribes in chapter 14.

13

Isaac and the
Death of Osiris

The murder and resurrection of Osiris constituted the most important myth in Egyptian life. It stood for the principle that any Egyptian could survive his death if only he lived and died in the right manner. Egyptians believed that Osiris weighed the deeds of each applicant for the afterlife and determined who would be allowed to enter the next life.

Egyptians also strongly believed in the practice of magic by imitation, in which the drawing, or modeling, of an image can help bring the idea behind the image into existence. Much tomb decoration derived from this idea, in the hope that in the afterlife the images in the tomb would become real for the deceased. Consistent with these magical beliefs, funerary rituals revolved around the attempt to identify the deceased with the god Osiris: What was done to Osiris was done to the deceased.

Since Osiris was both hacked up and reconstituted, funerary rituals featured symbolic attempts to duplicate both events. For example, in an inscription from the tomb of the Fifth Dynasty's king Teta, we find:

Rise up, O thou Teta! Thou hast received thy head, thou hast knitted together thy bones, thou hast collected thy members.[1]

The Book of the Dead has similar examples. In one passage meant to be recited by the deceased in an effort to identify with Osiris, the text reads, "My head shall not be separated from my neck."[2] Another, from a chapter entitled "The Chapter of not letting the head of a man be cut off from him in the underworld," says:

I am the Great One, the son of the Great One; I am Fire, and the son of Fire, to whom was given his head after it had been cut off. The head of Osiris was not taken away from him, let not the head of the deceased be taken away from him. I have knit myself together (or reconstituted myself); I have made myself whole and complete; I have renewed my youth; I am Osiris, the lord of eternity.[3]

The introduction of fire in the resurrection process reminds us of Isis's behavior toward the queen's child. Each night she passed the child through the fire and burned away its mortal parts, but she was interrupted before the process was complete.

Linked to the concept of resurrection was the belief that Osiris and Horus were different aspects of a single god. Horus, as the living king, ruled over the living world, and Osiris, as the deceased king, ruled over the afterworld. When the Horus king died he became the Osiris king.

With such a belief system, the Egyptians were especially devoted to Osiris, and he became one of the most popular and important of all deities. But Akhenaten did not believe in Osiris and attempted to abolish his role in Egyptian funerary practices. This presented the early Atenist-Genesis scribes with a difficult problem in transforming this god of resurrection into a simple human being. How they handled that problem is the subject of this chapter.

The Isaac Cycle

The Isaac cycle in Genesis is relatively brief, consisting of only a couple of episodes. These are: the story of his birth; Abraham's offering (at God's request) of Isaac as a human sacrifice; a brief account of how his father obtained a wife for him; one of the wife/sister stories; and the passing of the birthright to Jacob. We have considered the passing of the birthright and the wife/sister stories in previous chapters. Here we will look at the story of his birth and how he was later offered as a human sacrifice.

In the last chapter we saw that Jacob corresponded to Horus and Rebekah corresponded to Isis. Therefore Isaac, as husband of Rebekah and father of Jacob, ought to correspond to Osiris, husband of Isis and father of Horus. But the circumstances of his birth don't seem to match that genealogical relationship.

Isaac is the younger half-brother (by thirteen years) of Ishmael. Ishmael, as we shall see below, corresponds to Set, sharing that role with Esau. As in the Jacob-Esau conflict, Isaac's father appears to favor his older brother while the mother favors the younger son and aids him in acquiring the birthright.

In the genealogical relationships, we then have another variation of the Horus-Set conflict, with Isaac in the role of Horus. Later, however, as husband of Rebekah and father of Jacob, he functions in the role of Osiris.

It should be noted, though, that simultaneously with his role of Osiris, Isaac also plays the role of Re in that he favors Esau's (Set's) claim over Jacob's (Horus's). This dual identity was necessitated by the merger of the Horus identities within Jacob. However, in Egyptian myth, both Re and Osiris functioned as Horus's father, so Isaac's dual role as Re and Osiris within the Jacob cycle does not actually conflict with the Egyptian tradition.

That said, why in the Isaac cycle does he first appear in the role of Horus? On the surface this seems unnecessary. The answer is that in Genesis the Isaac cycle fulfills a different function than does the Jacob cycle. Its purpose is to undermine the anti-Atenist theological underpinnings of Osiris in Egyptian religion.

In the Egyptian tradition, Osiris survived his own death and determined who would live in the afterlife. The living king represented Horus, son of Osiris; the deceased king represented Osiris. The merger of Osiris and Horus within the body of a single being identified the two deities as part of a single continuum. Horus and Osiris were aspects of one god, inhabiting two different worlds at the same time.

The Atenists needed to break this link between Horus and the resurrected Osiris, and they did so in Genesis with the story of Abraham's sacrifice of Isaac. This is perhaps the most puzzling story in the Bible and has caused commentators no end of difficulty in explaining why the Hebrew God would ask Abraham to offer up his son as a sacrifice. But by placing the story in the context of the Osiris myth we can resolve the moral dilemma.

Isaac's Sacrifice

At some point in Isaac's youth, God asked Abraham to slay his son and offer him up as a sacrifice. Abraham, without question, obediently accepted God's request and prepared to kill his son on an altar. At the last moment, as Abraham made ready to take Isaac's life, God intervened and stayed Abraham's hand. God then placed a ram close by as a substitute offering.

Genesis does not give Isaac's age at the time of the incident. The opinion of biblical scholars ranges from a child of perhaps only a couple of years old to a man in his twenties. Josephus thought that he was twenty-five years old at the time.[4] Interestingly, Plutarch is also unclear as to how old Osiris was when he was killed by Set. He says the murder occurred either in Osiris's twenty-eighth year of life or twenty-eighth year of rule.

The story of the sacrifice appears in Genesis 22 and goes as follows:

And it came to pass after these things, that God did tempt Abraham, and said unto him, Abraham: and he said, Behold, here I am. And he said, Take now thy son, thine only son Isaac, whom thou lovest, and get thee into the land of Moriah; and offer him there for a burnt offering upon one of the mountains which I will tell thee of. And Abraham rose up early in the morning, and saddled his ass, and took two of his young men with him, and Isaac his son, and clave the wood for the burnt offering, and rose up, and went unto the place of which God had told him. Then on the third day Abraham lifted up his eyes, and saw the place afar off. And Abraham said unto his young men, Abide ye here with the ass; and I and the lad will go yonder and worship, and come again to you. And Abraham took the wood of the burnt offering, and laid it upon Isaac his son; and *he took the fire in his hand, and a knife;* and they went both of them together. And Isaac spake unto Abraham his father, and said, My father: and he said, Here am I, my son. And he said, Behold the fire and the wood: but where is the lamb for a burnt offering? And Abraham said, My son, God will provide himself a lamb for a burnt offering: so they went both of them together. And they came to the place which God had told him of; and Abraham built an altar there, and laid the wood in order, and bound Isaac his son, and laid him on the altar upon the wood. And Abraham stretched forth his hand, and took the knife to slay his son. And the angel of the LORD called unto him out of heaven, and said, Abraham, Abraham: and he said, Here am I. And he said, Lay not thine hand upon the lad, neither do thou any thing unto him: for now I know that thou fearest God, *seeing thou hast not withheld thy son, thine only son from me.* And Abraham lifted up his eyes, and looked, and behold behind him a ram caught in a thicket by his horns: and Abraham went and took the ram, and offered him up for a burnt offering in the stead of his son. And Abraham called the name of that place Jehovahjireh: as it is said to this day, In the mount of the LORD it shall be seen. And the angel of the LORD called unto Abraham out of heaven the second time, And said, By myself have I sworn, saith the LORD, for *because thou hast done this thing, and hast not withheld thy son,* thine only son: That in blessing I will bless thee, and in multiplying I will multiply thy seed as the stars of the heaven, and as the sand which is upon the sea shore; and thy seed shall possess the gate of his enemies; And in thy seed shall all the nations of the earth be blessed; because thou hast obeyed my voice. *So Abraham returned unto his young men,* and they rose up and went together to Beersheba; and Abraham dwelt at Beersheba. [Emphasis added.]

This story presents a number of problems. For one, it refers to Isaac as Abraham's only son, ignoring the existence of Ishmael, whom Abraham perhaps loved more than Isaac. More important, though, is the whole question of God asking for a human sacrifice and Abraham dutifully obeying. Both actors are out of character. Earlier in Genesis, when God told Abraham of the plan to destroy Sodom, Abraham argued and negotiated with the deity on behalf of the innocent people who would be killed. How could a man who argued with God about matters of justice not even raise a question about God's request for a human sacrifice? And how could a god concerned with the taking of innocent life make such a request? That he was testing Abraham's loyalty somehow doesn't ring true.

Many commentators have interpreted this story as an explanation for the banning of human sacrifice among the Hebrews, a widespread practice among the Canaanite neighbors. But Speiser, among others, finds that explanation wanting. "If the author had intended to expose a barbaric custom, he would surely have gone about it in a different way."[5]

Complicating the discussion is the question of whether or not, in the original story, Abraham actually killed Isaac. A number of commentators have noted that in the final scene it is only Abraham that returns from the mountain; no mention is made of Isaac accompanying him. Friedman also notes that the sacrifice story belongs to the E source, and that Isaac makes no further appearance in E after this incident.[6]

Although at one point the text says that an angel stopped Abraham from completing the act, Friedman notes the ambiguity of a later passage that attributes to God the statement "because thou hast done this thing, and hast not withheld thy son."[7] This passage could be taken to mean either that the act was completed or that it was only offered.

We should also take note of a later midrashic tradition that holds that Abraham actually did kill Isaac in the original version of the story.[8]

A comparison between these events and the Osiris myths provides the answer to the difficult moral and ethical problems preserved in this strange episode.

The Osirian Iconography in Isaac's Sacrifice

Consider the iconography in the story of Isaac. He was bound to an altar for the purpose of becoming a burnt sacrifice. Abraham approached carrying both fire and a knife. Prior to setting the wood aflame, Abraham was ready to slay Isaac. (Note, also, that in traditional Jewish slaughter one slits the throat, in effect separating head from body.) God stopped Abraham's act at the last moment, suddenly a ram appeared, and Abraham placed the ram in the fire. In sum, Isaac, like Osiris and the deceased Egyptian kings in imitation of Osiris, was about to have his head severed from his body and his body passed through fire. (The ram will be discussed below.)

I suggest that the sacrifice of Isaac was derived from a ritual reenactment of Egyptian funerary services which identified the deceased with Osiris, but to undermine the connection between Osiris and resurrection, the symbolism had to be altered. Therefore, in the Atenist version, the ritual dismemberment was terminated. A similar disruption of the sacrifice occurs in the Plutarch story, when the Canaanite queen interrupts Isis as she passes the child through fire for the purpose of conferring immortality. This suggests the possibility that the interruption of Isaac's sacrifice may have also had an Egyptian source.

That this event originally served as a funerary ritual related to Osiris's resurrection receives confirmation through the sudden appearance of the ram. One of the most sacred animals in ancient Egypt was Ba-Neb-Djet, the ram of Mendes. In the Middle Kingdom, Egyptians identified it as the *ba*, or soul, of Osiris.[9] After death, they thought, the *ba* of the deceased visited the tomb where its body lay.[10] In the Isaac story, the ram, Osiris's *ba*, appears at the altar where the deceased is laid out. As the soul of Isaac (Osiris), it replaces Isaac on the funeral pyre.

In this story, the Genesis author has taken the ritual through which the deceased Horus becomes Osiris and given it a new meaning. It is no longer necessary for Horus to die in order to become Osiris; Osiris is simply Horus as an adult. What was originally cast in Egyptian religion as a distinction between this world and the next has been converted into a separation between child and adult. Horus and Osiris still remain part of an ongoing continuum, but the deistic nature of that relationship has been abolished. Osiris no longer rules the afterworld as the god of resurrection; only the one true god decides issues of life after death.

Circumcision

Circumcision as a biblical practice began with the birth of Isaac, when God advised Abraham that the covenant would pass not to Ishmael but to the child about to be born, Isaac. Circumcision of males signified acceptance of the covenant; uncircumcised males were cut off from Abraham's seed. Abraham and Ishmael were both circumcised on the same day, Abraham being ninety-nine and Ishmael thirteen. I suggest that the practice of circumcision is derived from Osirian ritual and that its institution in the story of the birth of Isaac is because of Isaac's identification with Osiris.

According to Herodotus, circumcision was originally practiced by the Egyptians, Ethiopians, and Colchians, the latter allegedly the remnants of an Egyptian colony.[11] He adds that the practice is also found among the Phoenicians and Syrians of Palestine, who, he says, admit that they learned of the practice from the Egyptians.[12] His reference to the Phoenicians and Syrians can only mean the Jews, as they were the only people in those regions to practice circumcision. The question that arises is: How did the Egyptians come to adopt this practice?

I strongly suspect that it was closely associated with the efforts of the Egyptian people to identify with Osiris so that they could be assured of resurrection. When Set scattered Osiris's parts around the country, Isis recovered all but the penis. Through magic, Isis created a substitute. Since it would be impractical for Egyptians to remove the penis, the idea of circumcision was developed, in which a piece of the penis was cut off to symbolize that Osiris was less than whole.

Ishmael and Set

In examining the story of Isaac's sacrifice I have argued that it depicts the transformation of Isaac as Horus into Isaac as Osiris. Aside from the iconography in that story, our identification of Isaac as Osiris depends on his role as husband of Rebekah (Isis) and father of Jacob (Horus).

However, we have also argued that Isaac corresponded to Horus and that his identity as Horus can be seen in his relationship to Ishmael, who, I have suggested, represents Set. So far, the identification of Ishmael with Set has relied only on his role as Isaac's older half-brother, who was a rival for the birthright. At this point we should examine some additional evidence for Ishmael's role as Set.

According to the Bible, Sarai had trouble conceiving a child and urged Abram to have a child by Hagar, her servant, so that there would be an heir. Both were quite elderly at the time, Abram in his eighties and Sarai in her seventies. When Hagar became pregnant, she recognized that she had special status in the household and behaved in an insulting manner towards Sarai. Sarai responded angrily, and drove Hagar from the house.

Hagar wandered into the Wilderness of Shur, a territory that lies on the Egyptian border, where an angel found her by a fountain. After inquiring as to why she fled from Abram's house, he said to her, "I will multiply thy seed exceedingly, that it shall not be numbered for multitude."[13] (The "I" suggests that the being is actually God, not an angel.)

The angel then told her, "thou art with child, and shalt bear a son, and shalt call his name Ishmael . . . *And he will be a wild ass of a man; his hand will be against every man, and every man's hand against him;* and he shall dwell in the presence of all his brethren."[14] [Emphasis added.]

Returning to Abram's household, she gave birth to Ishmael, and remained there for over thirteen years, at which time Isaac was born. Abram (whose name changes to Abraham after the birth of Isaac) greatly loved Ishmael, and Hagar continued to believe that her son would be Abraham's heir. Therefore she remained contemptuous towards Sarai (whose name changes to Sarah after Isaac is born.)

Sarah could not tolerate Hagar's behavior and demanded that Abraham "cast out this bondwoman and her son: for the son of this bondwoman shall not be heir with my son, even with Isaac."[15] Sarah's request upset Abraham terribly, but God consoled him, telling him to follow Sarah's direction and be assured that Ishmael would become a nation.[16]

The next morning, Abraham sent Hagar on her way, and again she returned to the wilderness. Before long, she ran out of water. Afraid that she and her son would die of thirst, she placed him under a bush and then went off a distance, unable to face the prospect of the child's death. But God heard the voice of the child and placed a well in the ground. Then he promised Hagar that Ishmael would be a great nation. "And God was with the lad; and he grew, and dwelt in the wilderness, and became an archer."[17]

In keeping with the promise to make Ishmael a great nation, God gave Ishmael twelve sons, and they became princes who ruled in the territory "from Havilah unto Shur, that is before Egypt."[18]

Although Ishmael lacks the telltale red hairy hide of Esau, the biblical evidence does contain other indications of his relationship to Set. To begin with, he is the older brother and favored by the head of the clan, while the younger brother has the support of his mother, reflecting the basic Set-Horus conflict. And, Ishmael as the older half-brother more closely parallels the genealogical relationship between Set and Horus than do Jacob and Esau. Here, of course, Isaac corresponds to Horus.

Perhaps the most conspicuous connection of Ishmael and Set is the description of him as "a wild ass of a man, his hand against every man, and every man's hand against him, and he shall dwell in the presence of all his brethren." (The King James Version translates "wild ass of a man" as "wild man," but most other translations use "wild ass of a man" or "wild colt of a man." Speiser notes that the Hebrew word used, *pere'*, could stand for "wild ass" or "wild horse."[19]

Ishmael, as the "wild ass," corresponds to Set's donkey image, and his depiction as a threat against all others recalls that Set, too, threatened the other gods if he didn't get his way in the dispute with Horus. To quote from *The Contendings of Horus and Set:*

> Seth, the son of Nut, became furious at the Ennead when they had said these words to Isis the Great, the God's mother. So Seth said to them: I shall take my scepter of 4,500 *nemset*-weight and kill one of you a day.[20]

And elsewhere in *The Contendings,* Re declares:

> Let Seth, son of Nut, be delivered to me so that he may dwell with me, being in my company as a son, and he shall thunder in the sky and be feared.[21]

Ishmael and Set also ruled over the same territory—the Wilderness of Shur, to where Horus banished Set and where Ishmael became a mighty nation. Additionally, like Esau and Jacob, he had twelve children.

At this point we should also recall that in the Genesis chronology Ishmael's date of birth coincides with what may have been the founding date of Avaris, the city the Hyksos dedicated to Set.

The Parents of Isaac and Osiris

Isaac was the son of Abram and Sarai, but after Isaac's birth God changed their names to Abraham and Sarah. As with the name change of Jacob, I suspect that these also signify the merger of multiple deities into single identities. More specifically, I believe the name changes for Abram and Sarai signify the confusion over the identity of Osiris's parents.

In the ancient Heliopolitan tradition, Osiris was the son of Geb and Nut. In Plutarch, however, we saw that Osiris and Horus the Elder were thought to be the sons of Re and Nut. In other ancient traditions Horus was also identified as the son of Re and Hathor. Egyptian kings, for instance, often thought of themselves simultaneously as the sons of both Re and Osiris.

Given this confusion over Osiris's parentage, I would like to briefly explore a couple of incidents in Genesis that seem to draw from these contradictory ideas in Egyptian myth.

Abram and Sarai/Re and Hathor

When God told Abram about the forthcoming birth of his son Isaac:

> *Abraham fell upon his face, and laughed,* and said in his heart, Shall
> a child be born unto him that is an hundred years old? and shall
> Sarah, that is ninety years old, bear? *And Abraham said unto God,
> O that Ishmael might live before thee!* And God said, Sarah thy wife
> shall bear thee a son indeed; and *thou shalt call his name Isaac:*
> and I will establish my covenant with him for an everlasting
> covenant, and with his seed after him. And as for Ishmael, I
> have heard thee: Behold, I have blessed him, and will make him
> fruitful, and will multiply him exceedingly; twelve princes shall
> he beget, and I will make him a great nation. But my covenant
> will I establish with Isaac, which Sarah shall bear unto thee at
> this set time in the next year.[22] [Emphasis added.]

The image of Abram falling on his face, laughing in reaction to
God's announcement brings to mind a startlingly similar incident
between Re and Hathor in *The Contendings of Horus and Set.* In the
Egyptian story, Re, against the wishes of the other gods, strongly
supported Set's claim to succeed Osiris. In his zeal on behalf of Set,
he turned to Horus and accused the young god of being "despicable
in your person, and this office is too much for you, you lad, the flavor
of whose mouth is (still) bad."[23]

This angered the other gods, and one of them rashly insulted Re.
"Your shrine," the god cried, "is vacant."[24]

This created a great commotion and the gods all departed the
chamber, leaving Re very saddened by what had transpired. The
following excerpt tells what happened next:

> And so the great god spent a day lying on his back in the pavil-
> ion very much saddened and alone by himself. After a consider-
> able while Hathor, Lady of the Southern Sycamore, came and
> stood before her father, the Universal Lord, and she exposed
> her vagina before his very eyes. Thereupon the great god
> laughed at her. Then he got right up and sat down with the
> Great Ennead. He said to Horus and Seth: Speak concerning
> yourselves.[25]

The story then proceeds to the incident on the Island in the Middle, in which Isis tricks Set into uttering the words that undermine his claim to the leadership.

There are several intriguing parallels between the story of Abram and the story of Re. In the Egyptian story Re supports the claim of Set while the other gods support the claim of Horus; in Genesis Abram supports the claim of Ishmael but God favors Isaac. In both stories we find the Set supporter on the ground laughing. In both cases the laughter results from an implied sexual act, in Abram's case with Sarai and in Re's with Hathor. In both stories, each leader falls to the floor almost immediately after declaring a preference for the older brother's claim.

The above parallels suggest that Abram and Sarai originally represented the gods Re and Hathor, which would make Re and Hathor the parents of Osiris. Since Isaac represents both Horus and Osiris, and Egyptians identified both as the sons of Re, Genesis conveniently integrates Re into the story of Isaac's birth. The connection between Sarai and Hathor is somewhat more difficult to establish.

In Plutarch it is Nut who gives birth to both Osiris and Horus the Elder, but in other traditions Horus is the son of Hathor. Since both Hathor and Nut are sky goddesses they are easily interchangeable. I suggest that in associating Abram with Re the Genesis author associated Hathor, instead of Nut, with Sarai.

That the Re-Hathor incident immediately precedes the Island in the Middle story, both of which involve an argument over who is heir to Osiris's title, reinforces the argument that Genesis refers to both stories, and supports the idea that the patriarchal narrative drew upon Egyptian literature for its historical information.

Abraham and Sarah / Geb and Nut

Isaac's other set of parents are Abraham and Sarah, who, I suggest, correspond to Geb and Nut. The name changes from Abram and Sarai to Abraham and Sarah were an attempt by the Genesis author to merge Re with Geb and Hathor with Nut. In this regard both Re and Geb, in the Plutarch account, are the fathers of the children in Nut's womb.

Also, according to Plutarch, Re had ordered Nut to stay away from Geb, and when he discovered her disobedience he punished her by denying her the ability to bear children. It was only through divine intervention that Nut gave birth.

By the age of ninety, Sarah, too, was unable to conceive, suggesting that God didn't want her to have children either. And here, too, it took divine intervention to enable her to give birth. These parallels, however, are admittedly weak, and the connection to the Egyptian story would be significantly enhanced if we had some direct evidence that Sarah's inability to conceive stemmed from God's anger.

We lack such direct evidence, but there are hints in the Genesis story that God and Sarah may have had a troubled relationship. Not only couldn't she conceive, when Sarah overheard God tell Abraham that Sarah would give birth to a child she found this amusing and began to laugh at the improbability. God was angry at her reaction, taking her laughter as a sign that she lacked faith in his powers. He then asked why she laughed. Sarah became frightened, and denied laughing, in effect lying to God.[26]

In this story we see that God's anger at Sarah was connected to her giving birth. Her secret laughter, signifying her lack of faith in God's powers, was akin to Nut's rejection of Re's injunction. And Sarah, like Nut, feared that God would know what she had done in secret.

That some sort of distortion occurred in the telling of Sarah's story seems evident from how differently God reacted to her laughter than he did to Abraham's. Both found it humorous that Sarah, at the age of ninety, could bear a child. God had no problem with Abraham's reaction but became angry at Sarah's. Why should that be?

I strongly suspect that the redactors heavily edited the original story in order to minimize Sarah's (i.e., Nut's) sin. By late biblical times, Sarah had become a heroine to the Children of Israel. Her story must have evolved to the point where only faint traces of the original Nut story remain.

Abraham's identification with Geb is similarly weak, the evidence being mostly contextual. Egyptians identified Geb as the "Father of the Gods" because of his role in the birth of the Osirian family. According to the Pyramid Texts, Atum appointed Geb to rule over the Ennead. When he stepped down, Geb appointed Osiris as his successor.

The names Abram and Abraham are both derived from the Hebrew root *ab*, meaning "father." Biblical scholars tend to translate Abram as "exalted father," and Abraham filled approximately the same role in Hebrew history that Geb performed in Egyptian mythology: He served as head of the first family.

Abraham's family, as we have seen from the earlier evidence, corresponds in large measure to the Osirian family. While initially Isaac corresponds to Horus, his marriage to Rebekah, the Isis figure in the last chapter, shows that he was also identified with Osiris.

Egyptians identified both Re and Geb as the father of Osiris, often holding both genealogies to be true. In Genesis, Isaac is the son of both Abram and Abraham. Abram, as we have seen above, appears to correspond to Re, and despite the weak evidence, there does appear to be traces of a link between Sarah and Nut. This would suggest that Abraham corresponds to Geb.

It is not difficult to see how a deity known as the Father of the Gods and the first ruler can become identified with the Hebrew "exalted father" who ruled over the first family of the Hebrew people.

14

The Twelve Tribes Myth and the Canaanite Conquest

One of the most persistent traditions in biblical history is that the nation of Israel was founded by twelve tribes descended from the twelve sons of Jacob. Yet, for the time between the Exodus and the end of the united monarchy (approximately four hundred years when the tribes supposedly flourished), not a single shred of evidence outside the Bible corroborates their existence. At most, we have the thirteenth-century Merneptah victory stele that mentions the existence of an entity known as Israel, and evidence from the middle of the first millennium B.C. that the Hebrew monarchy split into two kingdoms, Israel in the north and Judah to the south. Also, some place names correspond to the names of some of Jacob's sons and some of their descendants, but place names offer no proof of Hebrew tribal origins. It was quite common in ancient times for groups to identify the names of places with a mythological ancestor. In Genesis 10 the Table of Nations provides a good example of such a practice.

Biblical scholars generally cite two historical events to explain this lack of tribal evidence. First, according to the Bible, King Solomon divided the country into twelve districts with boundaries that differed from the tribal boundaries. On a rotating basis, each district was to provide one month's labor to the government. Scholars believe that after these reforms the tribal boundaries ceased to exist.[1] But that seems unlikely.

Solomon was very unpopular in the north, and after his death the Bible alleges that ten tribes severed their relationship with Judah and formed the kingdom of Israel. If this happened, Solomon's reforms would have been too short-lived and too unpopular to have had any lasting effect on boundaries with centuries of tradition.

The second historical factor involved the conquest of the northern kingdom in 722 B.C. by the Assyrians. The Bible alleges, and Assyrian records confirm, that many of the captured people were forcibly removed from Israel and resettled in other areas, with Assyria moving other people in as a replacement.[2] After this, the northern kingdom of Israel ceased to exist. Since the northern kingdom allegedly consisted of ten tribes that were forcibly removed, scholars believe that these tribes became assimilated in their new homeland and were no longer identifiable as Hebrew tribes. Thus, for at least this later period, tribal evidence shouldn't exist.

There are some problems with this view also. Despite the split between Israel and Judah, not all the citizens of Israel were located in the north. Many continued to live in the south, and "the children of Israel which dwelt in the cities of Judah, Rehoboam reigned over them."[3] Furthermore, in Chronicles, a late composition written after the Babylonian exile, there is an allegation that when the Hebrews returned from Babylon, Benjamin, Ephraim, and Manasseh came to Jerusalem.[4] At least two of these tribes, and perhaps all three, belonged to the northern kingdom, and if they came out of Babylon after the Hebrew captivity they couldn't have been eliminated by the earlier Assyrian exile.[5]

Both of these explanations, however, focus on the period following the united monarchy, and neither explains the lack of evidence during the four hundred years preceding it. Few historians, though, take the claim literally that an individual named Jacob had twelve sons, each fathering his own tribe and all coming together as the nation of Israel. What most scholars do believe is that the tribal structure, built around families and clans, is a well-documented feature of Palestinian society; at some point in history a group of Palestinian tribes, perhaps twelve in number, came together in a religious or political coalition; some, if not all of these tribes, spent some time in Egypt and left under hostile circumstances. Subsequently, most of them faded from the scene.

The tribal structure, however, was not an Egyptian phenomenon. If the Exodus resulted from a religious confrontation between the pharaoh and the Aten cult, pitting Egyptian against Egyptian, as argued in the preceding chapters, then the great majority of those who left Egypt with Moses were not organized into tribes. This does not mean that there were no prominent and influential families among the leaders of the departing Egyptians or that there weren't alliances made with local kings and princes, but the idea of a tribal confederation based on family clans presents an erroneous picture of how the Hebrew nation developed. The notion of twelve tribes is a myth, and the ten lost tribes are equally fictitious. Even Joshua's conquest of Canaan is mostly a late invention.

How Many Tribes?

The identification of Israel with twelve tribes is long-standing. Jesus, for example, says to the Apostles: "Verily I say unto you, That ye which have followed me, in the regeneration when the Son of man shall sit in the throne of his glory, ye also shall sit upon twelve thrones, judging the twelve tribes of Israel."[6] And today, we still use the Twelve Tribes as a synonym for Israel. But an examination of biblical evidence casts great doubt on whether such an entity or anything like it ever existed after the Exodus.

At the very outset, for example, we have confusion over whether there were twelve or thirteen tribes. When Jacob handed out blessings to his sons he granted independent status to the two sons of Joseph—Ephraim and Manasseh: "as Reuben and Simeon, they shall be mine."[7] Ephraim, the younger of the two, became heir to Joseph's birthright, and about him Jacob forecast that "his seed shall become a multitude of nations."[8]

This leaves Manasseh as a separate entity from Ephraim, and when the tribal territories were allotted, Manasseh received two territories while Levi received none. (Levi, as the priestly class, was allowed the use of particular cities within the other tribal allotments.) So thirteen allotments (two for Manasseh) were made to twelve tribes (counting Ephraim and Manasseh), and one tribe received no territory. Do we have twelve tribes or thirteen?

Other inconsistencies in the Bible also cast doubt on the Twelve Tribes' structure. When Jacob acknowledged Joseph's two children as separate tribes, the twelve become thirteen. When land was distributed, the Calebites (a branch of Judah) and the Kenites (a non-Hebrew group related to Moses through marriage) also received separate portions, increasing the number of tribes by two.

Judges 1 presents a particularly puzzling problem. It lists Joseph, Ephraim, and Manasseh as three separate tribes and omits four other tribes from the Hebrew roster. Since Joseph is the father of Ephraim and Manasseh, he should not be listed as a separate tribe from his two sons. The missing tribes include: Levi, Issachar, Gad, and Reuben. The omission of the last two might be explained by the fact that Judges 1 describes the conquest of Canaan while Reuben and Gad settled in Jordan. But if Levi and Issachar participated in the conquest, why omit them?

In another inconsistency, Moses blessed the tribes but omitted Simeon from the list.[9] Elsewhere, the Song of Deborah recognizes only ten tribes and some of them have names other than those given to Jacob's sons.[10] And in the account of the split between Judah and Israel, the number of tribes fluctuates between twelve and eleven.

The Song of Deborah

Judges 4 and 5 tell the story of Deborah, a Hebrew judge who rallied several Israelite forces against an oppressive Canaanite king. Judges 5 provides a poetic account of the battle, telling of how ten Hebrew groups responded to the call. Most biblical scholars accept this poem as one of the oldest passages in the biblical text, perhaps contemporaneous with the events recounted.[11] Judges 4, written in prose much later, describes the same battle but only mentions two of the tribes.

We first meet Deborah near Bethel sitting under the "palm of Deborah," where the people of Israel would come to her for judgment.[12] At the time, Israel was suffering under the dominion of Jabin, the Canaanite king of Hazor. Deborah called upon the Hebrew people to rise up against Jabin and liberate the nation.

Geographically, Hazor lies way up near the northern tip of Israel in the territory associated with the tribe of Naphtali. Bethel is in central Palestine in the territory associated with Ephraim. Judges 4 places the battleground in the vicinity of Mount Tabor, close to the common borders of three tribal territories—Naphtali, Issachar, and Zebulun.[13] Judges 5 puts the battle elsewhere, near Megiddo, in the territory of Manasseh, a short distance from the borders of Zebulun and Issachar but away from Naphtali.

The political picture painted by this geographical distribution shows a Canaanite king from the far north of Palestine militarily dominating all of the northern and central part of the country, and a revolt by the people of central Palestine. The status of the south is unclear.

It is interesting to note that according to the Book of Joshua, in describing events that preceded the Song of Deborah but written much later, the king of Hazor is also named Jabin and his kingdom is also depicted as the most powerful and influential force in northern Canaan.[14] However, in Joshua, after the Israelites captured Hazor they burned it to the ground and all its inhabitants were killed. How, then, at the time of Deborah, only a few decades later, did a new king—Jabin—come to rule such a vast empire from Hazor? Since the Song of Deborah appears to be contemporaneous with the events described within the poem, or at least close to them in time, we can only conclude that the account in Joshua borrowed heavily from the story of Deborah's battle but it made Joshua the central military figure. (See *The Conquest,* below, for a discussion of problems with the Book of Joshua.)

The Song of Deborah contains significant information about the constituent members of the Hebrew nation, and a roll call of who responded to Deborah's rallying cry and who didn't:

> Out of Ephraim was there a root of them against Amalek; after thee, Benjamin, among thy people; out of Machir came down governors, and out of Zebulun they that handle the pen of the writer.
>
> And the princes of Issachar were with Deborah; even Issachar, and also Barak: he was sent on foot into the valley. For the divisions of Reuben there were great thoughts of heart.
>
> Why abodest thou among the sheepfolds, to hear the bleatings of the flocks? For the divisions of Reuben there were great searchings of heart.
>
> Gilead abode beyond Jordan: and why did Dan remain in ships? Asher continued on the sea shore, and abode in his breaches.
>
> Zebulun and Naphtali were a people that jeoparded their lives unto the death in the high places of the field.[15]

The roster of names is interesting both for whom it names and whom it leaves out. Answering the call in the first listing are Ephraim, Benjamin, Machir, Zebulun, and Issachar. A little farther down, the text refers to Zebulun and Naphtali as participating in the fighting. Not answering the call are Reuben, Gilead, Dan, and Asher. Not named at all are Judah, Simeon, Levi, Manasseh, and Gad.[16]

Machir and Gilead

Machir and Gilead, both mentioned as among the affiliated groups, are not sons of Jacob or Joseph. But Machir appears in Genesis as the son of Manasseh, and that may account for why Manasseh doesn't appear in Deborah's list.[17] And Gilead is later named as a son of Machir.[18] Gilead, however, was also a territory conquered by Machir and given to him by Moses.[19] If Machir was the conqueror of Gilead, as depicted in the story of the Canaanite conquest, why is he listed in the Song of Deborah as separate from Gilead, with Machir answering her call and Gilead rejecting it?

And where is Gad? The Jordanian side of the confederation, running from north to south, consisted of the half tribe of Manasseh, Gad, and Reuben.[20] The city of Gilead is located in the territory of Gad.

However, at some point Gilead was believed to be a large territory, not merely a city, and its size appears to have been approximately equivalent to Jordan. In both Joshua and Deuteronomy, for example, Gilead is considered a territory large enough to distribute to all three tribes on the Jordanian side of the confederacy—Reuben, Gad, and Manasseh.[21]

If Deborah is giving us an accurate picture of political geography, then we can conclude that at the time of the battle in question Manasseh and Gad did not exist. In its place were the two kingdoms of Machir and Gilead. In later times, (rather than at the time of Moses), Machir conquered part of Gilead, and the combined territories came to be known as Manasseh. The remaining part of Gilead came to be called Gad.

Naphtali

The existence of Naphtali at the time of Deborah also raises a question. Although a passage in the poem indicates that Naphtali participated in the rebellion, it has the sense of being a later insert.

First of all, it appears out of sequence, not with the list of participants but after the list of nonparticipants. Also, the verse couples Naphtali with Zebulun, a group already mentioned in the prior listing. Why should its name be repeated later in connection with Naphtali? Also, in the Judges 4 account of the battle (a later version of the story) only Zebulun and Naphtali take part, the same two tribes as in the questioned passage in Judges 5.

Judges 4 places the battle close to the common border of Naphtali, Issachar, and Zebulun, while Judges 5 places it in Manasseh, near Issachar and Zebulun but away from Naphtali. And, as already noted, the Canaanite enemy was the king of Hazor, one of the chief cities of the territory associated with Naphtali. The insertion of Naphtali into the poem strongly suggests that it was not part of Israel at the time of the Song of Deborah and was integrated into the empire at a later date, perhaps through conquest by either David or Solomon. At that time Naphtali scribes must have attempted to enhance the territory's image from one in which the enemy king ruled to one in which the local people rebelled.

The Omitted Tribes

In addition to Gad and Manasseh, the Song of Deborah also omits Judah, Simeon, and Levi. If these tribes were part of a tribal confederation, why don't we have their response to Deborah's call to arms? Were they in or out? Benjamin, a very small territory on Judah's border, responded.

In the case of Judah and Simeon, logic suggests that they weren't part of the Hebrew confederation until later. (We will have more to say on this.) Levi, on the other hand, never functioned as a tribe; it simply encompassed the priest class and didn't appear in the text because the priests would not be among the political entities making up the confederation. However, priests were integral to ancient war efforts. In the poetic version, two other craft groups, the governors and writers, appear at the scene. Under these circumstances the absence of Levi is puzzling.

From the examination of the Song of Deborah, then, we can conclude the following: In the twelfth century Israel did not constitute a tribal confederation of twelve tribes, nor was it even a tribal confederation. It was an alliance of nine city-states—Ephraim, Machir, Benjamin, Zebulun, Issachar, Reuben, Dan, Asher, and Gilead—encompassing central and northern Canaan, and Jordan. Next we must ask whether all nine city-states were controlled by the Egyptians who left Egypt with Moses or if some of them were controlled by allies who joined up with the Hebrews after the Exodus.

The Sea Peoples

Under the reign of Merneptah in the late thirteenth century B.C., and the reign of Ramesses III in the early twelfth century, Egypt was invaded by a somewhat mysterious coalition of forces known to the Egyptians as the Sea Peoples. The Egyptians identified them as northerners who "made a conspiracy in their islands" and who engaged in "the Great Land and Sea Raids."[22] Other inscriptions indicate that the Sea Peoples waged violent and aggressive war against the Hittites and Syrians as they trekked down into Canaan.[23]

Egyptian paintings show not only battle scenes between Egypt and the Sea Peoples, but also depict, among the Sea Peoples, women and children in ox carts.[24] As many commentators have noted, ox carts are the type of conveyance used by people who plan to farm land on a permanent basis, they are *not* war vehicles. Their presence in the pictures, along with women and children, signify that the Sea Peoples were involved in a mass population movement in search of a new homeland.

The first raid by the Sea Peoples on Egypt took place during the time of Merneptah. Descriptions of what occurred appear on the same stele that indicates that Israel was a strong military force but not yet associated with a particular territory. Among the invaders named by Merneptah were the Shardana, Shekelesh, Ekwesh, Teresh, and Lukka.[25] In the second wave of invasions, under Ramesses III, the groups identified by name are the Peleset, Tjeker, Shekelesh, Denyen, and Weshesh.[26] Pictorial evidence shows that the Shardana and the Teresh also joined the second wave of invaders.[27]

The national identities of these groups have been the subject of much speculation, but one equation seems certain. Most scholars believe that the Peleset were the Philistines. Many also identify the Denyen with Homer's Danoi, the name Homer used for the Greek invaders of Troy, but such identification is speculative. Some scholars have also suggested that the Denyen may have been the forerunners of the Hebrew tribe of Dan.

The evidence in support of this last view comes primarily from the Song of Deborah, which depicts Dan as staying by his ships. Scholars argue that at this time the Hebrews were not known to be seafarers. So, they ask, how did Dan come to own a fleet of ships? According to this view Dan arrived in Canaan with the Sea Peoples and became assimilated into the Hebrew nation. In this regard, we should note that the most prominent Danite in Hebrew history was Samson and that he seemed to have more of an affinity with the Philistines than with the Israelites.

Geographically, Dan had two locations in Israel. Initially, it lay on the Palestinian shore, continuing north from where the Philistines left off. Later, according to the Bible, enemies drove Dan from that location and they relocated in the far north. Dan's location on the coast, just north of the Philistines, and its connection to ships certainly gives a strong indication that the Danites were part of the Sea Peoples' confederation.

At the same time that the Song of Deborah places Dan by his ships it also places the Hebrew tribe of Asher by the seashore, indicating that it, too, was a seagoing people. Geographically, Asher encompassed the territory that coincided with the southern part of Phoenicia, a nation well-known for and strongly identified with seafaring skills. Some information about the Shardana, another member of the Sea Peoples' confederation, strongly suggests that Asher and the Shardana were one and the same.

The earliest evidence of the Shardana, dating to the fourteenth century B.C., indicates that they lived in the vicinity of Byblos, which was only a few miles north of the territory associated with Asher.[28] Beginning with the reign of Ramesses II, they served as mercenaries in the Egyptian army and during the Sea Peoples' raid on Merneptah the Shardana fought on both sides.[29] Historians generally believe that the Shardana originated either in Sardinia or Sardis, but there are some doubts about this.[30] N. K. Sandars, who has written extensively on Mediterranean and Middle Eastern history, argues that the Egyptian pictures of the Shardana with horned helmets and short kilts point to an origin not far from the northern Syrian coast.[31]

Given the similarity between the names Asher and Shardana, and the proximity of both groups to Byblos and the northern Syrian coast, there seems little reason to doubt that the territory of Asher was a Shardana stronghold at the time of Deborah's rebellion.

Linguistic evidence also suggests a link between the Shekelesh and the tribe of Issachar. Unfortunately, we have little evidence of what land the Shekelesh inhabited. A Hittite text refers to the Sikala "who live in ships," but gives no indication of where they were from.[32]

They first appear on the Egyptian scene in the raid against Merneptah and they returned during the second round of attacks, during the reign of Ramesses III. Because of their name, historians believe they have a connection to Sicily, but the evidence is an eighth-century B.C. reference to the *sikels* in that region. Therefore, we cannot say if they originally came from Sicily or left for Sicily after their arrival in Canaan.

In considering the connection between Issachar and the Shekelesh, we have to recognize that the Egyptians didn't use the letter *L* and substituted the letter *R* when transliterating foreign words. For example, Egyptian texts refer to the Peleset as the Pereset and to the Shekelesh as the Sekeresh (Skrs in ancient Egyptian).[33] Issachar (Ysskr in Hebrew), then, would be an Egyptian pronunciation of Ys-skl, suggesting a linguistic connection between Issachar and Sekeresh. (The final *S* in the Egyptian Skrs is a grammatical ending and not part of the name proper.)

Then there is the matter of Zebulun. In the tribal allotments Zebulun resides east of Asher and Manasseh, and south of Naphtali, away from the coast. According to Jacob's blessing to his children, though, Zebulun dwelled "at the haven of the sea; and he shall be for an haven of ships; and his border shall be unto Zidon."[34]

Zidon (Sidon) was one of the chief cities of the seafaring Phoenicians and had political associations with the territory immediately north of Naphtali and Asher. Jacob's blessing apparently preserves an earlier tradition in which Zebulun was not only a seafaring nation but also bordered on Zidon, in the territory later occupied by Naphtali and Asher, which suggests that Zebulun was either a native Canaanite people from before the Exodus period or one of the Sea People groups that arrived after it.

Dan, Asher, Zebulun, and Issachar, all northern Canaan territories, lie along the path taken by the Sea Peoples on their land invasion route. The Sea Peoples were fierce fighters and at least one group, the Philistines, established such a strong presence in Canaan that in ancient times the country was named Philistia after them. Deborah's rebellion occurred not long after the second invasion, and the remaining Sea Peoples couldn't have disappeared in such a short time. Therefore, the evidence suggests that at the time of Deborah the territories of Dan, Asher, Zebulun, and Issachar were inhabited and dominated by Sea Peoples. This suggests that these four political entities were not Hebrew tribes and did not participate in the Exodus. The Hebrews and Sea Peoples in the northern territories were probably part of a military-political alliance bound together by a common need for protection against Egyptian, Hittite, and Philistine encroachment.

If this is the case, then of the ten territories named in the Song of Deborah, four did not participate in the Exodus. Of the six remaining tribes, four belong to the Rachel group: Benjamin, Ephraim (the son of Joseph), Machir, and Gilead (the last two descending from Joseph through Manasseh). The other two are Reuben and Naphtali. As discussed before, however, the reference to Naphtali appears to be a late insert.

Omitting Naphtali gives us a much more compact Hebrew grouping in central Canaan and Jordan. The Canaanite component would consist of the three Rachel tribes, Ephraim, Machir, and Benjamin, all bunched together in central Canaan. And in Jordan, directly east of these kingdoms, would be Gilead (also a Rachel tribe) and Reuben. This coincides with the route followed by the Exodus peoples, beginning in Jordan and moving into central Canaan.

Reuben is the most southerly of the Jordanian territories, and according to the Bible it was the first stop along the route of conquest. Reuben, however, would not have been a tribe. It was simply the territory where Israel first dwelled after the Exodus. For this reason Reuben came to be thought of as Jacob's firstborn son.

Israel eventually spread out from its initial homeland and colonized or conquered other territories. Because the Dead Sea separates Reuben from Canaan, the Israelites would have first moved north into Gilead and then west to Ephraim. From there they would have spread south to Benjamin and north to Machir. Logically, therefore, we are left only with Rachel tribes as the Exodus contingent—Benjamin, Ephraim, Machir, and Gilead.

The Conquest

The story of Israel's conquest of Canaan appears primarily in the Book of Joshua, and describes the armies of Israel successfully engaging one powerful kingdom after another, bringing the land under their dominion. It also describes the division of land among the tribes. Experts believe that the account compiles several stories brought together after the split between Israel and Judah. Albright, for example, maintains that in its present form Joshua dates to the seventh century B.C. and that some parts were written as early as the tenth century B.C.[35]

Because of the importance of this story in Israel's history, archaeologists have spent a good deal of time studying the conquest, and their findings generally demonstrate that Joshua is an unreliable source. Two of the key battles in Joshua's campaign were at Jericho and Ai. Excavations have demonstrated that Jericho was destroyed around 1500 B.C. and remained unoccupied for several centuries thereafter.[36] The evidence compels most scholars to conclude that the story of Joshua's conquest of Jericho is pure fiction. As for Ai, the city was destroyed around 2400 B.C. and remained unoccupied until at least the twelfth century, when little more than a village was established in the vicinity.[37] For this reason many scholars, hoping to rekindle the credibility of Joshua, have proposed that the conquest of Ai was confused with the capture of nearby Bethel.

For a different view of the military-political relationship between Israel and its neighbors after the Exodus, there is the Book of Judges. In it, Israel is far from the dominant force in Canaan. Throughout we see that the nation is frequently ruled by Canaanite kings, and only on occasion does it manage to shake off these bonds. From the Song of Deborah, which shows a Canaanite king ruling over central and northern Palestine, we can see that Judges preserves the more accurate tradition.

Judges 1 also gives us a different view of the conquest than the one presented in Joshua. Contrary to Joshua, it implies that the territories were allotted to the tribes before the conquest, and that each of them then set out to reduce the assigned territories to submission. However, almost all the tribes failed in that effort. Only Judah and Simeon, the two southern tribes, succeeded.

This chapter of Judges has the air of propaganda written after the split of the monarchy, designed to enhance Judah at the expense of Israel. That it was written at a late date is suggested by its omission of Issachar (who answered Deborah's call) as one of the tribes in the Canaanite campaign, an omission that indicates it was written well after the Song of Deborah.

Another indication that the story of Judah's successful campaign was a propaganda insert comes from the treatment of the campaign against Jerusalem. In Judges 1:8 we are told:

> Now the children of Judah had fought against Jerusalem, and had taken it, and smitten it with the edge of the sword, and set the city on fire.

Contrast this with Judges 1:20:

> And the children of Benjamin did not drive out the Jebusites that inhabited Jerusalem; but the Jebusites dwell with the children of Benjamin in Jerusalem unto this day.

And with Joshua 15:63:

> As for the Jebusites the inhabitants of Jerusalem, the children of Judah could not drive them out: but the Jebusites dwell with the children of Judah at Jerusalem unto this day.

Jerusalem was part of Benjamin's allotment. The claim that Judah took Jerusalem and set it afire contradicts both Joshua 15:63 and Judges 1:20. In both of these passages the Jebusites remained in control of the city "unto this day" (obviously a time well after the events described). In Joshua, however, Judaean propagandists inserted Judah into the forefront by substituting Judah for Benjamin. This was no doubt necessitated by the need to bring the Benjaminite city of Jerusalem under Judaean control.

Proof that Israel never conquered Jerusalem in the age of Judges and that it remained a Jebusite stronghold throughout that period can be found in the following biblical passage describing King David's campaign against the city:

> And the king and his men went to Jerusalem *unto the Jebusites, the inhabitants of the land:* which spake unto David, saying, Except thou take away the blind and the lame, thou shalt not come in hither: thinking, David cannot come in hither. Nevertheless David took the strong hold of Zion: the same is the city of David.[38] [Emphasis added.]

Here, in the time of David, Jerusalem has no Judaeans and no Benjaminites. The city was still occupied by the Jebusites, which confirms that the earlier passages about Judah or Benjamin living in Jerusalem with the Jebusites "unto this day" were written in the monarchical period, after the conquest of Jerusalem. It is also consistent with the opinion that Judah didn't exist at the time of Deborah's rebellion.

The Division of Judah and Israel

The division of the House of Israel into two separate kingdoms, Israel in the north and Judah in the south, was one of the most tragic events in that nation's history. The two kingdoms allegedly divided along tribal lines. If ever there were an entity known as the twelve tribes, one would think that an event of such proportions would be well remembered and documented in the country's history. But that is not the case. How the tribes were divided is quite confusing.

Northern Israel supposedly consisted of ten tribes, as indicated by the following passage:

> And it came to pass at that time when Jeroboam went out of Jerusalem, that the prophet Ahijah the Shilonite found him in the way; and he had clad himself with a new garment; and they two were alone in the field: And Ahijah caught the new garment that was on him, and rent it in twelve pieces: And he said to Jeroboam, Take thee ten pieces: for thus saith the LORD, the God of Israel, Behold, I will rend the kingdom out of the hand of Solomon, and will give ten tribes to thee: (But he [Rehoboam, Solomon's heir] shall have one tribe for my servant David's sake, and for Jerusalem's sake, the city which I have chosen out of all the tribes of Israel:)[39]

Ahijah may have rent his garment in twelve pieces, but he handed out only eleven fragments, ten for Israel and one for Judah. Other passages add to the confusion. At one point we are told that "there was none who followed the house of David, but the tribe of Judah only."[40] And in the very next verse we are told "he [Rehoboam] assembled all the house of Judah, with the tribe of Benjamin."[41] Was Benjamin with Israel or Judah?

Who Simeon sided with also presents a problem. In the division of territory Simeon's lot fell "within the inheritance of the children of Judah"[42] to Judah's south and completely cut off from the north. It seems inconceivable that Simeon could have joined with Israel against Judah. Yet nothing indicates that it remained loyal to the southern monarch.

Next, we must consider Levi. Ahijah ripped his garment into twelve strips, but there were thirteen tribes. Joseph's sons Manasseh and Ephraim were each separate tribes with separate inheritances. Levi, on the other hand, had no separate allotment. It had sanctuaries within the other territories and, as the priestly class, would have had large holdings in Judah. Levi would not have received any of the ten fragments; it would have kept its openings to both sides.

This leaves Simeon and Judah in the south, Benjamin up for grabs, Levi on the sidelines, and eight or nine tribes in northern Canaan and Jordan (depending upon whether Ephraim and Manasseh constitute one Joseph tribe or two separate tribes). Proponents of the tribal theory believe this difficulty can be resolved by an early disappearance of Simeon, an event that receives some support from its omission in Moses's blessing. However, 1 Chronicles, written after the Babylonian exile, says that the Simeonites were still around at the time of the writing and dwelling in the vicinity of Mount Seir.[43] Therefore, Simeon didn't disappear; it would have to have been aligned with Judah.

This would imply that Benjamin formed the tenth tribe of Israel, but this also seems unlikely. The capital of the southern kingdom was Jerusalem, located in Benjamin's territory. This indicates that Benjamin joined with Judah, giving us a tally of three tribes for Judah and either eight or nine for Israel (depending upon whether the two Joseph tribes were counted separately or together), with the thirteenth tribe of Levi unaligned—a very different arrangement than the one-and-ten division alleged in the story of Ahijah.

The Evolution of the Twelve Tribes Myth

Although the twelve tribes existed only as myth, it is worth spending some time on some Egyptian traditions that may have been responsible for this belief. As noted in chapter 12, the frequency of groups of twelve probably derives from the daily battle between Horus the Elder and Set. This solar imagery could have been important factors that led to the idea that there was a House of Israel with twelve sons. But some other Egyptian influences may also have played a role.

The Bronze Cup

Consider, for instance, a story preserved by Herodotus that tells of an alliance among twelve Egyptian kings:

> After the reign of Sethos, the priest of Hephaestus, the Egyptians for a time were freed from monarchical government. Unable, however, to do without a king, for long they divided Egypt into twelve regions and appointed a king for each of them. United by intermarriage, the twelve kings governed in mutual friendliness on the understanding that none of them should attempt to oust any of the others, or to increase his power at the expense of the rest. They came to the understanding, and ensured that the terms of it should be rigorously kept, because, at the time when the twelve kingdoms were first established, an oracle declared that the one who should pour a libation from the bronze cup in the temple of Hephaestus would become master of all Egypt.[44]

Herodotus then goes on to discuss other events in the history of Egypt, but after a while he returns to the above story.

> Now as time went on, the twelve kings, who had kept their pact not to molest one another, met to offer sacrifice in the temple of Hephaestus. It was the last day of the festival, and when the moment for pouring the libation had come, the high priest, in going to fetch the golden cups which were always used for the purpose, made a mistake in the number and brought one too few, so that Psammetichus, finding himself without a cup, quite innocently and without any ulterior motive took his helmet off, held it out to receive the wine, and so made his libation. The other kings at once connected this action with the oracle, which had declared that whichever of them poured their libation from a bronze cup, should become sole monarch of Egypt. They proceeded to question him, and when they were satisfied that he had acted with no malice, they decided not to put him to death, but to strip him of the greater part of his power and banish him to the marsh-country, forbidding him to leave it or have any communication with the rest of Egypt.[45]

Eventually, Psammetichus returned and became king over all of Egypt.

Before commenting on the story itself, we should take note of some chronological problems in Herodotus. Initially he says that a king Sethos ruled and that after his reign followed a period of kinglessness, after which the alliance of twelve kings was formed. Who was this King Sethos?

Herodotus places him three rulers after the Fourth Dynasty pharaoh Mycerinus. But Herodotus has also placed kings of the Twelfth Dynasty earlier than kings of the Fourth Dynasty. Additionally, he refers to an Ethiopian king named Sabacos having temporarily ruled Egypt during the reign of Sethos's predecessor.[46] Sabacos, he indicates, was a contemporary of Psammetichus, mentioned in the above story.[47]

The problem is that Sabacos and Psammetichus are very probably identified with Shabako, a Twenty-fifth Dynasty Ethiopian king who ruled in Egypt during the eighth century B.C., almost two thousand years after the Fourth Dynasty, and Psammetichus, an Egyptian king of the Twenty-sixth Dynasty. It seems highly unlikely that there would have been a king Sethos so late in Egyptian history, given that the god Set had become a symbol of evil in the first millennium.

Herodotus's history of Egypt has a very confused chronology, and he has gotten many details wrong. For instance, as previously noted, he placed the Twelfth Dynasty prior to the Fourth Dynasty. An important clue to the historical context of Herodotus's story is that Sethos was followed by a period of kinglessness. This may be an oblique reference to the Hyksos period, when Set was the chief deity and Thebes was in retreat. However, we need not resolve the question. The story is a folk legend, and it bears some similarity to the story of Joseph.

In both stories twelve persons share dominion. In both stories a prophesy indicates that one of the twelve will rule over the other eleven. In both stories the other eleven become fearful of the twelfth, planning at first to kill him but changing their minds and just banishing him. Finally, the twelfth person becomes king over the other eleven.

An interesting detail in the Psammetichus story is the role played by the bronze cup, which forms the dramatic focus: It singles someone out for special attention. In the story of Joseph a silver cup plays a similar role.

As part of the testing of his brothers, Joseph hid a silver cup in Benjamin's bag and then later accused the brothers of having stolen the cup. After the brothers offered to let Joseph search their belongings they were shocked to find the cup in Benjamin's bag.

Although the Joseph cup story does not quite agree with the Psammetichus cup story in all details, in both the dramatic crux is the same. Each of the two cup holders was shocked to find himself possessing a special cup, and its owner posed a threat to the safety of the eleven rivals.

Scholars do not mention the Herodotus story when analyzing Joseph's tale, but they have acknowledged that other Egyptian literary influences have been incorporated into the biblical account. Perhaps the most significant borrowing involves the seduction of Joseph by the wife of the nobleman who obtained Joseph as a servant. A similar event occurs in the Egyptian story known as the "Tale of the Two Brothers." I suggest that the story of twelve kings and a bronze cup also found its way into the story of Joseph. For our purposes, its importance is that it tells of twelve Egyptian kings bound together by a covenant, much like the idea of the twelve tribe confederation, and of how eleven challenged the one, just as in the biblical version.

The Body of Osiris

As noted earlier, the Hebrews were confused as to whether there should be twelve tribes or thirteen. I suspect this was due to an Egyptian tradition separate from that of Horus's twelve sons, this one involving the body of Osiris. When Set found Osiris's corpse, he hacked it into fourteen pieces and distributed them around the country. Thirteen of the pieces were recovered, but the fourteenth, the penis, had been swallowed by a fish and was never found.

The thirteen parts of Osiris became associated with sacred territories. Abydos, for example, chief center of the Osiris cult, maintained that the god's head had been buried there. Over time, a tradition would have developed that the country had thirteen sacred territories, one for each part of Osiris's body that was recovered.

Although the idea of thirteen sacred territories would have been popular, the Atenists could not tolerate its connection to Osiris. Since Osiris could no longer be openly worshiped, the images associated with his body were transferred to Jacob and his family. This required that a thirteenth son be introduced, causing Joseph's inheritance to be divided between two tribes.

In addition to twelve (thirteen?) sons, Jacob also had a daughter, Dinah. I suggest that she was added to Jacob's family as a symbol of the missing fourteenth part of Osiris's body, the penis.

Conclusions

The Merneptah victory stele shows the existence of Israel in the late thirteenth century B.C. From the Song of Deborah, we have a roster of the Hebrew alliance that existed about a century after Merneptah, and it differs substantially from that of the traditional twelve tribes. Missing from the list are Manasseh, Simeon, Judah, Levi, and Gad. Although Manasseh is omitted, the roster does contain two subdivisions of that tribe, Machir and Gilead.

The poem does mention Naphtali, but the context suggests that in the time of Deborah Naphtali was a Canaanite kingdom ruled by the king of Hazor. From Jacob's blessing we can assume that Zebulun originally encompassed the territory belonging to Naphtali (i.e., up to the borders of Zidon), and that later Naphtali became a separate entity. This led to the subsequent insertion of Naphtali's name into the Song of Deborah.

Reuben is also mentioned in the poem, but Reuben was not originally a tribe. It was the territory where Israel first settled after the Exodus, and for this reason Reuben was thought of as the first son of Jacob.

Historical evidence also shows that at the time of Deborah the Sea Peoples were active on the Palestinian coast and in the northern part of Canaan. Four tribes mentioned in the Song of Deborah—Dan, Asher, Zebulun, and Issachar—all lie across the territories dominated by the Sea Peoples and all seem to have some connection to the Sea Peoples' confederation. Both Dan and Zebulun are clearly linked to ships, and Dan is also linguistically related to the Denyen, one of the Sea Peoples groups. Asher and Issachar also seem to have names that share linguistic roots with the Sea Peoples tribes of Shardana and Shekelesh.

This leaves a base group of Benjamin, Ephraim, Machir, and Gilead. Neither Machir nor Gilead were among the children of Jacob, and in later times the two were absorbed under the name of Manasseh. Their presence in the list suggests that the naming of Jacob's sons occurred at a later time. Benjamin and Ephraim are both Rachel tribes, and the integration of Machir and Gilead into Manasseh indicates that they originally belonged to the Rachel grouping. This strongly suggests that the original Exodus group consisted primarily of a Rachel confederation.

Although the Book of Joshua describes "twelve tribes" sweeping across Canaan and establishing a powerful military presence, such a picture is inconsistent with the archaeological evidence and contradicts the viewpoint in the Book of Judges, which shows Israel to have been only a minor player on the scene, for the most part incapable of displacing the Canaanite kings and constantly subjected to Canaanite domination. The conquest by twelve tribes is also inconsistent with the evidence from the Song of Deborah, which shows that several of the more powerful tribes didn't yet exist.

The falseness of the conquest picture is demonstrated by the various accounts of the conquest of Jerusalem. In Joshua, it is alleged that the Judaeans couldn't drive out the Jebusites but lived there with them "unto this day," while in Judges 1 Judah is depicted as defeating the city and torching it. Elsewhere in Judges 1 it is claimed that the Benjaminites couldn't drive out the Jebusites, and it was they who lived with them "unto this day." Finally, in the story of David we learn that Jerusalem was completely in the hands of the Jebusites, and neither Benjaminites nor Judaeans were living there. The conquest stories were propaganda accounts designed to enhance the claims of the united monarchy, and later of Judah, to the various territories brought under its dominion. To some extant, the conquest stories may have been borrowed accounts of the Sea Peoples' invasion of Canaan.

The question over whether there were twelve or thirteen tribes originated in Egyptian mythology. The notion of Jacob's twelve sons ruling over twelve territories was derived from the myth of Horus the Elder ruling over the twelve daylight hours while his brother Set ruled over the twelve nighttime hours. There was also a folk tradition indicating that at one time Egypt was ruled by twelve kings. Coinciding with the idea of twelve kings ruling twelve territories was the idea that there were thirteen sacred territories, each representing the final resting place of one of the parts of Osiris's body. This accounted for some of the confusion over the total number of tribes. When Israel moved into Canaan and over the years formed various political alliances, the names of the allies became identified with the twelve sons of Jacob.

So, Israel was not created out of a confederation of twelve tribes. Joshua did not conquer Canaan. And there were no ten lost tribes.

15

Rewriting the History of Ancient Israel's Origins

In the preceding chapters we have looked at a variety of sources concerning the origins of ancient Israel—biblical, historical, and literary. Taken together and placed in historical and chronological context, the evidence is centered around some common themes: The patriarchal history drew primarily on Egyptian mythological cycles about Osiris and Horus; the Twelve Tribes never existed; Moses served as chief priest in the court of Pharaoh Akhenaten; the Exodus took place during the coregency of Ramesses I and Sethos I; and the first Israelites were Egyptians, the persecuted remnant of Akhenaten's religious devotees.

As to the life of Moses in the Egyptian court, the Bible is mostly silent. Nor does it tell us the identities of the pharaoh who raised him, the pharaoh who oppressed Israel, or the pharaoh of the Exodus. A connection between Moses and Akhenaten requires no challenge to fundamental biblical history. Nor is there anything inconsistent or historically incoherent in placing the Exodus during the coregency of Ramesses I and Sethos I, nor in making Horemheb the pharaoh who died during the exile of Moses. Only those with a strong personal or ideological antipathy to the Moses-Akhenaten connection will have any deep-seated problems with these conclusions. This does not mean others would necessarily agree that Moses and Akhenaten were allies, but at least they would acknowledge the possibility.

With regard to many other matters, however, the biblical history regarding the emergence of ancient Israel has to be rewritten. As we have seen in our examination of the patriarchal history, in the stories of the Twelve Tribes and the account of the Canaanite conquest the Bible itself is extremely inconsistent and contradictory, and frequently draws on myths and traditions rather than actual history. Much of the writing of biblical history by the Hebrew scribes has been heavily affected by the passage of time and tremendous local cultural influences, including such traumatic events as the destruction of the northern kingdom of Israel and the Babylonian captivity of the southern kingdom of Judah. Therefore, let me set forth a simple narrative of what I believe to be the true story of the origins of ancient Israel.

When Akhenaten came to the throne at about 1374 B.C., Egypt's stranglehold over Canaan started to loosen. Pressures from the Hittites in the north emboldened many of the local Canaanite rulers to challenge Egypt's political authority. In the forefront of this rebellion stood Labaya, the king of Shechem, who, with his sons, established a modest empire that dominated much of central Canaan, loosely corresponding to what later came to be known as the Joseph territories of Ephraim and Manasseh. The House of Israel did not yet exist.

Remarkably, Akhenaten did little to counteract the foreign revolts and generally ignored his allies' calls for help. Under his reign, Egypt's Canaanite empire collapsed. This state of affairs continued throughout the balance of the Eighteenth Dynasty. Although many Egyptologists assume that Horemheb, the last king of the dynasty, reinstituted much of Egypt's authority in Canaan, no evidence to that effect exists. Indeed, shortly after his death, records depict Sethos I attempting to recapture control all along the routes leading from Egypt into Canaan.

More important than Akhenaten's inattention to foreign affairs was the domestic religious revolution wrought in his name. Ill prepared to be king after his father's designated heir died prematurely, Akhenaten assumed the throne under the name Amenhotep, a name that recognized the Theban view of Amen as chief deity in Egypt. Beginning in the fifth year of his reign, life in Egypt changed. Akhenaten launched a religious revolution that had a profound impact on Egypt's religious affairs.

This new religion held that only one deity existed, Re-Herakhty, manifest in the form of Aten, the sun disk. No other gods were to be worshiped and graven images of deity were banned. Representations of Amen, the chief deity of Thebes, were not only prohibited, but the god's name and image were physically removed from monuments all over Egypt. Akhenaten also downplayed the role of Osiris in funeral rituals, a central feature of Egyptian life. Understandably, Akhenaten's reforms greatly disturbed the Theban establishment that until then controlled Egypt.

The chief priest of Akhenaten's new cult may have been named Osarseph, but in conformity with the pharaoh's directive prohibiting the use of personal names containing the name of an unacceptable deity as an element, Osarseph changed his name to either Hormose (Hrms) or Ramose (Rms). In this important role, Osarseph administered the religious reforms that so offended the Theban establishment and its national network. No doubt, the Thebans saw in him the cause of all that angered them. He became the focus of their wrath.

As part of his break with Theban tradition, Akhenaten expended much of his energy on building a new capital city, Akhetaten. Like any capital, it became an important residential section for the new political and religious establishment. The city provided economic benefits to tens of thousands of Egyptians. It housed soldiers, priests, a massive civil service, laborers for the ongoing construction projects, merchants, important families, and the commercial network for such a city to survive. In order to control the rest of Egypt, he needed tens of thousands of additional personnel serving around the country and under his control, especially troops to put down resistance, priests to manage the religious reforms, and civil servants to do his bidding.

Akhenaten showed little genius for administrative skills, and whatever success he enjoyed stemmed from the abilities of his civil service, with Osarseph at its head. Another power behind the throne was Ay, an ambitious general and social climber with close ties to Akhenaten. In about his sixteenth year on the throne, the pharaoh appointed Smenkhkare, a blood relative, as his coregent. Akhenaten died a year later and Smenkhkare succeeded to the throne. Two years later, he also died.

We do not know much about the internal politics behind the succession, but it led to the elevation of the young child Tutankhaten as pharaoh. Although a blood relative to Akhenaten, he served as a pawn of the Theban establishment. Upon taking the throne, he changed his name to Tutankhamen, thus signaling the ouster of the Aten cult and the return of the Theban establishment to power. In all likelihood, this arrangement arose from a deal with Ay, the military power behind Tutankhamen, who carefully sought to placate any threats to his own power base and personal political agenda.

The reemergence of the Theban establishment meant the immediate diminution in authority of the Aten cult. Osarseph, now the de
facto, and perhaps de jure, head of Akhenaten's priesthood, represented the main threat to continued Theban prominence: They had
to eliminate him and he knew it. He fled Egypt, probably at first to
Ethiopia, since he was not only already situated far to the south but
also because the way to Canaan would have been more heavily
guarded and more difficult to pass through.

The Bible does say that Moses had an Ethiopian wife, and this may
have been one of Osarseph's links to that country. Or he may have
met her after he arrived there. Osarseph may also have had connections with Ethiopians anxious to weaken Egyptian authority. That
nation had been an independent territory subjected to Egyptian
domination for centuries. In the Hyksos period it appears to have
been more closely allied with the foreigners than with the Thebans,
despite its southern location below Thebes.

At first the Thebans allowed the Aten cult to continue, albeit without anything resembling its earlier role. No doubt some degree of
caution prevailed. Too swift a retribution could have provoked a
counter-revolution, and Thebes needed time to consolidate.

Tutankhamen died after nine years, and Ay emerged from behind
the throne to the front seat. He served four years and left no heir of
royal blood. This opened the way for the popular general Horemheb
to become king. Close to the Theban establishment, he had little
hesitation about taking on the Aten cult, launching a systematic
campaign to eliminate every trace of the Atenist heresy. He demolished the capital city of Akhetaten, chiseled out all references to the
Aten and Akhenaten in monuments all across the country, and insti-
gated a campaign of persecution against the more influential elements of the cult.

Such an effort had a devastating impact on the followers of
Akhenaten. The loss of their capital city with its attendant financial
resources, the loss of contributions to their priesthood, forced labor,
the confiscation of property, the punishment of leaders, the banishing of soldiers, all worked to create a permanent underclass seeth-
ing with anger.

Osarseph, like Moses in the Bible, heard the cry of suffering from
his people and could only wait for his god to deliver them from
oppression. And, as in the Bible, the pharaoh of oppression died.
Horemheb ruled for about twenty-seven years, dying at about 1315

B.C., and in his final days he appointed Ramesses I to the throne. Shortly thereafter, Ramesses I appointed his son Sethos I as coregent.

Ramesses I, like Horemheb, was a general without royal blood. But he was a northerner, not from Thebes, and he was from a family of Set worshipers, as signified by the name of his son and his celebration of the foundation of Avaris, the Hyksos capital.

The elevation of a northern, Set-worshiping, Hyksos-appeasing pharaoh could not have occurred without some difficulty in Thebes and other parts of Egypt and its empire. Perhaps this was the sign Osarseph waited for.

Sensing the opportunity for rebellion and a rehabilitation of the Atenist cult, Osarseph organized a military alliance aimed at overthrowing Ramesses I. In the north he induced the kingdom of Shechem to join him. In the south he probably had Ethiopian contingents. And throughout the country were the remnants of the Aten cult, the displaced allies who wanted revenge. To these we must add disparate groups of resenters, power seekers, mercenaries, and opportunists, a "mixed multitude" of non-Atenists.

Osarseph launched a two-front attack, from the Shechemites in the north and his own troops in the south. Soon after, the Shechemites were stopped at the Egyptian borders, but Osarseph had a large enough force to hold his ground in the south. Eventually, the two sides negotiated a peace treaty, granting safe passage out of Egypt for Osarseph, his army, and their families.

This negotiated departure from Egypt constituted the Exodus. The civil war between the forces of Osarseph and the armies of the pharaoh appear in the Bible, along with the negotiations for safe passage, as the story of the Ten Plagues, an epic account drawing upon Egyptian literary conventions to describe events.

Osarseph, or Moses, to use the shortened form of his adopted name (Ramose or Hormose), settled his entourage in the area associated with the tribe of Reuben. As was common in ancient times, people tended to identify foundation settlements with a mythical ancestor, and in later Israelite writings this mythical ancestor came to be known as Reuben. Because this territory served as the first homeland of Israel, Reuben, according to conventional mythological grammar, came to be known as the firstborn son of Jacob.

The armies of Moses probably continued to have a close relationship with the kingdom of Shechem. But as Sethos I and then

Ramesses II brought much of Canaan back within the sphere of Egyptian influence, Shechem ceased to be the large kingdom that it had been in the time of Akhenaten. Genesis 34 even hints at a political break between Israel and Shechem sometime in the course of their alliance.

Over time the Israelites in Reuben spread out into central Jordan and then across the river into the largely unoccupied hills of central Canaan, establishing many small communities throughout the land. From the hills in Canaan further settlements spread north and south.

At the same time that Israel moved into the central highlands, Canaan experienced several waves of invasion from the powerful Sea Peoples' confederation, chief of which were the Philistines. Led by Greek warrior castes, the Sea Peoples established strong roots in this new territory and on several occasions, most notably during the reigns of Merneptah (c. 1239–1229 B.C.) and Ramesses III (c. 1197–1166 B.C.), they battled fiercely against Egypt itself. The pressures exerted by the Sea Peoples in Canaan and against Egypt may have provided the cover that allowed the Israelites to smoothly cross over the Jordan and easily settle in the central highlands.

Despite the biblical allegations, at this time Israel had no tribal structure. They may have had influential families, political factions, and some settlements with special military strengths, but there were no tribes. As evidenced by the Song of Deborah, the subsequent tribal divisions reflected the growth and merger of territorial bases.

As was common in Canaan and throughout the Middle East, occasionally one king or another became more powerful than his neighbors and flexed his military muscle and political power. One such person in this premonarchical period, mentioned both in the Song of Deborah and the Book of Joshua, appears to have been a north Canaanite king named Jabin, who may have dominated much of the north and central Canaanite territories.

Simultaneous rival pressures came from the coastal territories associated with the Philistines. The evidence suggested by the Song of Deborah indicates that the Israelites in central Canaan formed an alliance with the leaders of several northern city-states, some of which may have been Sea Peoples' strongholds. Out of this alliance grew the entity of a "Greater Israel," which served as the model for what later came to be known as Israel's tribal confederation.

While Israel's allies shared political and military allegiances, they did not share religious views. In addition, many of the Egyptians who left Egypt with Moses did not subscribe to Atenist orthodoxy. The presence of Canaanite, Greek, and Egyptian deities and priests within the Israelite ranks fueled dissension among the mainstream Atenists, leading to a variety of conflicts, intrigues, and schisms.

It is at about this point in history that our inquiry into Israel's origins ends. Shortly thereafter the monarchy emerged. Under King David, a fusion of ideals seems to have taken place. On the one hand, he established the orthodox Atenist view as the central religion of ancient Israel. On the other, however, he (and Solomon after him) seems to have encouraged all the other factions to worship in their own way, as long as they recognized the fundamental supremacy of the Atenist priesthood. Much of the subsequent Israelite writing about this time revolves around these religious feuds and schisms.

Postscript: A Note on the Genesis and Egyptian Chronologies

In chapters 4 through 7 I have spent a good deal of time demonstrating the cross-references between the Genesis birth-and-death chronology and Egyptian dynastic history. This material, although sufficient to prove the point, is an abbreviated account of a very much larger study that provides much more corroboration for my arguments. Unfortunately, space limitations make it impossible to include that full study here.

As we noted in those chapters, Egyptologists strongly disagree even on such fundamental issues as what year a Sothic date represents. As you can imagine, scholars have a great many more areas of disagreement, some major and some minor.

Because many Egyptologists have a strong attachment to their own positions on these issues, it should not be surprising that many might vehemently oppose any suggestion that they made a mistake. Critics of my chronological arguments will no doubt pick and nibble at the evidence presented here in an effort to discredit my overall argument. But they will do so by dropping context and failing to place the issues in proper perspective.

For example, if I should tie a date in Genesis to a date in the Egyptian chronology that depends upon the early Sothic date for Amenhotep I instead of the later date, advocates of the later date will no doubt point out my lack of detailed evidence for the earlier one. They also might argue that many Egyptologists support the later date and that therefore my argument falls apart. Of course, the fact that many Egyptologists disagree with one another does not prove that one side or the other is correct. Truth is not a matter of majority vote.

In making this argument, the critics will ignore a number of factors. First, they will overlook the evidence that so many other dates in Genesis also coincide with Egyptian dynastic dates, something that couldn't happen unless the two chronologies were based on a common history. Second, they will also fail to note how the selection of a particular Egyptian date requires that several others fall at a particular time and that the Genesis dates align with the required sequence, a coincidence that can't be dismissed as random chance.

Other critics might argue that I simply pick a date here and there and that by sheer coincidence I am bound to find a couple of random correspondences between a Genesis date and any number of randomly chosen Egyptian events. Such arguments will overlook that I am talking about only a particular type of Egyptian event—when particular kings came to the throne. And again, the critics will overlook the very high number of correlations between Genesis and the Egyptian king lists, a set of correspondences so large that the coincidences are mathematically improbable except as a deliberate relationship.

Therefore, I think it appropriate to briefly describe what is in that longer study and what is left out of the present manuscript.

In the materials not published here I present a far more detailed examination of the many pieces of evidence used to reconstruct the dynastic chronology. In numerous cases I examine the archaeological record relating to particular kings, showing what we know about them and what we don't. For each dynasty examined, I set forth all the important issues that deal with the chronological calculations. I place the issues in context and cross-reference them with the Turin Canon, Manetho, other king lists, and the Genesis birth-and-death chronology. Of the many conclusions reached in my examination, several stand out and should have a substantial impact on biblical and Egyptological studies.

First, I show that Manetho's original history, before it was redacted by subsequent editors, contained an accurate chronological account of Egyptian dynasties, one that is consistent with present

Egyptological opinion. In connection with this point, I also provide a detailed arithmetic pattern analysis of the figures used in Manetho's troubling Second Intermediate Period, showing how his original dynastic chronology was distorted, what chronology he originally used for the Second Intermediate Period, and how Genesis has the same dynastic date sequence as Manetho for the Second Intermediate Period.

Second, I compare Manetho's reconstructed history with the Genesis birth-and-death chronology, demonstrating that dynasties One through Eighteen both contain virtually the same chronological history.

Third, I show that the predynastic chronology in Genesis (from the birth of Adam to the birth of Methuselah) is derived from the same source as Manetho's chronology of the Egyptian gods, and that both are based on the Theban doctrine of Creation. The examination shows that the Bible's seven days of Creation derive from Egyptian theology and that the story of Noah's Flood revolves around Egyptian calendar cycles.

Fourth, the precise alignment between the Genesis and Manetho chronologies enables us to resolve almost every major chronological dispute about Egyptian dynastic history prior to the Nineteenth Dynasty.

At the core of my study is a comparison of the many inconsistencies in the different versions of Manetho. By comparing them in each of their sources and placing them in the context of the archaeological record, I am able to reconstruct what Manetho must have originally written. The evidence shows that Manetho's redactors made two particular errors over and over, leading to a badly mangled version of what he wrote.

First was the failure of the redactors to properly account for coregencies. Second was the constant misreading of lines of summation as descriptions of additional lines of kings, causing either dynastic totals to be double-counted or consecutive dynasties to be added together.

I hope to publish the complete study at a later date under the probable title *Creation and Chronology*.

Notes

1. The Problem of Israel's Origins

1. The term "of the Chaldees" refers to either Chaldaea, a province of Babylon, or Babylon itself. The Chaldaeans rose to prominence in 614 B.C., when they defeated the Assyrians and made Babylon the capital of their empire. The claim that Abraham came from Ur of the Chaldees is anachronistic, suggesting that it was inserted into the biblical text by the redactor sometime after the Babylonian conquest of Israel in the sixth century B.C.

2. Hershel Shanks, "Israel's Emergence in Canaan; *BR* interviews Norman Gottwald," *Bible Review* (October 1989): 26.

3. The starting date for Akhenaten's reign falls somewhere between 1379 and 1350 B.C. The chronological issues dividing Egyptologists on this question will be more fully explored in later chapters, at which time 1374–73 will be offered as the correct solution.

4. Donald B. Redford, *Akhenaten: The Heretic King* (Princeton: Princeton University Press, 1984), 176.

5. Cyril Aldred, *Akhenaten: King of Egypt* (London: Thames and Hudson, 1988), 7.

6. Redford, *Akhenaten*, 232.

7. Exod. 1:11.

8. Exod. 3:23.

9. Gen. 47:11. While the English transliteration varies slightly from that in Exodus 1:11, the Hebrew spelling is the same and scholars treat both names as identical.

10. Walter Sullivan, "Ice Data Upset Timetable on Ancient Disaster," *New York Times*, August 6, 1989.

11. Gen. 25:26.

12. Gen. 47:9.

13. 60+130+430=620.

14. 400–130–60=210.

15. Solomon was also called Jedidiah. 2 Sam. 12:24–25.

16. James Barr, *Biblical Chronology: Legend or Science* (London: University of London, 1987), 7.

17. Sir Alan Gardiner, *Egypt of the Pharaohs* (Oxford: Oxford University Press, 1978), 273.

18. This second occurrence of the name Israel appears on what archaeologists dub the Moabite Stone. Discovered in 1868, it is attributed to King Mesha of Moab and details conflicts between his kingdom and Israel. Mesha is mentioned in 2 Kings 3:4.

19. James P. Pritchard, ed., *The Ancient Near East: An Anthology of Texts and Pictures*, 2 vols. (Princeton: Princeton University Press, 1958), 1:231.

20. Wente and Van Siclen III, 223.

21. Ibid.

22. Gardiner, 273.

23. It should be noted that the non-Semitic Sea Peoples, whose defeat is celebrated in this stele, were a large immigrant population that suddenly appeared in the region and raised a military challenge to the Egyptians. Theoretically, Israel's status in the inscription is consistent with it being one of these immigrant groups. However, the name is not recorded among those of the Sea Peoples. Its listing in a separate portion of the text from that dealing with the Sea Peoples enables us to reject the idea that Israel's status, as depicted in the inscription, was due to its participation in the Sea Peoples' immigration. A subsequent connection between Israel and the Sea Peoples will be explored in chapter 14.

24. Gardiner, 157.

25. See, generally, Genesis 49 for Jacob's blessings of his children.

26. Some scholars have suggested that in the story of Esther, which takes place in the Persian court, Esther and her uncle Mordecai represent the important Babylonian gods Ishtar and Marduk, and that the two villains in the story, Vashti and Haman represent two other important Babylonian gods, also named Vashti and Hammon. At about the time of the Esther story, Marduk and Ishtar may have displaced Vashti and Hammon as chief deities in the Babylonian capital of Susa, then under Persian control.

2. The Genesis Birth-and-Death Chronology

1. For one example of such an approach see John Walton, "The Antediluvian Section of the Sumerian King List and Genesis 5." *Biblical Archaeologist* (Fall 1981): 207.

2. For the history of biblical textual analysis, I draw primarily upon Richard Elliot Friedman's *Who Wrote the Bible* (New York: Summit Books, 1987).

3. See, for example, Genesis 19:37–38, 22:14, 26:30, 35:20, Deuteronomy 3:14, 10:8, and 34:6.

4. Friedman, 256.

5. Ibid., 28.

6. *Harper's Bible Dictionary*, 8th ed., s.v. "sources."

7. Friedman, 87. After the reign of Solomon, the kingdom of Israel split into two separate kingdoms, Israel in the north and Judah in the south.

8. Ibid.

9. Ibid., 116.

10. Ibid., 210.

11. Robert Graves and Ralph Patai, *Hebrew Myths: The Book of Genesis,* 1963 reprint (New York: McGraw-Hill, 1966), 132.

12. 1755=2705–950.

13. 1715=1815–100.

14. 1729=1815–86.

15. 1655=1715–60.

16. 1564=1655–130+39.

3. The Throne of Horus

1. W. G. Waddell, ed., *Manetho* (1940: reprint Loeb Classical Library, 1980), xxi.

2. Ibid.

3. Gardiner, 440.
4. Waddell, op. cit.
5. Gardiner, 50.
6. Waddell, op. cit.
7. Gardiner, 50.
8. Ibid., 63.
9. Waddell, op. cit.
10. Ibid.
11. Gardiner, 48.
12. Ibid., 51.
13. Ibid., 91.
14. That is Africanus's description. Eusebius gives five kings ruling for seventy-five days.
15. That is Africanus's description. Eusebius gives five kings ruling one hundred years.
16. Gardiner, 109.
17. Ibid., 67.
18. Ibid., 112.
19. Ibid., 438.
20. Some Egyptologists identify this king as Menthotpe I, others as Menthotpe II. There was an earlier Menthotpe in the Theban line, but because of his slight political power, Egyptologists disagree as to which of these Menthotpes should be identified as Menthotpe I. In this work, the king who unified Egypt will be identified as Menthotpe II.
21. Gardiner, 147.
22. This high-year mark is controversial in that it is from graffiti rather than an official record.
23. Gardiner, 243.
24. Waddell, op. cit., 75.
25. Gardiner, 148.
26. Ibid., 64.
27. The Egyptians knew the star as "Spdt," but the Greeks pronounced it "Sothis," which pronunciation has been adopted by Egyptologists. Sothis is now known as Sirius and has been nicknamed the Dog Star. Each year, there is a period of seventy days in which the star is blocked out by the sun's light, leaving it invisible in the sky. The first appearance of Sothis after this disappearance is the heliacal rising.
28. 1,460 solar years equaled 1,461 Egyptian civil years.
29. Richard A. Parker, "The Sothic Dating of the Twelfth and Eighteenth Dynasties," *Studies in Honor of George R. Hughes, January 12, 1977, Studies in Ancient Oriental Civilization. No. 39* (Chicago: Oriental Institute, 1977), 182.
30. The year immediately before *A.D.* 1 is 1 B.C. There is no year 0.
31. Parker, 182, n. 17, citing M. F. Ingham, "The Length of the Sothic Cycle," *JEA* 55 (1969), 36–40.
32. Parker, 182.
33. Gardiner, 65.
34. Parker, 183.
35. Edward F. Wente and Charles C. Van Siclen III, "A Chronology of the New Kingdom", *Studies in Honor of George R. Hughes, January 12, 1977, Studies in Ancient Oriental Civilization. No. 39* (Chicago: Oriental Institute, 1977), 233. This essay, which appears in the same volume that contains Parker's essay dating the Sothic cycle to 1314 B.C., notes that many scholars still prefer 1318 as the beginning of the Sothic cycle.

36. Ibid.
37. Ibid.
38. Ibid.
39. Ibid.
40. Ibid.
41. Ibid.
42. Ibid.
43. Ibid., 250.
44. Ibid.
45. Ibid., 249.
46. Gardiner, 445.
47. Ibid., 249.
48. Ibid.
49. Ibid.
50. Ibid.
51. *Cambridge Ancient History* (also cited as *CAH*), 2:2B, 1038.
52. There are a small number of scholars who challenge the dating of the seventh year of Senwosre III to the period between 1872 and 1877 B.C.,but the nature of their disagreement with the majority view does not affect the issue of how many Sothic cycles intervened between the Twelfth and Eighteenth Dynasties.
53. Gardiner, 66.
54. Ibid.

4. Enoch and Sothis: A Solar Clue

1. The life spans for Noah and Shem are omitted from table 2.1 because that information is omitted from Genesis 5. Noah lived 950 years and Shem lived 600 years.
2. E. A. Speiser, The Anchor Bible, vol. 1, *Genesis, A New Translation With Introduction and Commentary* (New York: Doubleday, nd), 43. The coincidence in names referred to by Speiser is between Enoch and Enmeduranna. Earlier in the same commentary, Speiser notes that the initial *H* in the Hebraic spelling of Enoch (i.e., Hanoch) precludes any etymological connection between Enoch and Enmeduranna.
3. Alexander Heidel, *The Gilgamesh Epic and Old Testament Parallels* (Chicago: University of Chicago Press, 1949), 248.
4. The Semitic lunar calendar consisted of alternating months of twenty-nine and thirty days. The lunar cycle is approximately twenty-nine and a half days long. The Egyptians also used a lunar calendar, but it used a twenty-five-year cycle.

5. Eber and Thebes

1. William C. Hayes, "The Middle Kingdom in Egypt," in *Cambridge Ancient History,* 3rd ed. (Cambridge, England: Cambridge University Press, 1971), I:2A, 479.
2. Gardiner, 439.
3. Turin Canon data taken from Gardiner, 439.
4. Egyptians didn't write their numbers in the same way that we do. They had separate signs for 1, 10, 100, and so forth. To write the number "34" they would use four "one" signs and three "ten" signs.
5. Waddell, op. cit., 63–73. The Manetho lists place the first king, Amenemhe I, between the Eleventh and Twelfth Dynasties and give him a reign of sixteen years.

The 176-year total includes the sixteen years, although the Manetho text excludes
Amenemhe I from the total and gives 160 years as the total.

6. Ibid.
7. Gardiner, 442.
8. Gen. 10:25.
9. Speiser, 70.
10. J. H. Hertz, ed., *The Pentateuch and Haftorahs,* 2nd ed. (London: Soncino Press, 1976), 38.
11. Gardiner, 151.
12. Ibid., 165.
13. Ibid.
14. Waddell, op. cit., 95.

6. Methuselah and Memphis

1. Gardiner, 430.
2. Ibid., 430–31.
3. Ibid., 420.
4. William C. Hayes, "Chronology: I. Egypt—To the End of the Twentieth Dynasty," in *Cambridge Ancient History,* 3rd ed. (Cambridge, England: Cambridge University Press, 1970), I:1, 175.
5. Ibid.
6. Gardiner, 431–33.
7. Ibid., 73.
8. Ibid., 433.
9. W. Stevenson Smith, "The Old Kingdom in Egypt and the Beginning of the First Intermediate Period," in *Cambridge Ancient History,* 3rd ed. (Cambridge: Cambridge University Press, 1971), I:2A, 147.
10. Gardiner, 75.
11. Smith, *CAH,* 1:2A, 148.
12. Hayes, *CAH,* 1:1, 176.
13. Gardiner, 75.
14. Smith, *CAH,* 1:2A, 150.
15. Ibid., 147.
16. Ibid.
17. Ibid., 161.
18. Ibid., 162.
19. Gardiner, 434. See his note 5.
20. Ibid.
21. Ibid., 82.
22. Ibid., 434.
23. Ibid., 83.
24. Ibid., 434.
25. Smith, *CAH,* 1:2A, 172.
26. Ibid.
27. Ibid., 145.
28. Ibid., 172.
29. Ibid.
30. Ibid.
31. Ibid.
32. Ibid.

33. Donald B. Redford, *Pharaonic King Lists, Annals, and Day Books* (Mississauga: Benben Publications, 1986), 237.
34. Ibid.
35. Herodotus, *The Histories,* Translated by Aubrey de Selincourt, (Middlesex, England: Penguin Books, 1978), 180.
36. Smith, *CAH,* 1:2A, 174.
37. Herodotus, 180.
38. Hayes, *CAH,* 1:1, 178.
39. Smith, *CAH,* 1:2A, 185.
40. Gardiner, 435.
41. *CAH,* 1:2B, 995.
42. Smith, *CAH,* 1:2A, 180–88.
43. Ibid., 183.
44. Hayes, *CAH,* 1:1, 178.
45. Ibid.
46. Ibid., 179.
47. Smith, *CAH,* 1:2A, 192–93.
48. Ibid.

7. Joseph and the Eighteenth Dynasty

1. Gardiner, 443.
2. Waddell, 101, 115. In the Josephus version Manetho lists the first king as Tethmosis.
3. Gardiner, 443.
4. Ibid., 443, 445.
5. Wente and Van Siclen III, 218.
6. Gardiner, 248.
7. Wente and Van Siclen III, 231.
8. Ibid.
9. Ibid.
10. Ibid.
11. Ibid.
12. Exod. 1:8.
13. Gen. 41:1–4.
14. Gen. 41:5–7.
15. Gen. 41:34–36.
16. Gen. 41:46.
17. Hans Goedicke, *Egyptological Studies in Honor of Richard A. Parker,* ed. Leonard H. Lesko (Hanover and London: Brown University Press, 1986), 39.
18. Goedicke, 42.
19. Wente and Van Siclen III, 223.
20. Ibid.
21. Redford, *Akhenaten,* 13.
22. Wente and Van Siclen III, 218.
23. Gardiner, 443.
24. Ibid.
25. Wente and Van Siclen III, 225.
26. William C. Hayes, "Egypt: Internal Affairs From Thutmose I to the Death of Amenophis III," in *Cambridge Ancient History,* 3rd ed., (Cambridge: Cambridge University Press, 1973), II:1, 315.

27. Waddell, 101. In all three versions of Manetho—Josephus, Africanus, and Eusebius—Amenhotep I is listed in third position and Chebron (i.e., Thutmose I) is listed in second position. Why these two kings were listed in reverse order is not known, but there are other instances in Manetho's Eighteenth Dynasty chronology in which the sequence of kings is out of order.

28. Wente and Van Siclen III, 226.

29. Hayes, *CAH*, II:1, 317.

8. Dating the Exodus

1. Hertz, 213, n. 23.
2. Deut. 8:2.
3. Deut. 34:7.
4. Gardiner, 443.
5. Ibid., 274.
6. Ibid., 258.
7. If you add up the lengths of reign for each of Solomon's successors as king of Judah, the total time from the year he began building the Temple to its destruction is 430 years. Since independent sources permit us to date the destruction of the temple to 587 B.C., the biblical account would date Solomon's initial building program to 1017 B.C.
8. Exod. 6:16.
9. Exod. 6:18.
10. Exod. 6:20.
11. Gen. 46:11.
12. Josephus, *Jewish Antiquities,* II.318.
13. Demetrius, quoted by Artapanus, who is quoted by Eusebius, in *Preparation for the Gospel,* vol. 1, trans. Edwin Hamilton Gifford (Grand Rapids: Baker Book House, 1981), 425d–26a.
14. Demetrius, 425d.
15. Ibid., 425d–26a.
16. Abraham arrived in Canaan in his seventy-fifth year (Genesis 12:4); Isaac was born in Abraham's one hundredth year (Genesis 21:5); Jacob was born in Isaac's sixtieth year (Genesis 25:26); and Jacob arrived in Egypt during his one hundred and thirtieth year (Genesis 47:9). Therefore, the total period is 215 years.
17. Josephus, op. cit., II.203.
18. Speiser, 113.
19. Ibid., 113.
20. Gen. 46.
21. Exod. 12:37.
22. Gen. 13:1.
23. This usage is similar to the American usage of the term "the South" to refer to the southeastern portion of the United States. When traveling to that part of the country, one claims to be headed to "the South," regardless of the direction the traveler is actually going.
24. Gen. 11:28–31.
25. Gen. 12:1–4.
26. Speiser, 80. J (28) and P (31) refer to Genesis 11:28 and 11:31.
27. *Harper's Bible Dictionary,* s.v. "Amorites."
28. Speiser, 113.
29. Waddell, 42.

30. Gardiner, 156.
31. Ibid.
32. Ibid.
33. Ibid.
34. Num. 13:29.
35. Gardiner, 157.
36. Demetrius, 424c.
37. Josephus, op. cit., I.346.
38. Artapanus, quoted by Alexander Polyhistor, quoted by Eusebius in *Preparation for the Gospel,* 436c.
39. Exod. 2:23.
40. Exod. 3.
41. Exod. 14:23.
42. Exod. 14:28.
43. Hertz, 213, n. 23.
44. Gardiner, 236.
45. Josephus, op. cit. II.250–55.

9. Egypt Under Akhenaten

1. Budge, *Egyptian Religion,* 37–40.
2. Ibid., 113.
3. Ibid., 127.
4. Ibid., 131.
5. Redford, *Akhenaten,* 176.
6. Some scholars have attempted to deny the monotheistic nature of Akhenaten's religious reform by pointing to the king's occasional references to the goddess Maat, but Maat is more an abstract goddess symbolizing correct and moral behavior, and the references to Maat are used in an idiomatic way to refer to the king being one who "stands in truth."
7. Gardiner, 216.
8. Aldred, 239.
9. Ibid.
10. Ibid.
11. Ibid.
12. Gardiner, 204.
13. Ibid.
14. Aldred, 239.
15. Ibid., 7.
16. Ibid., 259.
17. Ibid., 260.
18. Redford, op. cit., 233.
19. Ibid.
20. Ibid.
21. Aldred, 259.
22. Ibid.
23. Ibid., 261.
24. Ibid., 244.
25. Redford, op. cit., 172.
26. Ibid.
27. Ibid., 172–73.

28. Aldred, 262.
29. Redford, op. cit., 175.
30. Aldred, 245.
31. Redford, op. cit., 173.
32. Ibid.
33. Ibid.
34. Aldred, 240.
35. Ibid.
36. Redford, op. cit., 175.
37. Ibid.
38. Ibid., 176.
39. Ibid., 175.
40. Ibid., 175–76.
41. Aldred, 48.
42. Redford, op. cit., 179–80.
43. Ibid., 180.
44. Pritchard, 227.
45. Aldred, 243.
46. Ibid., 239.
47. Gardiner, 229.
48. Redford, op. cit., 178.
49. Aldred, 305.
50. *Who's Who in Egyptian Mythology*, s.v. "Negative Confessions."
51. Ibid.
52. Ibid.
53. *Harper's Bible Dictionary*, s.v. "Ten Commandments."
54. Diodorus Siculus, *Diodorus Siculus*, 12 vols., trans. C. H. Oldfather (1948; reprint, Loeb Classical Library, 1968), I.77.7–10.
55. Aldred, 305.
56. Ibid.
57. Ibid.
58. Ibid.
59. Genesis 12:6.
60. Genesis 33:19, 34.
61. Joshua 24:32.
62. Joshua 24.
63. Albright, *CAH*, II:2A, 114.
64. Ibid.
65. Ibid., 115.
66. Ibid., 116.
67. Ibid.
68. Ibid.
69. Ibid.
70. Gardiner, 236.
71. Redford, op. cit., 207.
72. Ibid., 208.
73. Ibid.
74. Ibid., 235.
75. Ibid., 213–14.
76. Ibid., 214.
77. Ibid., 215.
78. Ibid., 217.

79. Ibid., 218.
80. Ibid.
81. Ibid., 221.
82. Ibid.
83. Ibid.
84. Ibid., 227.
85. Ibid.
86. Ibid., 224.
87. Ibid.
88. R. O. Faulkner, "Egypt: From the Inception of the Nineteenth Dynasty to the Death of Ramesses III" in *Cambridge Ancient History*, 3rd ed. (Cambridge: Cambridge University Press, 1971), II:2A, 219.
89. Faulkner, *CAH*, II:2A, 219–20.
90. Ibid., II:2A, 219.
91. Exod. 2:23.

10. Exodus: The Egyptian Version

1. Exod. 12:37.
2. Exod. 12:38.
3. Waddell, 103. In the Manetho chronology Akhenaten appears under the name Amenophis and has a reign of nineteen years, but Akhenaten only served seventeen years. Smenkhkare, his designated successor, served up to three years, some unknown portion of which was as coregent with Akhenaten. Therefore, the total of nineteen years represents the combined reigns of both Akhenaten and Smenkhkare. Because Akhenaten and Smenkhkare served as coregents and were equally tainted by the Amarna heresy, the later scribes apparently combined the two reigns as if they were one period of rule.
4. Ibid., 121.
5. Ibid., 145.
6. Ibid., 121.
7. Ibid., 119–33.
8. Josephus would have to have double-counted the fifty-nine-year reign of Sethos to arrive at the sum of 518 years for the period from Tethmosis to the end of Ramesses II.
9. The 393-year period terminates at the end of the reign of Sethos.
10. Amenophis, son of Paapis, is the well-known Egyptian sage "Amenophis, son of Hapu," who served under both Amenhotep III and Akhenaten.
11. It may be just a coincidence, but according to the census figures in Numbers 26, at the time of the Exodus the two Joseph tribes, Ephraim and Manasseh, had a total of about 85,200 members.
12. Redford, *Pharaonic King Lists*, 293.
13. In the Manetho king list, King Or has a reign of thirty-six years and five months. Amenhotep III has a high-year mark of thirty-seven, indicating he completed at least part of his thirty-seventh year.
14. According to Exodus 8:22 and 9:26, during the confrontation between Moses and the pharaoh, the Israelites were located in Goshen, separate and apart from the Egyptians, and therefore not subjected to the plagues heaped upon the Egyptian people.
15. Josephus, *Against Apion*, from *Josephus*, 9 vols., trans., H. St. J. Thackery (1926; Cambridge, Mass.: Harvard University Press, 1976), I.288–92.

16. Redford, *Pharaonic King Lists*, 287.
17. Num. 12:1–2.
18. Waddell, op. cit., 85.
19. Albright, *CAH*, 2:2A, 116.
20. Josephus uses both Sethos and Sethosis as the name of this king.
21. Waddell, 103–105.
22. Herodotus, 168–69.
23. Diodorus Siculus, I.57.5–8.
24. Redford, *Pharaonic King Lists*, 258.
25. Ibid.
26. The sea battles at Medinet Habu depict the war against the Sea Peoples in the reign of Ramesses III, late in the twelfth century B.C.
27. Redford, *Pharaonic King Lists*, 258, n. 6.
28. Unless otherwise indicated, I follow the version of Danaus and Aegyptus appearing in *Apollodorus*, Loeb Classical Library edition, II.1.4–5.
29. Frank H. Stubbings, "The Rise of Mycenaean Civilization" in *Cambridge Ancient History*, 3rd ed. (Cambridge, England: Cambridge University Press, 1973), II:1, 635.
30. Ibid., 636.
31. Ibid.
32. Diodorus Siculus, XL.3.
33. Redford, *Pharaonic King Lists*, 281.
34. Josephus, *Against Apion*, I.183–84.
35. Bernard W. Anderson, *Understanding the Old Testament* (Englewood Cliffs, N.J.: Prentice-Hall, 1957), 32.
36. Exod. 2:10.
37. Anderson, 31.
38. Ibid., 32.
39. Gardiner cites instances of "Mose" alone as an Egyptian name. Gardiner, 268–69, 277.
40. Redford, *Akhenaten*, 175–76.
41. Aldred, 89.
42. Artapanus, 432c.
43. Waddell, 103, 121.
44. Redford, *Pharaonic King Lists*, 227.
45. Ibid., 276.
46. Ibid., 283.
47. Ibid., 283–4.
48. Ibid., 284.
49. Ibid.
50. Ibid.
51. Ibid.
52. Ibid., 285.
53. Josephus, *Against Apion*, II.15–19.
54. Ibid.
55. In Manetho, the king who precedes Ramesses I, corresponding to Horemheb, has the name Acencheres. It's not hard to see that name corrupted into Bocchoris, but I am not yet convinced that this occurred.
56. Josephus, op. cit., I.312.
57. Ibid., I.304–11.
58. Ibid., I.312–15.
59. Tacitus, *The Histories* (New York: Penguin Books, 1964), 5. 3.
60. Josephus, op. cit., II.20.

61. Ibid.
62. Apion, quoted by Josephus in *Against Apion,* II.8–11.
63. Both the Africanus and Eusebius versions of Manetho allege that a lamb spoke during the reign of the Twenty-Fourth Dynasty king identified as Bocchoris.
64. Redford, *Pharaonic King Lists,* 286.
65. Ibid., 277–81.
66. Waddell, op. cit., 145.
67. Ibid.
68. Redford, *Akhenaten,* 187.
69. Ibid.
70. Aldred, 283.
71. Redford, *Akhenaten,* 187.
72. Ibid.
73. Exod. 4:6.
74. Exod. 4:7.
75. Exod. 33:18.
76. Exod. 33:20.
77. Exod. 33:22–23.
78. Exod. 34:30.
79. Exod. 34:33–35.
80. The Hebrew words for *light* and *horn* are the same.
81. Friedman, 202.
82. Exod. 3:4.
83. Num. 12:1–2.
84. Num. 12:10.
85. Num. 12:13–14.
86. Num. 12:11.
87. Exod. 13:2. See also Exodus 13–15.
88. Lev. 13:45.
89. Lev. 22:4.
90. Redford, *Akhenaten,* 57–58.
91. Ibid., 58.
92. Aldred, 231.
93. Ibid., 232.
94. Ibid.
95. This is Josephus's Amenophis, son of Paapis, from the story of Osarseph.
96. Redford, *Pharaonic King Lists,* 250.
97. Ibid., 250.
98. Gardiner, 262.
99. Ibid.
100. Ibid., 261.
101. Ibid., 264.
102. Ibid., 263.
103. The controversial writer Immanuel Velikovsky has argued that this Egyptian manuscript actually describes the ten plagues of the Exodus. While I and virtually every Egyptologist disagree with Velikovsky's conclusion, I do acknowledge that his writings first drew my attention to some of the similarities between the Egyptian and biblical texts.
104. R. O. Faulkner, trans. "Admonitions of an Egyptian Sage" in *The Literature of Ancient Egypt,* ed. William Kelly Simpson (New Haven and London: Yale University Press, 1972), 210.
105. Faulkner, op. cit., 210.

106. All Papyrus quotes are from Faulkner, *The Literature of Ancient Egypt.*
107. Exod. 7:20–21.
108. Exod. 9:23.
109. Exod. 9:25.
110. Exod. 10:15.
111. Exod. 10:22.
112. Exod. 9:6.
113. Exod. 11:15.

11. Who Were the Genesis Patriarchs?

1. Friedman, 248.
2. Ibid., 71.
3. Ibid., 197.
4. Ibid., 191.
5. Gen. 21:32.
6. Gen. 21:22.
7. Gen. 26:2.
8. Gen. 26:1.
9. Gen. 26:26.
10. Gen. 26:18.
11. The Genesis chronology places Isaac's confrontation with Abimelech at approximately 1650 B.C. The Philistines arrived in Canaan during the late thirteenth century B.C. as part of the Sea Peoples' invasion.
12. *Harper's Bible Dictionary,* s.v. "Gerar."
13. Rudolf Anthes, "Mythology in Ancient Egypt," *Mythologies of the Ancient World,* ed. Samuel Noah Kramer (New York: Anchor, 1961), 69–70.
14. Ibid., 71.
15. Ibid., 34.
16. Ibid., 34.
17. Plutarch, *Plutarchi de Iside et Osiride liber : Graece et Anglice,* trans. S. Squire (Cambridge, 1744), reprinted in Budge, *Egyptian Religion,* 62–78. All references to Plutarch's story of Osiris are keyed to this translation. Summaries of it can be found in any general study of Egyptian mythology.
18. Plutarch, in Budge, *Egyptian Religion,* 63–64.
19. Ibid., 63.
20. Ibid., 64.
21. Ibid.
22. Ibid., 76.
23. *The Contendings of Horus and Set,* trans. E. F. Wente, in *The Literature of Ancient Egypt* (New Haven and London: Yale University Press, 1973), 108–26.
24. Wente, *The Literature of Ancient Egypt,* 111.
25. Ibid., 109.
26. Ibid., 123–24.

12. The Horus Cycle: Jacob and Esau

1. Gen. 25:26.
2. Gen. 25:25.
3. Gen. 25:27.
4. Gen. 25:28.

5. Gen. 27:41.
6. Budge, *Egyptian Religion*, 64.
7. *Who's Who in Egyptian Mythology*, s.v. "Set."
8. Gen. 25:32.
9. Gen. 27:11–12.
10. Gen. 27:13.
11. Wente, *The Literature of Ancient Egypt*, 114.
12. Ibid., 115.
13. Ibid.
14. A variation of this confrontation between Isis and Set appears in the story of King David and Bathsheba. David desired Bathsheba but she was married to Uriah the Hittite, a soldier in David's army. David arranged a mission designed to lead to Uriah's death, leaving him free to marry Bathsheba. After Uriah died in the encounter, Nathan the priest came before David and told him about an injustice in his kingdom involving a rich man with many cattle and a poor man with one ewe. The rich man was entertaining a traveler and wanted to feed him well, but didn't want to kill any of his own cattle, so he took the poor man's ewe and had it served up. David was greatly angered at the rich man's actions and declared that he should surely die for them. Nathan then told David, "Thou art the man." (See 2 Samuel 12:1–7.)
15. Gen. 27:2.
16. Gen. 36:1.
17. Gen. 36:20
18. Speiser, 283.
19. Ibid.
20. Gen. 36:24–25.
21. The Mazoretic text has "Anah daughter of Zibeon." The Septuagint version has "son of Zibeon." Speiser believes that the Mazoretic text confused *bt* (daughter) with *bn* (son) and that there was an error in transmission. Anah, according to all versions, was apparently the hero of some local folk legend having to do with the discovery of a hot spring. (Genesis 36:24)
22. Gen. 10:17.
23. Gen. 34:2.
24. Gen. 26:34, 28:9.
25. Gen. 36:2–3.
26. Gen. 25:30.
27. Speiser, 196.
28. Gen. 27:39–40.
29. Both Peniel and Penuel are given as the name of the place where this incident occurred.
30. Gen. 32:24–33:1.
31. Gen. 33:4–10.
32. Gen. 33:14.
33. Gen. 35:6–10.
34. Gen. 28:11–13.
35. Gen. 28:17–19.
36. Speiser, 218–220.
37. Budge, *The Egyptian Book of the Dead*, lxxi.
38. Ibid.
39. Gen. 34:31.
40. Strong's Dictionary, H2543, electronic version from Parsons Technology.
41. Gen. 49:5–10.

13. Isaac and the Death of Osiris

1. Budge, *Egyptian Religion,* 102.
2. Ibid., 101.
3. Ibid.
4. Josephus, *Jewish Antiquities,* I.227.
5. Speiser, 165.
6. Friedman, 257.
7. Ibid.
8. For a discussion of this tradition see Spiegel's *The Last Trial* (New York: Schocken, 1969; Hebrew edition, 1950) and Maccoby's *The Sacred Executioner* (New York: Thames and Hudson, 1982.)
9. Manfred Lurker, *Gods and Symbols of Ancient Egypt,* trans. Barbara Cummings (London: Thames and Hudson, 1980), s.v. "Ram."
10. *Who's Who In Egyptian Religion,* s.v. "Ba."
11. Herodotus, 167.
12. Ibid.
13. Gen. 16:10.
14. Gen. 16:11–12.
15. Gen. 21:12.
16. Ibid.
17. Gen. 21:20.
18. Gen. 25:18.
19. Speiser, 118.
20. Wente, *The Literature of Ancient Egypt,* 113–14.
21. Ibid., 125.
22. Gen. 17:15–20.
23. Wente, *The Literature of Ancient Egypt,* 112.
24. Ibid.
25. Ibid.
26. Gen. 18:11–15.

14. The Twelve Tribes Myth and the Canaanite Conquest

1. *Harper's Bible Dictionary,* s.v. "Tribes."
2. 2 Kings 17:23–24.
3. 1 Kings 12:17.
4. 1 Chron. 9:3.
5. Ephraim and Manasseh were part of the northern kingdom. Benjamin's allegiance is unclear from the biblical text. See the discussion of the split.
6. Matt. 19:28.
7. Gen. 48:5.
8. Gen. 48:19.
9. Deut. 33.
10. Judg. 5.
11. *Harper's Bible Dictionary,* s.v. "Deborah" and "Tribes."
12. Judg. 4:4.
13. Judg. 4:10–11.
14. Josh. 11.
15. Judg. 5:15–18.
16. Joseph is also excluded, but he was replaced by Ephraim and Manasseh.

17. Gen. 23.
18. Num. 26:29.
19. Num. 32:39–40.
20. Adding to the confusion among Manasseh, Machir, Gilead, and Gad is the frequent references in Joshua to half-Gilead as a territory and to the half tribe of Manasseh, when referring to the Jordanian portion of Manasseh.
21. Deut. 3:15–16, Joshua 22:9.
22. N. K. Sandars, *The Sea Peoples* (1978; London: Thames and Hudson, 1985), 119.
23. Ibid., 119.
24. Ibid., 120–124.
25. Ibid., 105–106.
26. Ibid., 119.
27. Ibid., 158.
28. Ibid., 106.
29. Ibid.
30. Ibid.
31. Ibid., 106–7.
32. Ibid., 112.
33. Ibid., 106.
34. Gen. 49:13.
35. *Harper's Bible Dictionary*, s.v. "Joshua, Book of."
36. Ibid., s.v. "Jericho."
37. Ibid., s.v. "Ai."
38. 2 Sam. 5:6–7.
39. 1 Kings 11:29–32.
40. 1 Kings 12:20.
41. 1 Kings 12:21.
42. Josh. 19:1.
43. 1 Chron. 4:42–43.
44. Herodotus, 188.
45. Ibid., 190.
46. Ibid., 184–85.
47. Ibid., 190.

Bibliography

Albright, William F. "The Amarna Letters From Palestine." In *Cambridge Ancient History*, II:2A, 3rd ed. Cambridge, England: Cambridge University Press, 1971.

Aldred, Cyril. *Akhenaten: King of Egypt.* London: Thames and Hudson, 1988.

Anderson, Bernard W. *Understanding the Old Testament.* Englewood Cliffs, N.J.: Prentice-Hall, 1957.

Anthes, Rudolf. "Mythology in Ancient Egypt." In *Mythologies of the Ancient World.* Edited by Samuel Noah Kramer. New York: Anchor, 1961.

Apollodorus, the Loeb Classical Library edition, 2 vols., trans. James George Frazier, 1921; Cambridge, Mass.: Harvard University Press, 1976.

Barr, James. *Biblical Chronology: Legend or Science.* London: University of London, 1987.

Bickerman, E. J. *Chronology of the Ancient World.* 2nd ed. Ithaca, N.Y.: Cornell University Press, 1982.

Budge, E. A. Wallis. *The Egyptian Book of the Dead.* New York: Dover, 1967.

———. *Egyptian Religion.* New York: Bell, 1959.

Clagett, Marshall. *Ancient Egyptian Science.* 3 vols. Philadelphia: American Philosophical Society, 1989.

Delaporte, I. *The New Larousse Encyclopedia of Mythology.* Translated by Richard Aldington and Delano Ames, revised by a panel of editorial advisers from the *Larousse Mythologie Generale,* edited by Felix Guirand. London: Hamlyn, 1968.

Egyptian Mythology. London: Hamlyn, 1963. Based on the text translated by Delano Ames from *Mythologie Generale,* Larousse, first published by Auge, Gillon, Hollier-Larousse, Moreau and Cie.

Emory, W. B. *Archaic Egypt.* Middlesex: Penguin Books, 1987.

Eusebius. *Preparation for the Gospel.* 2 vols. Translated by Edwin Hamilton Gifford. Grand Rapids, Mich.: Baker Book House, 1981.

Faulkner, R. O., trans. "Admonitions of an Egyptian Sage." In *The Literature of Ancient Egypt.* Edited by William Kelly Simpson. New Haven and London: Yale University Press, 1972.

Faulkner, R. O. "Egypt: From the Inception of the Nineteenth Dynasty to the Death of Ramesses III." In *Cambridge Ancient History*, 3rd ed., 2:2A, Cambridge, England: Cambridge University Press, 1971.

Friedman, Richard Elliot. *Who Wrote the Bible*. New York: Summit Books, 1987.

Gardiner, A. *Egypt of the Pharaohs*. Oxford: Oxford University Press, 1978.

———. *The Royal Canon of Turin*. Oxford: Griffith Institute, 1987.

Goedicke, Hans. "The End of the Hyksos in Egypt." In *Egyptological Studies in Honor of Richard A. Parker*. Edited by Leonard H. Lesko. Hanover and London: Brown University Press, 1986.

Graves, Robert. *The Greek Myths*. 2 vols. Baltimore: Penguin, 1955.

Graves, Robert, and Patai, Ralph. *Hebrew Myths: The Book of Genesis*. 1963 reprint. New York: McGraw-Hill, 1966.

Gray, John. *Near Eastern Mythology*. London: Hamlyn, 1969.

Greenberg, Moshe. *THE HAB/piru*. New Haven: American Oriental Society 1955.

Harding, A. F., and Tait, W. J. *Antiquity* 63 (1989).

Harper's Bible Dictionary, 8th ed.

Hayes, William C. "Chronology: I. Egypt—To the End of the Twentieth Dynasty." In *Cambridge Ancient History*. 3rd ed., 1:1. Cambridge, England: Cambridge University Press, 1970.

———. "Egypt: From the Death of Ammenemes III to Seqenenre II." In *Cambridge Ancient History*. 3rd ed., 2:1. Cambridge, England: Cambridge University Press, 1973.

———. "The Middle Kingdom in Egypt." In *Cambridge Ancient History*. 3rd ed., 1:2A. Cambridge, England: Cambridge University Press, 1971.

Heidel, Alexander. *The Gilgamesh Epic and Old Testament Parallels*. Chicago: University of Chicago Press, 1949.

Herodotus. *The Histories*. Translated by Aubrey de Selincourt. Middlesex, England: Penguin Books, 1978.

James, T. G. H. "Egypt: From the Expulsion of the Hyksos to Amenophis I." In *Cambridge Ancient History*. 3rd ed., 2:1. Cambridge: Cambridge University Press, 1973.

Josephus. *Against Apion*. 9 vols. From *Josephus*, vol. 1. Translated by H. St. J. Thackeray. 1926; Cambridge, Mass.: Harvard University Press, 1976.

———. *Jewish Antiquities*. 9 vols. From *Josephus*, vol. 4. Translated by H. St. J. Thackeray. 1991 reprint. Cambridge, Mass.: Harvard University Press, 1930.

Lurker, Manfred. *The Gods and Symbols of Ancient Egypt*. Translated by Barbara Cummings. London: Thames and Hudson, 1980.

Maccoby, H. *The Sacred Executioner*. New York: Thames and Hudson, 1982.

Mercatante, A. S. *Who's Who in Egyptian Mythology*. New York: Potter, 1978.

Neil, W. *Harper's Bible Commentary*. New York: Harper and Row, 1975.

Parker, Richard A. "The Sothic Dating of the Twelfth and Eighteenth Dynasties." In *Studies in Honor of George R. Hughes, January 12, 1977, Studies in Ancient Oriental Civilization. No. 39.* Chicago: Oriental Institute, 1977.

Pentateuch and Haftorahs, The. 2nd. ed. Edited by J. H. Hertz. London: Soncino Press, 1976.

Pritchard, James P., ed. *The Ancient Near East: An Anthology of Texts and Pictures.* 2 vols. Princeton: Princeton University Press, 1958.

Rainey, Anson F. "Rainey's Challenge." In *Biblical Archaeological Review,* November/December 1991.

Redford, Donald B. *Akhenaten: The Heretic King.* Princeton: Princeton University Press, 1984.

————. *Pharaonic King Lists, Annals, and Day Books.* Mississauga: Benben Publications, 1986.

Saggs, H. W. E. *Civilization Before Greece and Rome.* New Haven: Yale University Press, 1989.

Sandars, N. K. *The Epic of Gilgamesh.* London: Penguin, 1972.

————. *The Sea Peoples.* 1978; London: Thames and Hudson, 1985.

Shanks, Hershel. "Israel's Emergence in Canaan; *BR* interviews Norman Gottwald." *Bible Review,* October 1989.

Siculus, Diodorus. *Diodorus Siculus.* 12 vols. Translated by C. H. Oldfather. 1948; reprint Loeb Classical Library, 1968.

Smaller Classical Dictionary. Rev. from Sir William Smith, by E. H. Blakeney and John Warrington. New York: E. F. Dutton, 1958.

Smith, W. Stevenson. "The Old Kingdom in Egypt and the Beginning of the First Intermediate Period." In *Cambridge Ancient History.* 3rd ed., 1:2A. Cambridge: Cambridge University Press, 1971.

Speiser, E. A., ed. The Anchor Bible. Vol. 1. *Genesis, a New Translation With Introduction and Commentary.* New York: Doubleday.

Sullivan, Walter. "Ice Data Upset Timetable on Ancient Disaster." *New York Times,* August 6, 1989.

Tacitus. *The Histories.* New York: Penguin Books, 1964.

Waddell, W. G., ed. *Manetho.* 1940: reprint, Loeb Classical Library, 1980.

Walton, John. "The Antediluvian Section of the Sumerian King List and Genesis 5." *Biblical Archaeologist,* fall 1981.

Wente, E. F., and Van Siclen, C. "A Chronology of the New Kingdom." In *Studies in Honor of George R. Hughes, January 12, 1977, Studies in Ancient Oriental Civilization. No. 39.* Chicago: Oriental Institute, 1977.

Wente, E. F., trans. "The Contendings of Horus and Set." In *The Literature of Ancient Egypt.* Edited by William Kelly Simpson. New Haven and London: Yale University Press, 1972.

Wooley, C. Leonard. *The Sumerians.* New York: Norton, 1965.

Yurco, Frank J. "3,200-Year-Old Picture of Israel Found in Egypt." *Biblical Archaeological Review,* September/October 1990.

Index

303

Index

Genesis Chronology and Egyptian King-Lists:

The Egyptian Origins of Genesis History

Volume I: Egypt's Dynastic Period

BY

GARY GREENBERG

ISBN-13: 978-09814966-6-5

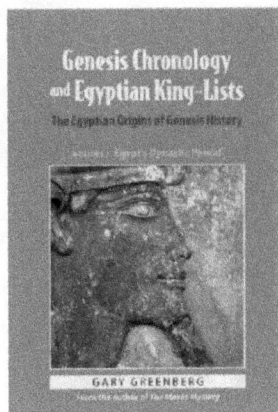

Based on a thorough examination of the archaeological and literary evidence for Egypt's chronological history, Greenberg looks at the birth and death dates of the Genesis patriarchs, from Adam to Joseph, to see what was going on in Egypt in the very same years that the biblical patriarchs were either born or died. The evidence shows that the biblical roster constitutes a disguised record of Egypt's dynastic history, and that many of the birth and death dates can be aligned on a precise one-to-one basis with Egypt's High Chronology starting dates for the first eighteen dynasties and many of the reigns of important Egyptian kings.

JUST SOME OF THE FASCINATING REVELATIONS

- The symbolic importance of Enoch's death after 365 years
- Methuselah's 969-year life span and a major contemporaneous political era of equal length in Egypt
- How the Joseph chronology identifies the pharaoh he worked for
- What was "divided" in the time of Peleg
- The Egyptian history behind the story of the sinful marriage between the sons of god and the daughters of men
- The importance of Egypt's 1460-year Sothic cycle in establishing anchor dates for Egyptian and Genesis chronology.

From the author of *The Moses Mystery: The Egyptian Origins of the Jewish People*

www.ingramcontent.com/pod-product-compliance
Lightning Source LLC
Chambersburg PA
CBHW070928150426
42812CB00049B/1599